IMAGES
*of America*

# SCOTTS VALLEY

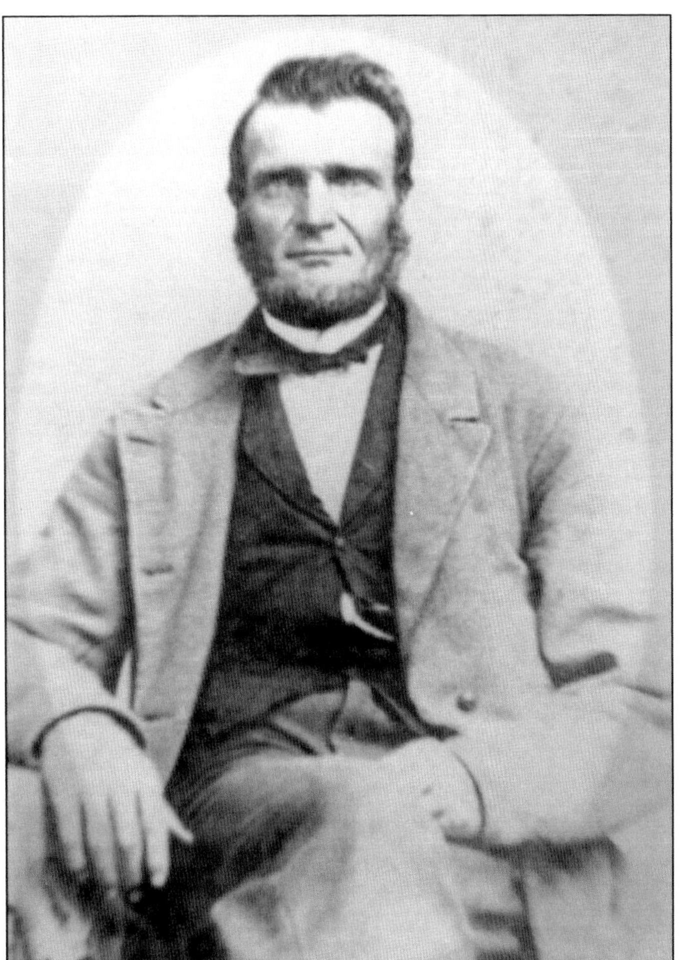

**Hiram Daniel Scott, 1860.** No one could have predicted the extraordinary life of Hiram Daniel Scott. He sailed to California as the eldest son of a Maine sea captain, made his fortune on a lucky gold strike in the Sierra foothills, and owned an entire Spanish Rancho, yet he ended life as a saloon owner on the remote frontier of the Arizona Territory. (Courtesy of the Leisz family.)

**On the Cover:** Built entirely with donations of land, money, materials, and labor, the first Scotts Valley School opened in 1872. Located on the same site as the present-day Scotts Valley Middle School, this building served as schoolhouse and community center for nearly 50 years, until a second school was built in 1923. Today's six-lane Scotts Valley Drive runs in front of the school, replacing the narrow country road shown in the photograph. (Courtesy of the Santa Cruz Museum of Art and History.)

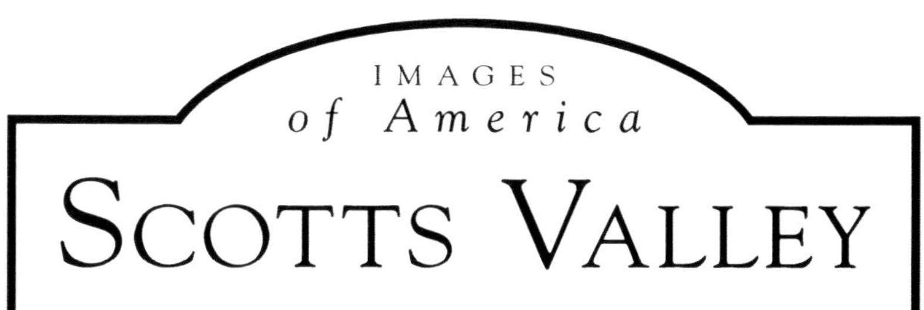


Deborah Muth

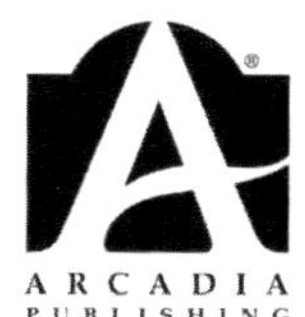

ISBN 978-1-4671-1571-1

Published by Arcadia Publishing
Charleston, South Carolina

Printed in the United States of America

Library of Congress Control Number: 2016935118

For all general information, please contact Arcadia Publishing:
Telephone 843-853-2070
Fax 843-853-0044
E-mail sales@arcadiapublishing.com
For customer service and orders:
Toll-Free 1-888-313-2665

Visit us on the Internet at www.arcadiapublishing.com

*This book is dedicated to the passionate, enthusiastic, and hardworking members of the Scotts Valley Historical Society.*

# Contents

# Foreword

As John W. Gardner once said, "History never looks like history when you are living through it." It is intriguing to think that we may be living through historical times or that some of us may be making history. Author Debbie Muth has an enthusiasm for preserving and recording the history of Scotts Valley. She has invested many years researching the city's history, collecting data, and interviewing individuals who have helped shape today's community. Her compilation of historic photographs, quotes from pioneer journals, newspaper archives, and interviews with people who made Scotts Valley history are captivating. Images of America: *Scotts Valley* invites the reader to discover why so many are drawn to the beauty of this city.

Debbie's passion for Scotts Valley goes beyond researching and recording history. In 2003, I was searching for an individual with an abiding interest in the city who would be willing to help shape our community. Debbie's enthusiasm for researching and studying history has made her an excellent planning commissioner, one who views Scotts Valley from a variety of perspectives. She serves on the Scotts Valley Planning Commission, is active in the Scotts Valley Historical Society, and supports our local schools and Scouting organizations. She holds a bachelor of arts in economics from the University of California, Santa Cruz, and she is a certified real estate appraiser. Debbie has a keen interest in preserving our city's natural and cultural resources. It is easy to understand why Debbie Muth was chosen to write a history of Scotts Valley. I can say that the rest is history!

In August 2016, Scotts Valley celebrates the 50th anniversary of its founding, yet Images of America: *Scotts Valley* reveals that the city's history is rich beyond those 50 years. The reader can journey through time and imagine Scotts Valley's past, from prehistoric archeological finds and how the area's indigenous Indian tribes lived to the development and manufacturing of disc drives, which were integral to the development of computer technology.

This volume helps us reflect on all that came before and consider what the future holds for our city. Perhaps inspired readers of this book will carry these impressions of our city's history in their hearts and, in so doing, help build the future of Scotts Valley—a future that honors not only who and what we were but also what we can become.

—Stephany E. Aguilar
Council Member, City of Scotts Valley

# ACKNOWLEDGMENTS

When I first took on the task of writing this book, I had no idea of the amazing journey that was ahead of me. My thanks first go to my family and friends who cheered me on when the task seemed overwhelming.

Next, I would like to acknowledge those individuals and organizations that so generously shared newspaper clippings, research materials, and photographs. All photograph credits are provided in the courtesy line at the end of each caption; the Scotts Valley Historical Society has been abbreviated as SVHS. To my regret, many contributed photographs could not be used because of space limitations or photograph resolution; however, I hope they can be used in the future. In this book, I have attempted to write about people and events in Scotts Valley in chronological order, with the exception of some structures that have changed usage over time.

My book is based in part on published and unpublished works from Richard Beal, Janice Bowman, Dr. Robert Cartier, Charlene Duval, Wilma Erlandson, Virginia Hooper, Margaret Koch, Glory Anne Laffey, Marian Leisz, David Outerbridge, Marion Pokriots, Dr. Donald Seapy, Jennice Singer, Eric Taylor, Mary Telles, and Dr. Everett Wilson. My sincere gratitude goes to the above authors for their dedication and love of Scotts Valley.

Every attempt has been made in the accuracy of names, facts, and dates; however, mistakes do happen. Corrections, additions, or comments can be directed to me below. Lastly, photographs and items pertaining to the history of Scotts Valley are always welcome for inclusion in a future Scotts Valley History Museum and archives. Please write to me at Debbie Muth, P.O. Box 66254, Scotts Valley, CA 95067. If you have purchased this book, many thanks! All author royalties will go to the Scotts Valley Historical Society to promote Scotts Valley history.

# INTRODUCTION

A visitor driving along the busy thoroughfares and quiet residential streets of Scotts Valley might not suspect our town contains much history. Few physical reminders of the past remain, with the exception of the archeological exhibit at city hall, the Scott House, and a few trees left from the Tree Circus. However, with just a little bit of research, an astonishing amount of history can be uncovered.

Like all cities, Scotts Valley was shaped by both the broad events of history and the people who settled here. Seeking religious converts, the Spanish missionaries claimed vast amounts of former native land, including Scotts Valley. With the end of the missions, José Antonio Bolcoff and then Joseph Ladd Majors became owners of the area of Scotts Valley then known as Rancho San Agustin. Frontiersmen and fur trappers, such as Isaac Graham and Charles McKiernan, left their established settlements for the open space of the West. They shaped the history of the area by building sawmills, tanneries, and gristmills. Lured by tales of easy riches, Hiram Scott and other pioneers came to Scotts Valley during the Gold Rush, thereby discovering the area's excellent soil and temperate climate.

While national and world events had some influence on local history, it was the rise of farm mechanization, the growing use of automobiles, and an improved road system that had the most influence in shaping Scotts Valley. Roadside attractions, including the Beverly Gardens, Camp Evers, the Tree Circus, Lost World, and Santa's Village, attracted tourists who stayed in the roadside hotels and ate at the local cafés. Further development included the Sky Park Airport and Bethany Bible College, and local celebrity property owners Marion Hollins and Alfred Hitchcock. As Scotts Valley matured into a city, new traditions of Scotts Valley Days and the Cavalcade were started. However, what has remained the same throughout Scotts Valley's history is the spirit of community involvement of the residents. Whether holding charity benefits for those in need or starting the first school in 1872 or the first high school in 1999, that same can-do spirit remains.

# *One*

# Early Beginnings

During the late Pleiocene to early Holocene epochs, some 5 million to 10,000 years ago, a vast inland sea covered parts of Santa Cruz County, Monterey County, Santa Clara County, and the San Joaquin Valley. In these warm, shallow waters, all manner of marine life and all types of fish and invertebrates lived and eventually died. The fossils of whales, sharks, stingrays, sea cows, sea lions, and many others were preserved because of strong tidal currents and narrow seaways, which deposited thick layers of sand and gravel. Over time, these layers were compacted into distinct layers, each with a rich variety of marine remains.

After the waters of the early sea receded, ancient peoples began to inhabit the densely forested mountains and marshy valleys. They were drawn by the mild climate, the abundant water from streams and artesian springs, and the wide variety of food sources, such as deer, elk, antelope, hare, geese, duck, quail, salmon, perch, abalone, mussels, clams, berries, tubers, nuts, and seeds.

Over many years, a succession of Indian peoples settled in the area, beginning with the Aruama, then the San Lorenzo, next the Umunhum, and finally the Ohlone. Archaeologists estimate that native peoples lived in Scotts Valley as far back as 10,000 to 12,000 years ago. These early residents lived on the shores of an ancient Pleistocene lake that covered an area near the present-day city hall and police station. Considered seminomadic, these "tribelets," as they are known, followed game and seasonal foodstuffs by establishing semipermanent sites according to the seasons. In addition, the prehistoric site may have served as a way station for travelers crossing the Santa Cruz Mountains. Scotts Valley's early role of linking the Santa Clara Valley to the Monterey Bay area would continue to shape the area in the decades to follow.

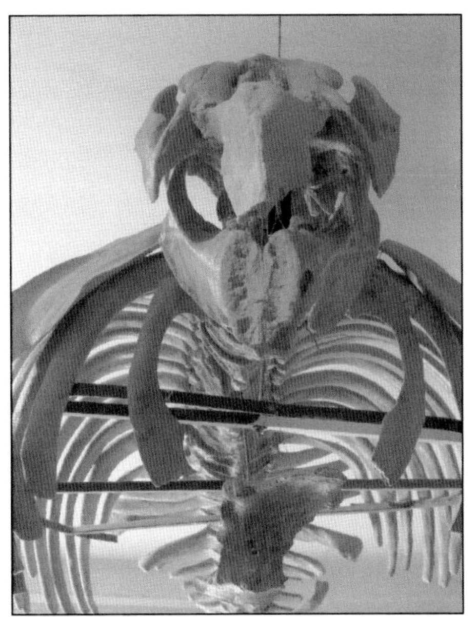

**Sea Cow Fossil.** In 1963, a team of scientists led by naturalist Frank Perry discovered the remains of an ancient 2,000-pound sea cow at the former Olympia Sand Quarry site. While the original fossil bones are kept at the University of California, Berkeley, plaster replicas, such as the one shown here, are on display at the Santa Cruz Natural History Museum and at the Takikawa Art and Natural History Museum in Japan. (Photograph by the author.)

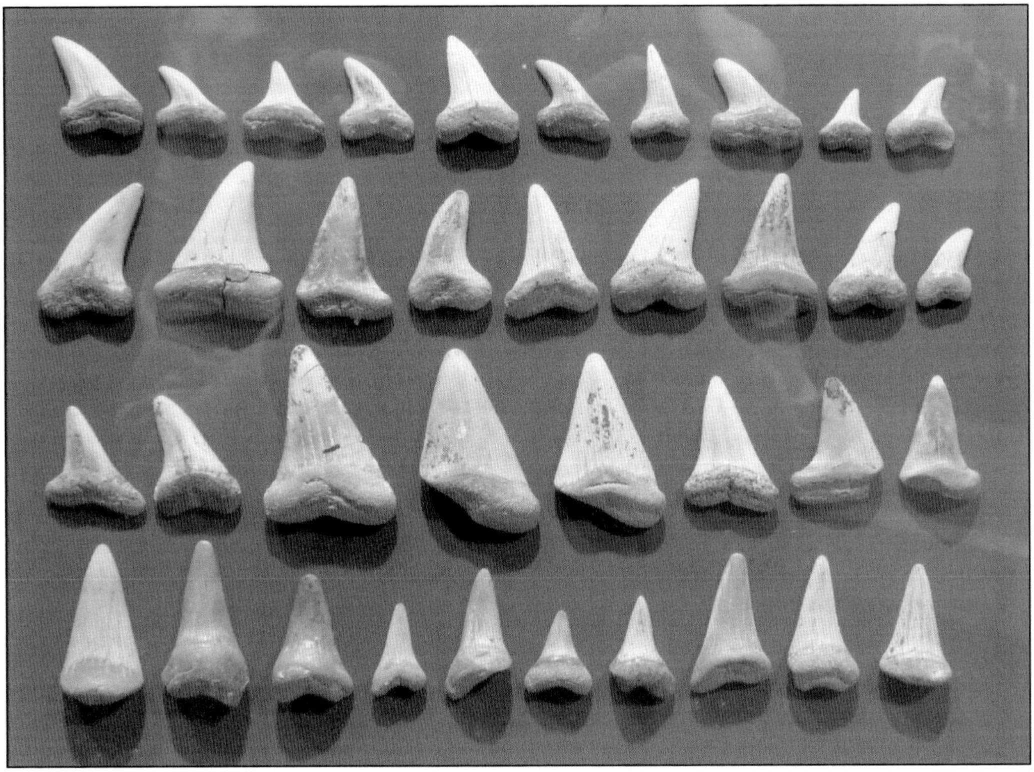

**Shark's Teeth.** As many as 19 different varieties of shark fossils have been discovered in and around Scotts Valley. Species range from small bottom dwellers to whale-sized specimens that ate plankton. Shark's teeth have been dug out of the sandy hills along Whispering Pines Drive and Lockhart Gulch. Whale fossils have also been found during the construction of the former Borland International headquarters and most recently near the former Polo Barn site. This image depicts an exhibit at the Santa Cruz Natural History Museum. (Photograph by the author.)

**THE RUINS, 1858.** Scotts Valley's first tourist attraction was known as "The Ruins." Gold-rush era descriptions of the formations hinted at a mysterious lost civilization and ancient buried treasure. This romanticized and inaccurate illustration of the Ruins is from *Frank Leslie's Illustrated Newspaper*, published in 1858. (Courtesy of SVHS.)

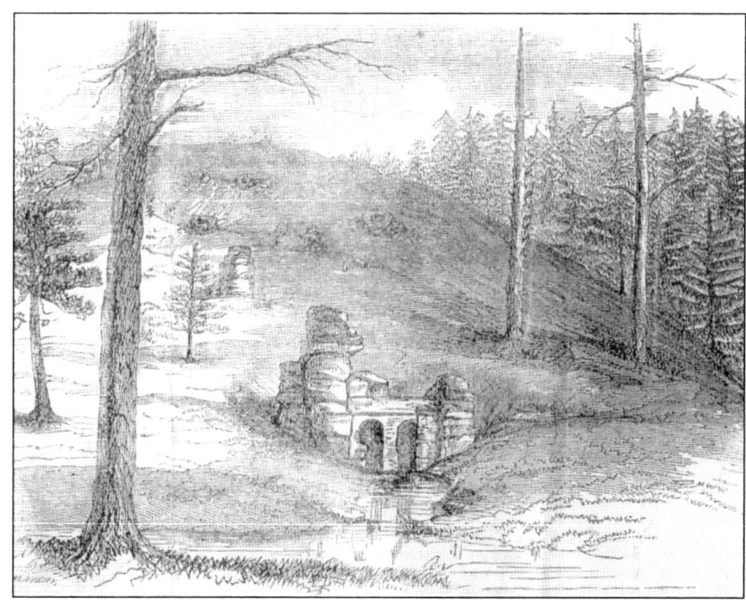

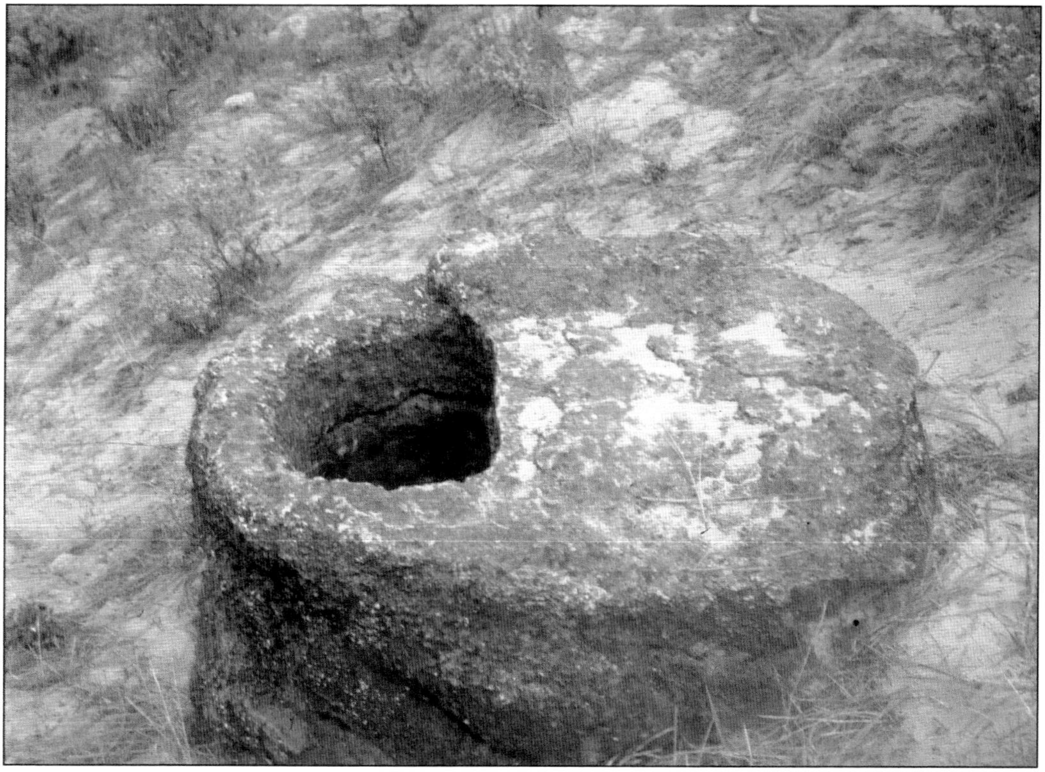

**ACTUAL RUINS FORMATION.** The columns are generally around four feet tall and range from two to six feet across. Scientists now believe the chimneys were formed by methane gas leaking from the seafloor when this part of California was underwater. Known as cold seeps, these areas can still be found in Monterey Bay. The formations, now considerably weathered, reside on property still owned by the Genn family, descendants of Ruth Delia Scott, Hiram Scott's sister. (Courtesy of Charlene Duval.)

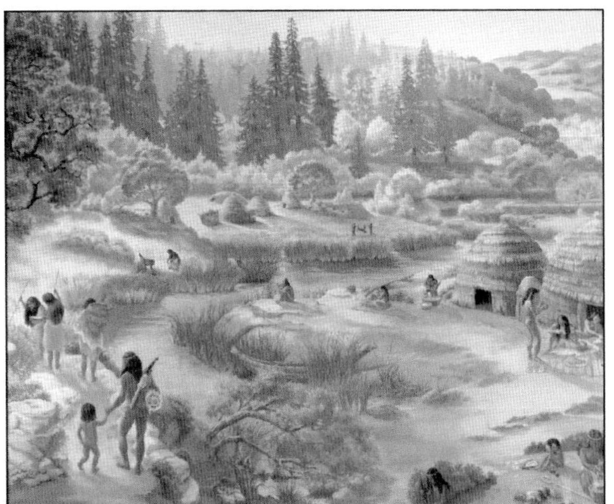

**Ohlone Life.** Ohlone villages were typically located near plentiful food sources and freshwater. Dwellings were constructed of tule reeds over a framework of willow poles. The men and boys used spears, not bows and arrows, for hunting and weapons. This mural by Ann Thiermann is on display at the Santa Cruz Natural History Museum. (Courtesy of the Santa Cruz Natural History Museum.)

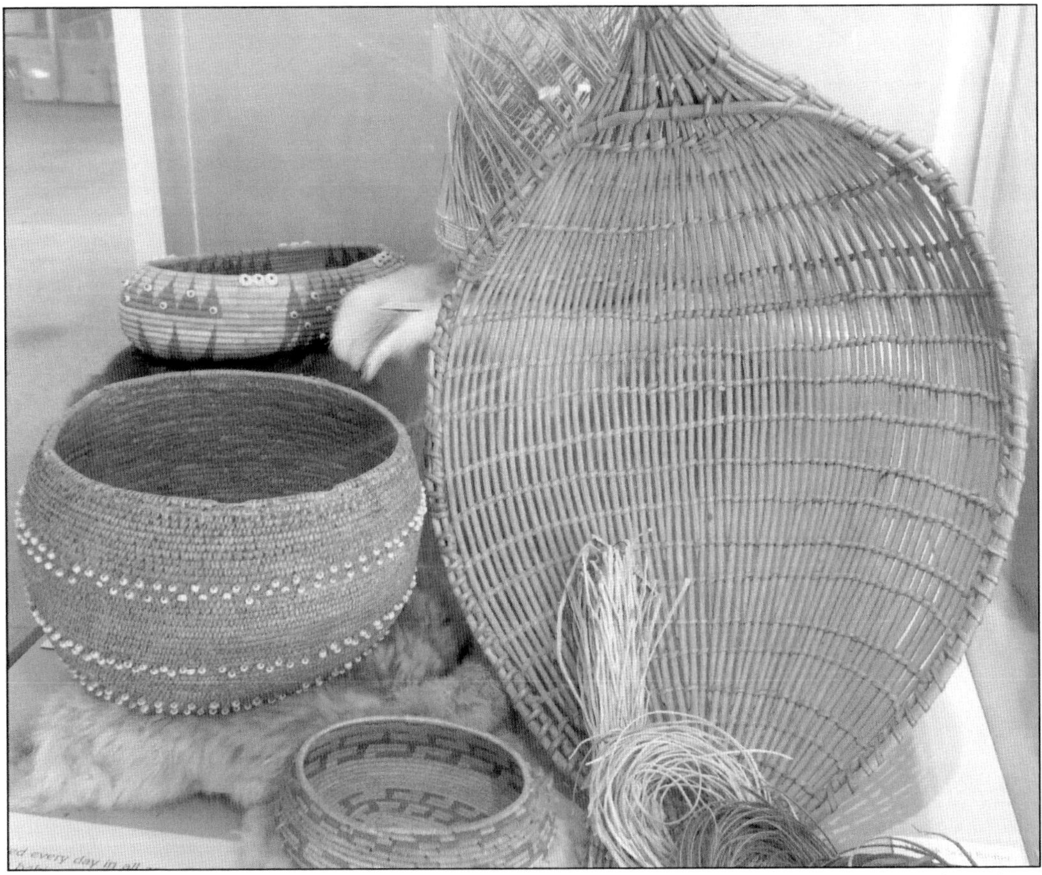

**Ohlone Basket Display.** The Ohlone women wove intricate baskets of willow, bracken fern, sedge, tule, and horsetail. Often, they were decorated with shells and feathers. Baskets were used for a wide variety of tasks, such as carrying, boiling, seed gathering, grinding, leaching, and storage. The Ohlone traded mussels, abalone products, and salt for cinnabar, obsidian, dogs, and tobacco. This basket display can be seen at the Santa Cruz Natural History Museum. (Photograph by the author.)

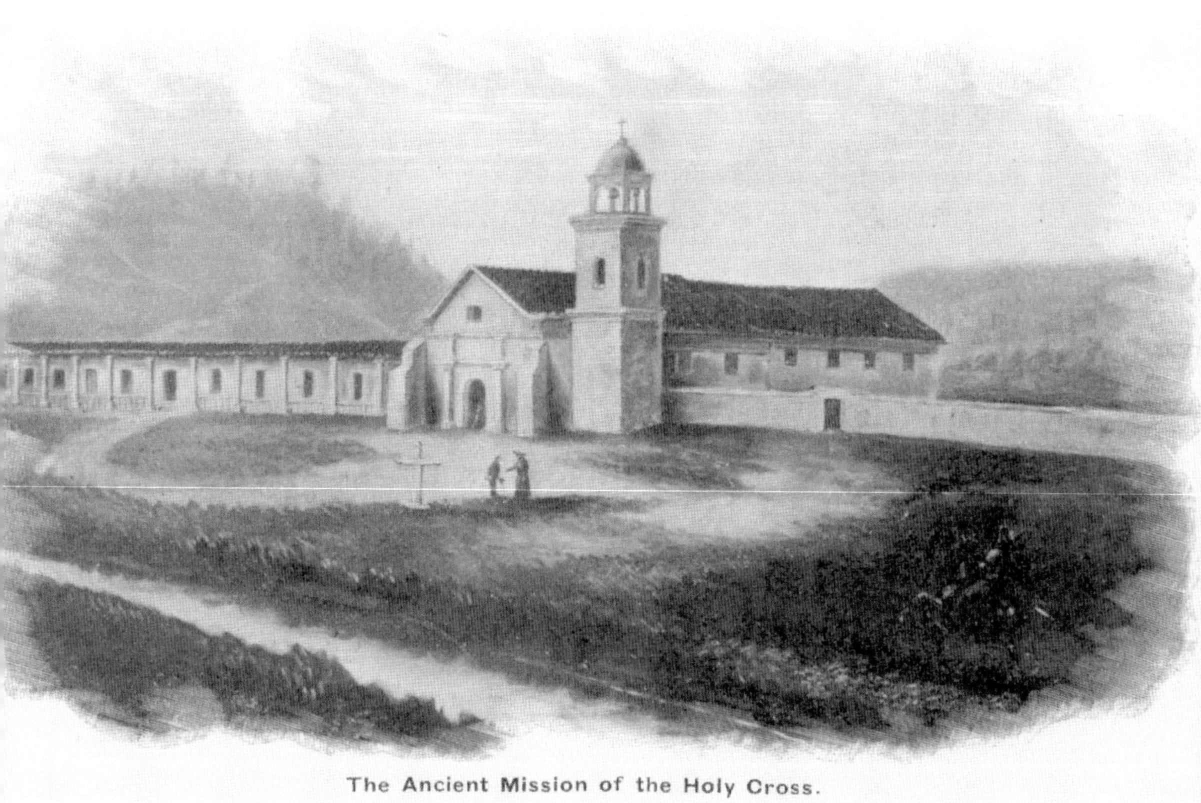

The Ancient Mission of the Holy Cross.

**The Santa Cruz Mission.** Founded by Friar Fermin Lasuén in 1791, La Misión de la Exaltación de la Santa Cruz was the 12th mission founded in California. Plagued by earthquakes, Indian unrest, and looting, the Santa Cruz mission had one of the lowest Indian populations of all the church settlements. Basketmaking and other traditional crafts and skills were lost as the Indians were forced to work at the mission holdings. The closing of the mission in 1834, combined with dramatic declines in the Indian population due to the introduction of European diseases, caused relocation to different areas other than the traditional settlements. The last reported native speaker of the Ohlone language died in 1935. (Courtesy of Eric Taylor.)

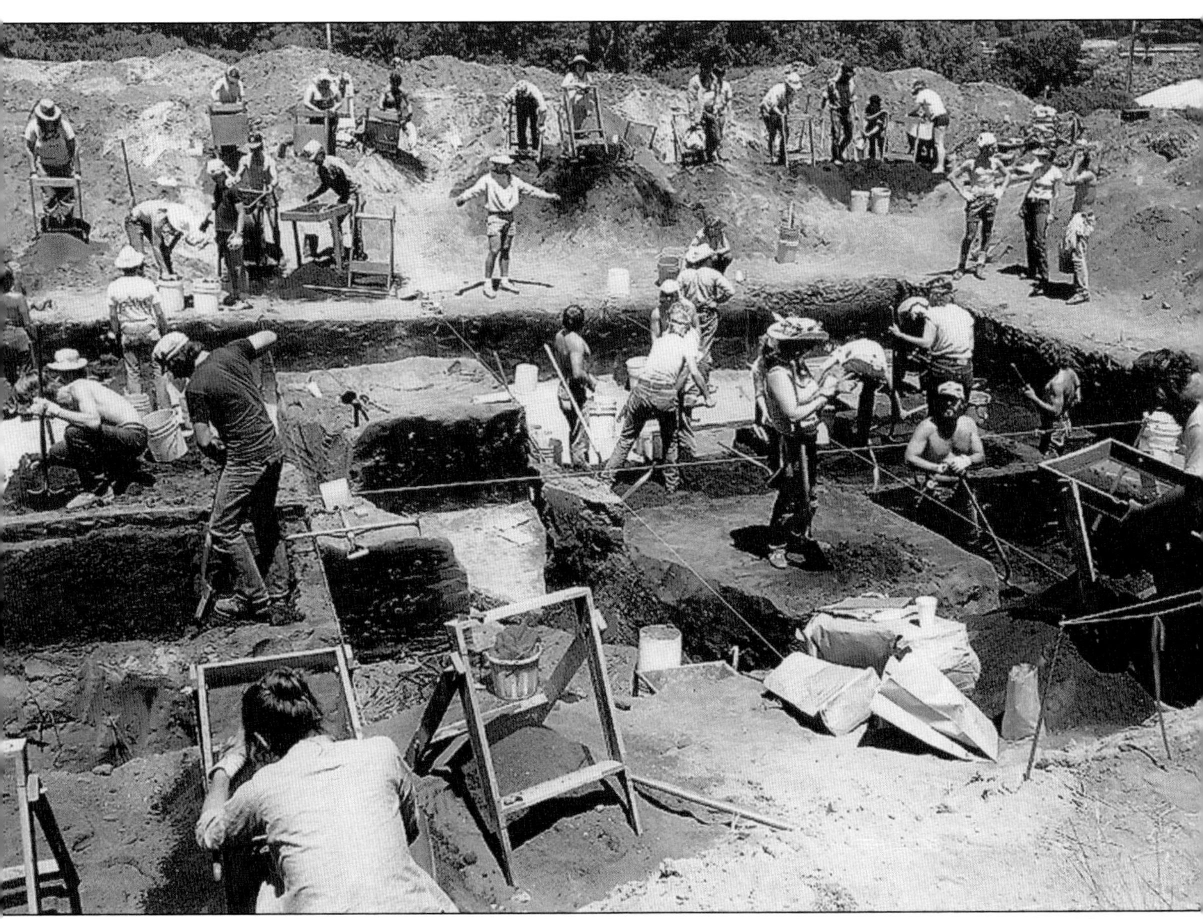

**Archeological Dig.** In 1980, the Santa Cruz Archeological Society and the Society of California Archeology filed a complaint in the Santa Cruz County Superior Court in response to grading done for Scotts Valley's new city hall parking lot without the presence of a qualified archaeological observer. A legal agreement was reached, and in 1983, an extensive three-day dig was undertaken over the Memorial Day weekend. An estimated 220 archaeologists, students, and other volunteers participated in the dig, which recovered over 11,505 artifacts and other related materials. Carbon 14, obsidian hydration, and artifact typing dating methods done on the artifacts indicated the city hall site to be one of the oldest continually occupied prehistoric sites on the West Coast, with evidence of human activity from 600 to 12,000 years in the past. A second dig was undertaken in 1987. (Courtesy of Dr. Robert Cartier.)

**Discovery of the Crescent.** One of the most unexpected discoveries to be uncovered from the 1983 archaeological dig was the Eccentric Crescent. Made from chert and an estimated 7,000 years old, the crescent-shaped stone is a believed to have been used as a cutting tool. Only 125 of these tools have been found in the United States. The discovery of the crescent caused considerable excitement among the participants and supplied additional support for the importance of the excavation. (Courtesy of Dr. Robert Cartier.)

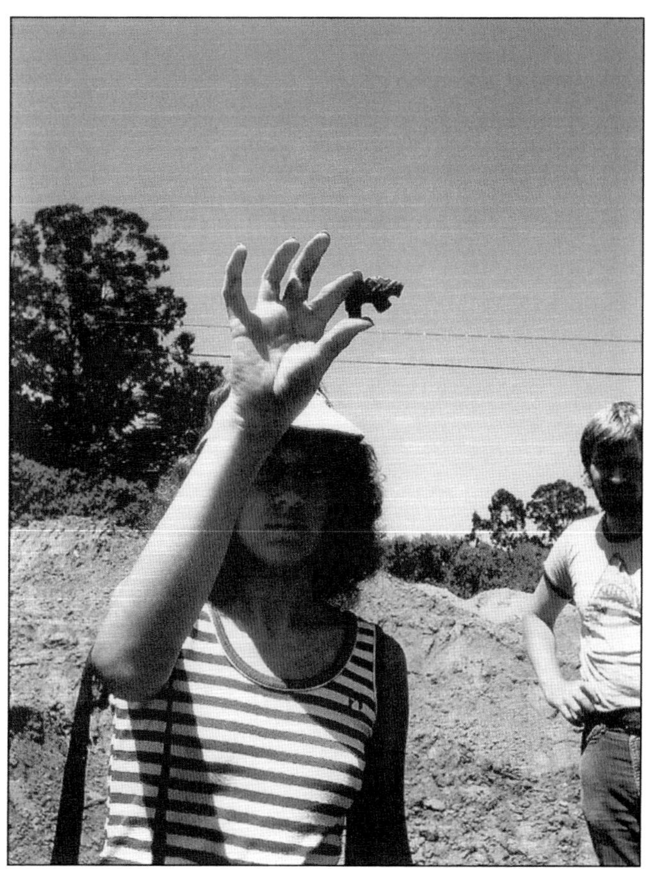

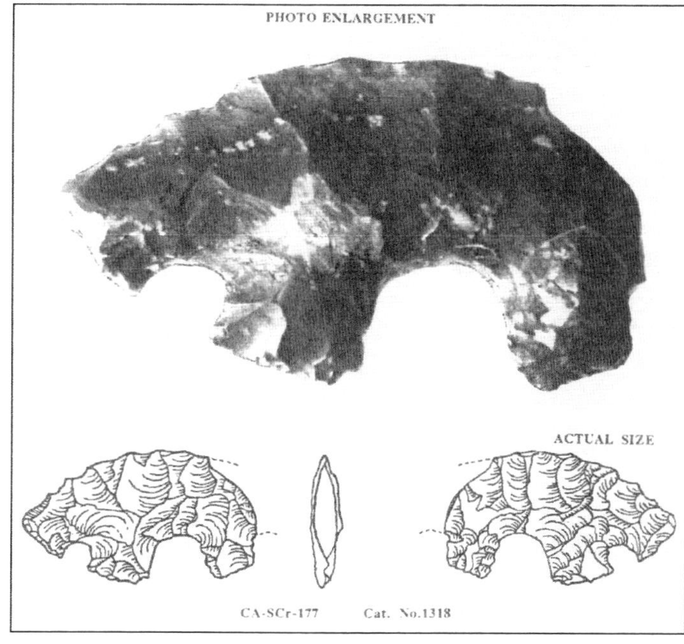


**The Eccentric Crescent.** Despite the presence of a large amount of artifacts, including spear points, knives, scrapers, and bifaces, no bones, shells, or teeth were found, perhaps due to the acidic soil of the area or the theory that the site was used only as a semipermanent campground with burial elsewhere. (Courtesy of Dr. Robert Cartier.)

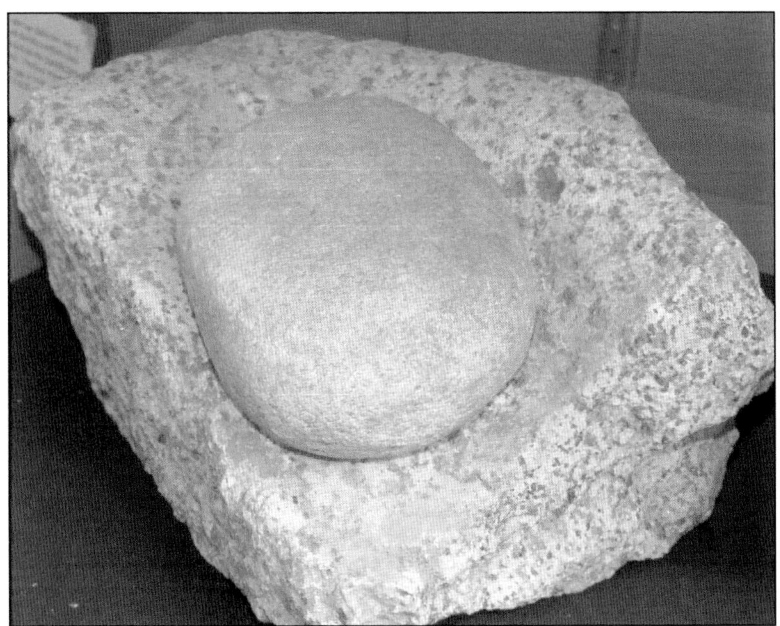

**GROUNDSTONE.** This artifact was found at the city hall site, officially known as CA-SCR-17. Well-compacted layers of earth aided in the preservation and identification of the artifacts. A display of some of the artifacts, along with descriptive explanations, can be viewed at the Scotts Valley City Hall. (Photograph by the author.)

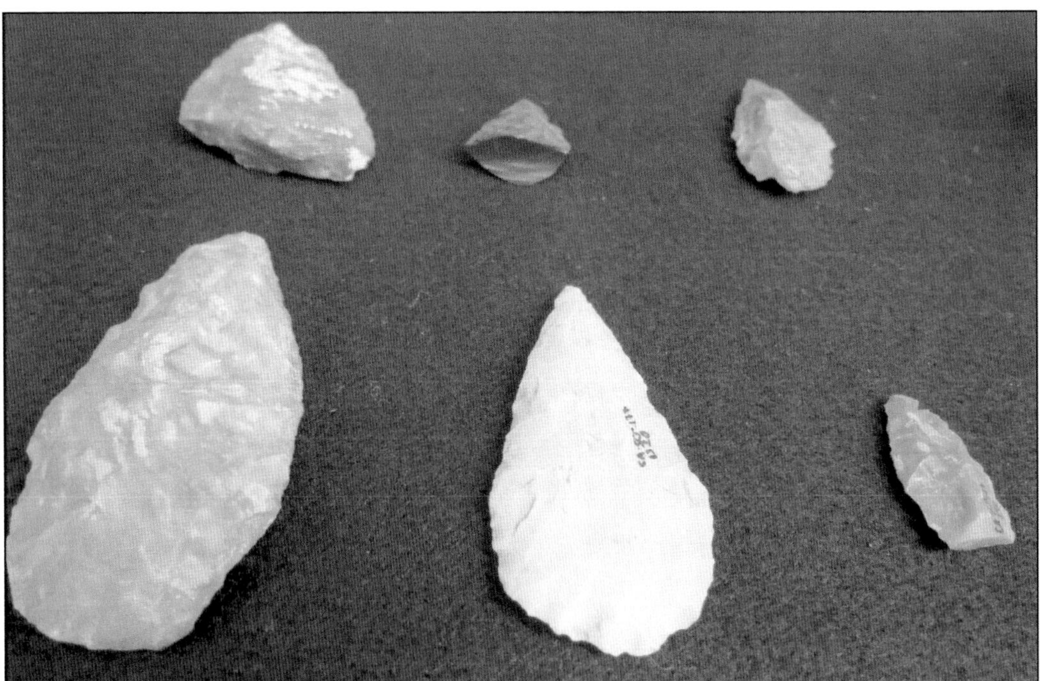

**DART, SPEAR, OR JABBING STICK POINTS.** Leaf-shaped bifaces, side-notched bifaces, an eccentric crescent, and quarry blanks were found at the city hall site. Analysis of the obsidian found indicates the Ohlone had a wide range of trading relationships, from Northern California to Nevada. Prior to Spanish contact, the native population was estimated at 7,000 to 10,000 people, with approximately 40 independent tribelets and 8 to 12 different yet related cultures and languages. This photograph shows a Scotts Valley City Hall exhibit. (Photograph by the author.)

## *Two*

# Hiram Scott's Valley

In the late 1700s, exploration and expansionary interests by European nations brought about permanent changes to the traditional Ohlone way of life. Although explorer Sebastián Vizcaíno had mapped most of the California coast in 1602, little was known of the regions north of Monterey. Spain, wanting to guard against competing British and Russian interests, sent four exploration parties to Alta California in 1769. Gaspar de Portolá and his men reached the Ohlone village of Chatu-Mu in present-day Santa Cruz on October 18, 1769. Portolá named the San Lorenzo River in honor of St. Lawrence and the rolling hills above the river Santa Cruz or Holy Cross. Soon after, many other people would follow, including military men, mission padres, vaqueros, fur trappers, hunters, frontiersmen, and foreign settlers from Mexico, Spain, the United States, England, and France.

Established by the Spanish government on February 2, 1797, the Villa Branciforte was located on a bluff above the San Lorenzo River. Intended to be a villa or soldier-settler community, it was one of only three nonchurch Spanish settlements established in California, the others being San José and Los Angeles. The settlement grew slowly as it struggled with problems of location, competition for land and labor with Mission Santa Cruz, a smallpox epidemic, and civil unrest. With the secularization of the Santa Cruz Mission in 1834, the Spanish government granted more than 150,000 acres of former church lands to private citizens as ranchos. Over time, Americans and other European immigrants came to own most of the former mission and Mexican lands. As more settlers arrived, the once vast and bountiful homeland of the Ohlone would be transformed into cities and towns with lumber mills, tanneries, farms, dairies, ranches, schools, businesses, and churches.

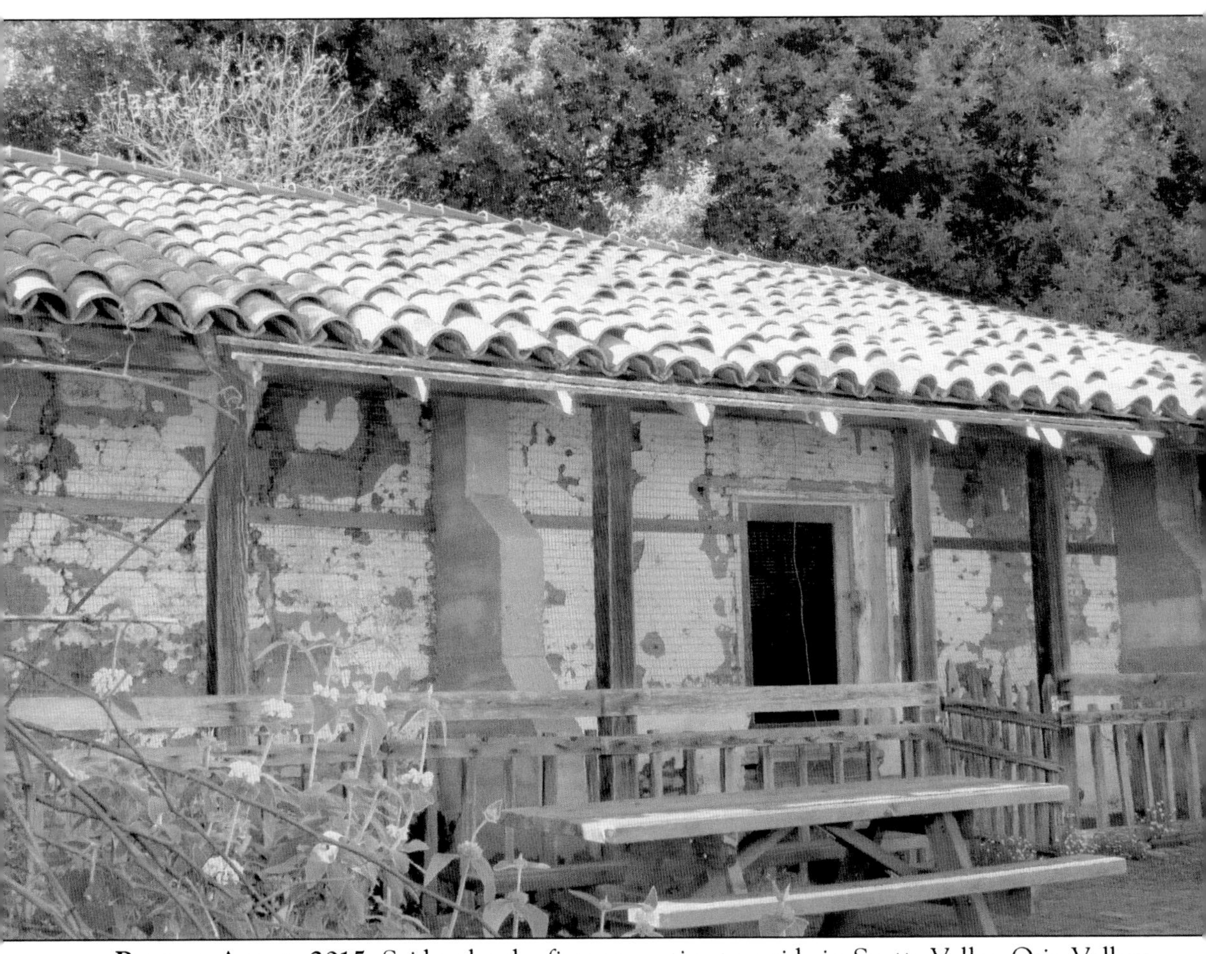

**Bolcoff Adobe, 2015.** Said to be the first nonnative to reside in Scotts Valley, Osip Volkov was born in a small seaport on the Russian peninsula of Kamchatka sometime between 1794 and 1798. In 1815, he jumped ship along the Monterey coast and found work as an interpreter and business agent for Spanish governor Pablo Vicente de Solá. Converting to the Catholic faith in 1817, El Ruso, or "the Russian," as he was also known, was given the Spanish name José Antonio Bolcoff. In 1822, he married María Candida Castro, the 14-year-old daughter of a prominent Villa de Branciforte family. Over time, Candida's father, Don Joaquin Castro, and his family would eventually become the recipient of eight major land grants in Santa Cruz County, including Aptos, Soquel, San Andres, Rodeo Gulch, and Refugio (north coast). In 1833, Bolcoff was granted the 4,437-acre San Agustin Rancho and the Zayante Rancho. The San Agustin Rancho, which includes most of present-day Scotts Valley, extended north from the Rancho La Carbonero to the top of Graham Ridge, east from the San Lorenzo River to Redwood Drive, then north and east to Canham and Vine Hill Roads. Bolcoff and his wife, Candida, along with her two sisters, María Jacinta and María de los Angeles, lived in an adobe home believed to have been located on an old Indian trail near the present-day King's Village Shopping Center. On January 14, 1839, Bolcoff, who had other more profitable business interests, relinquished his interest to the San Agustin Rancho for $400 to Joseph Ladd Majors, who was now both his godson and brother-in-law, and was later granted the nearby 12,147-acre Rancho Refugio. In 1866, Bolcoff died at the Castro Rancho San Andres in Watsonville having lost his Rancho Rufugio because of debts. Bolcoff's adobe, shown here, is now part of the Wilder Ranch State Park, located just north of Santa Cruz city limits. (Photograph by the author.)

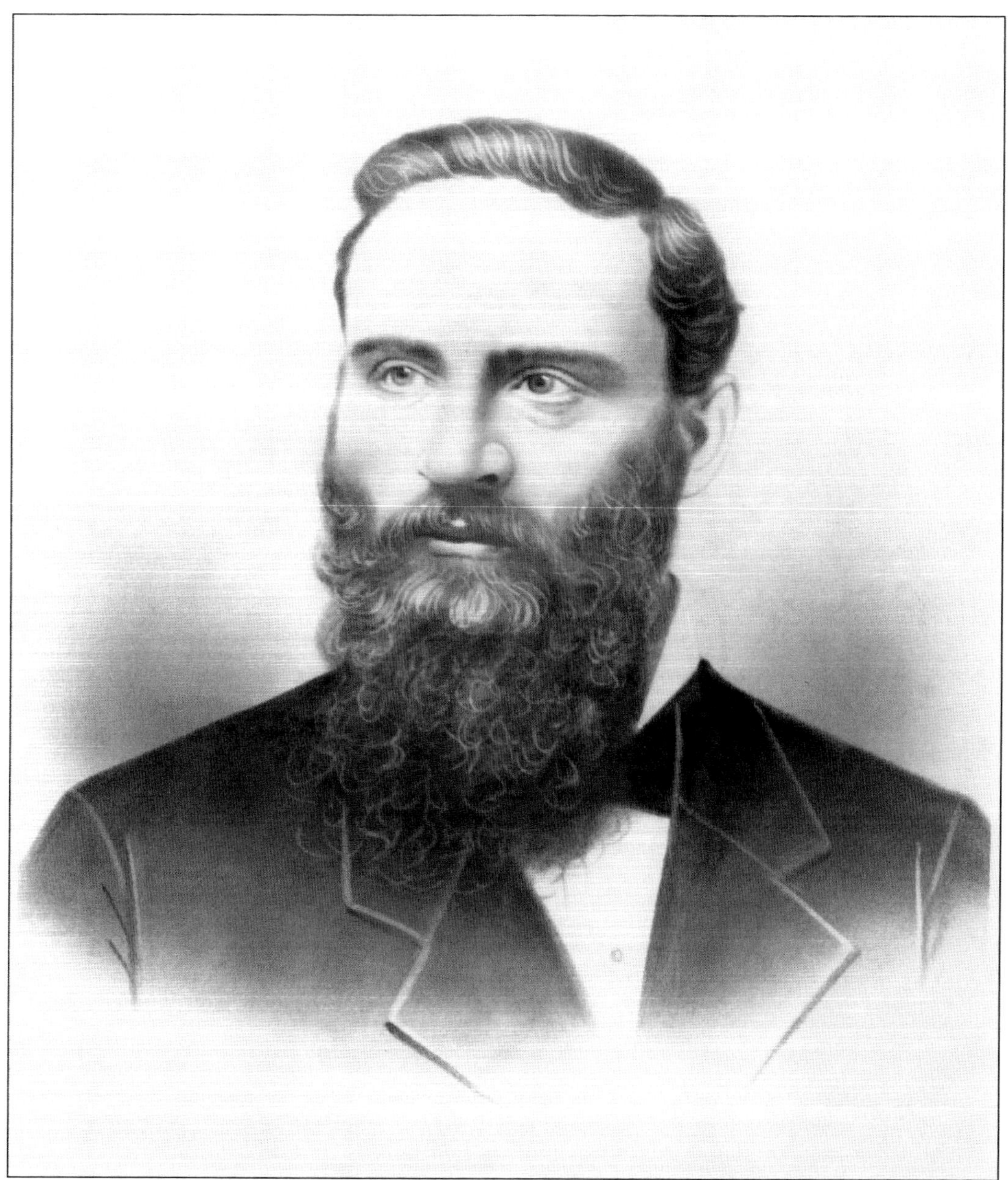

**Joseph Ladd Majors.** Born in 1806 in Bell Buckle, Bedford County, Tennessee, Joseph Ladd Majors came to California along the Santa Fe Trail and arrived in 1834, along with a group of other frontiersmen. Like Bolcoff, Majors became a naturalized Mexican citizen in 1838, taking the name Juan José Crisostomo Machos. In 1839, he married María de los Angeles Castro, sister to Candida Castro Bolcoff. In addition to raising cattle, opening a distillery, and growing wheat, Majors built one of the first nonchurch gristmills in California, believed to be located in the present-day Sky Park area. In 1852, Majors sold the San Agustin Rancho to Hiram Daniel Scott. The droughts of 1863 and 1864 greatly reduced Majors's wealth, and he died almost penniless in 1868. His widow, María de los Angeles Castro, slowly lost her large land holdings through lawsuits and eventually received county assistance before dying in 1903. (Courtesy of the Santa Cruz Museum of Art and History.)

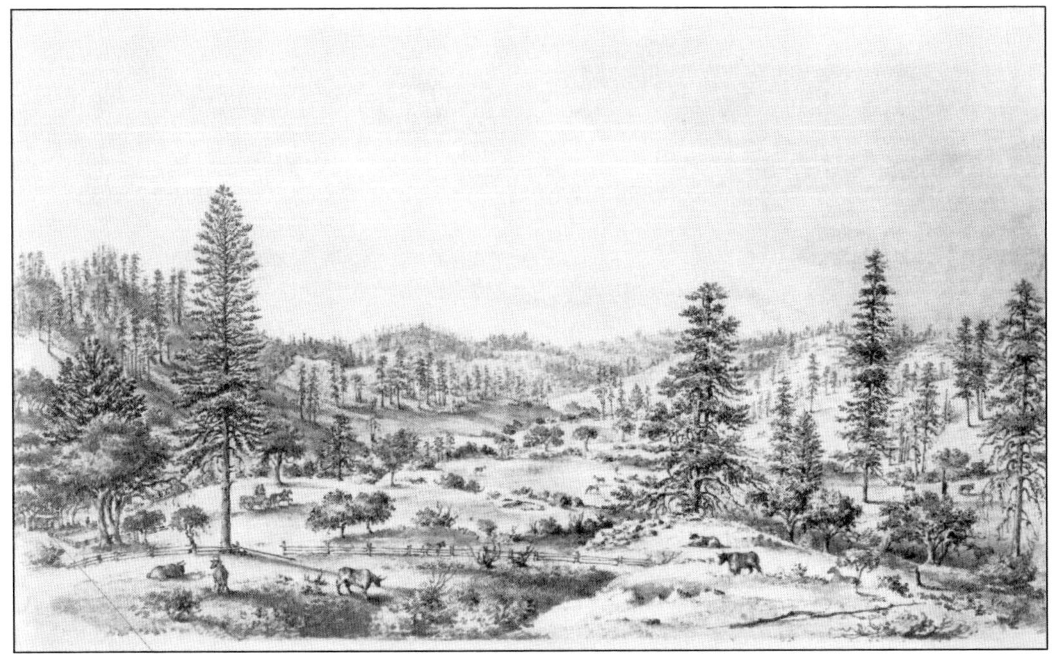

**Rancho Zayante.** In 1836, Isaac Graham led a group of foreigners in a revolt against then California governor Nicolás Gutíerrez. With the help of his friend Majors, Graham was able to purchase the 2,658-acre Rancho Zayante near present-day Felton. There, he established a distillery and sawmill. This photograph is from *Vischer's Pictorial of California: Sixty Views of Californian Landscape* by Edward Vischer, 1863. (Courtesy of Special Collections, Claremont College Library, Claremont, California.)

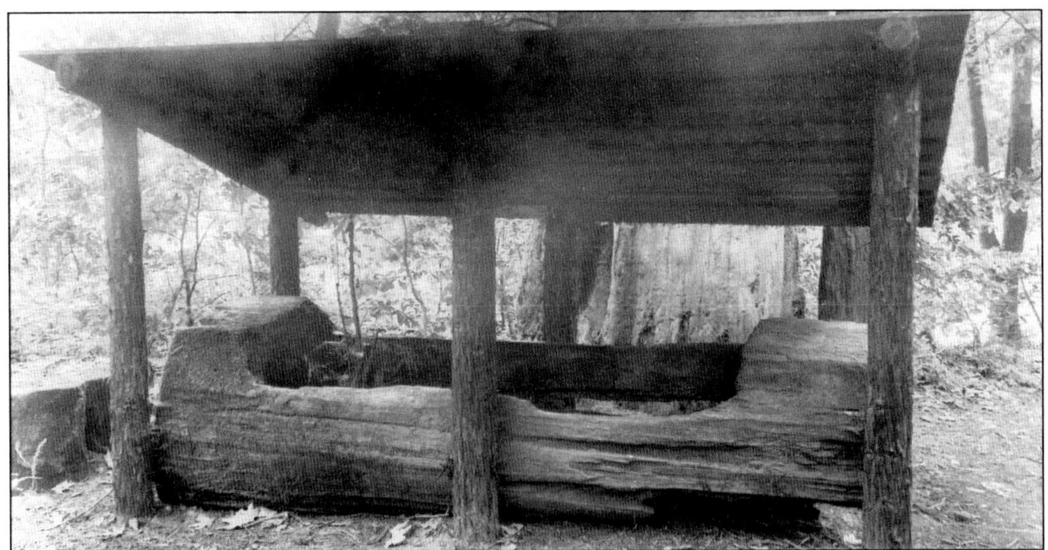

**Redwood Tanning Vat.** Leather tanning became one of the first commercial activities in Santa Cruz County because of the abundant supply of raw animal hides and tanbark from the native tan oak tree. Due to the high demand for shoes, saddles, and other leather goods, four local tanneries produced an estimated 10,000 hides in 1857. (Author's collection.)

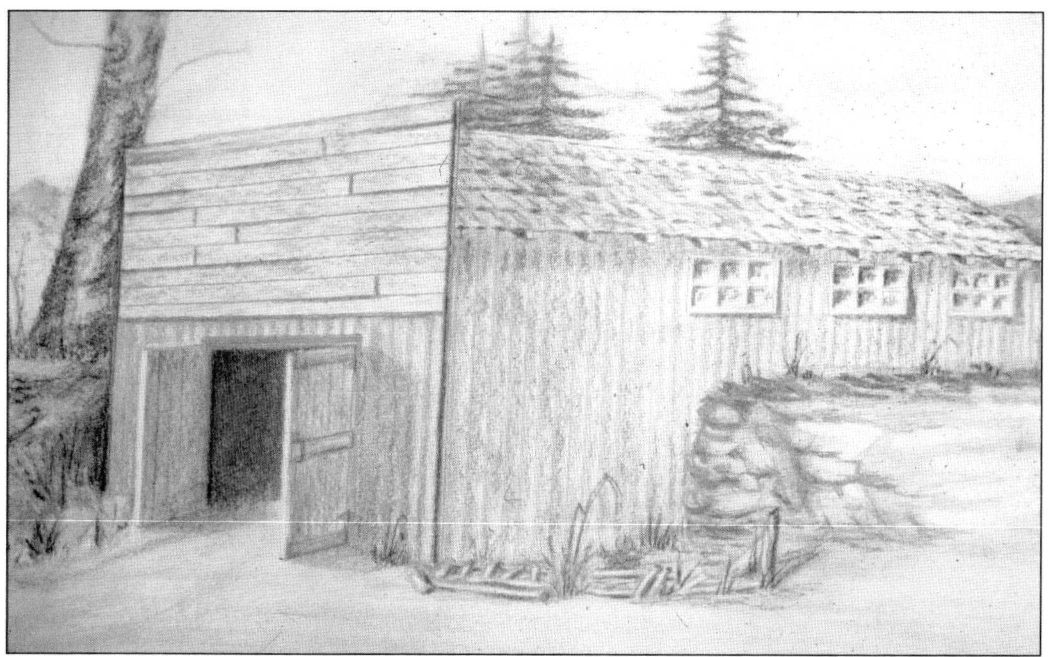

**Wagner, Anderson & Ziegler Tannery.** In 1843, Paul Sweet, a former Rhode Island sailor, was the second operator of one of the first commercial tanneries in California, located on Majors's land in today's Lockhart Gulch–Mount Hermon area. The tannery remained in operation until 1873. (Sketch by Agnes K. Lewis, courtesy of Charlene Duval.)

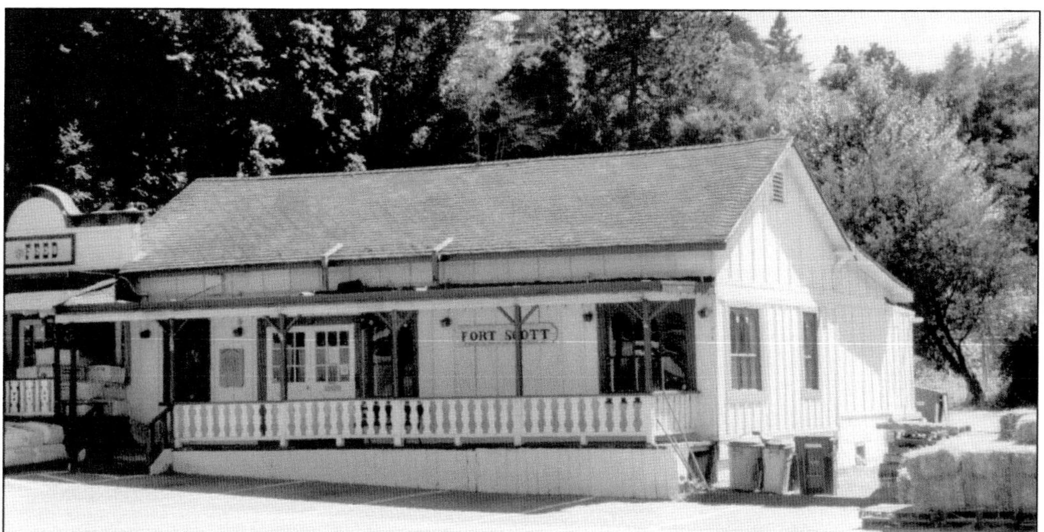


**Tannery Bunkhouse.** Remodeled, expanded, and twice relocated, the former bunkhouse went through a variety of owners and uses. The Locke family used the building as a residence until completion of their Victorian mansion. Sold to the Graham family in 1928, the building was the only tannery structure not destroyed in the Great Fire of 1929. New owners remodeled the building, which had been moved in 1969, into Cassidy's Pizza Parlor, part of the Pinnacle Pass Shopping Center at 75 Mount Hermon Road. Various businesses have since operated at this location. (Courtesy of Catherine Seapy.)

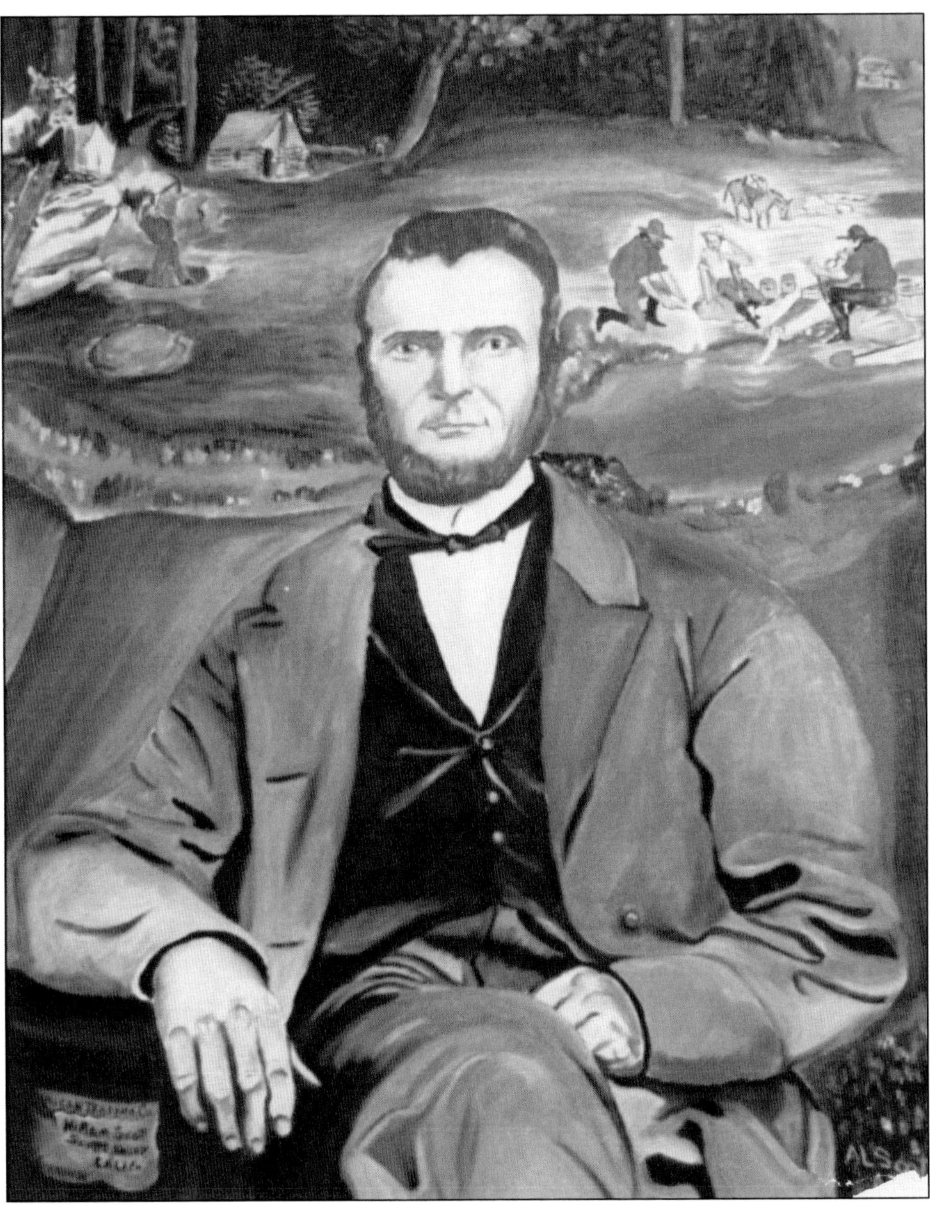

**Hiram Daniel Scott.** First noted in court records of 1642, the earliest North American Scotts resided in the Massachusetts Bay Colony of Cambridge. The Scotts were farmers, homebuilders, sawmill owners, and shipbuilders. One unfortunate ancestor, Margaret Stevenson Scott, was accused of witchcraft and hung in the Salem Witch Trials of 1692. In Maine, Captain Scott's family owned two schooners, the *Scott* and the *Hiram*. These schooners carried lumber, salt fish, boxboards, and barrel staves to the West Indies and returned with sugar, rum, and molasses. Hiram Scott was one of the lucky few prospectors who found gold in California. Born in Pittston, Maine, on January 29, 1822, Hiram Daniel Scott became a sailor. While off the coast of Monterey in 1846, he jumped ship and made his way to Santa Cruz. When news of John Marshall's discovery of gold at Sutter's Mill reached Santa Cruz, he quit his shipbuilding job and set out for the Sierra goldfields. This portrait of Hiram Scott was painted by Alfred Scott, a direct descendant of Hiram. (Courtesy of the Leisz family.)

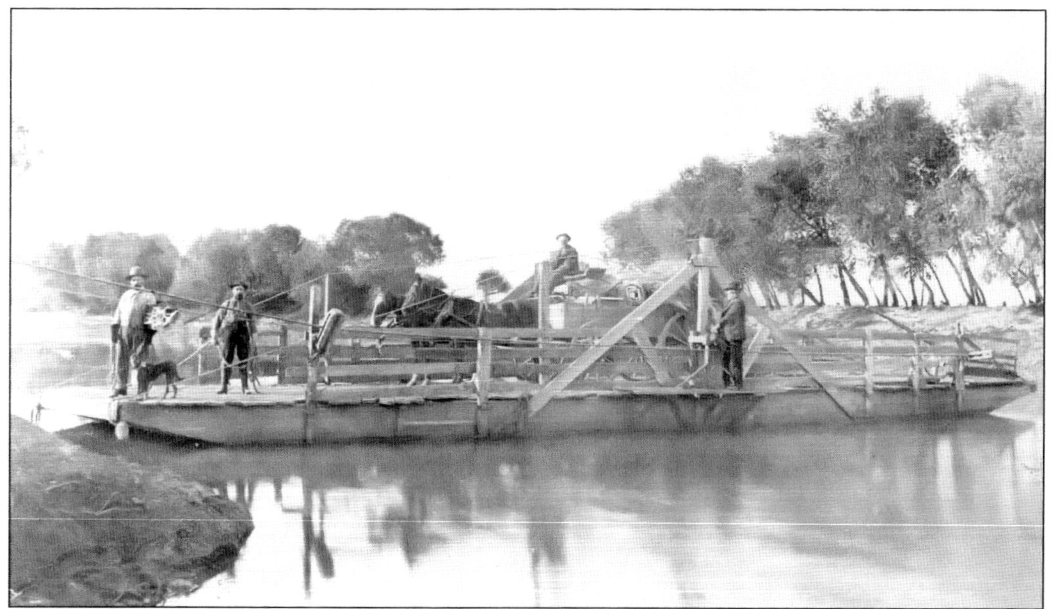

**River Ferry (Kingston).** No actual records can be found of the location of Scott's gold strike, but it is believed to have been near Placerville. Scott invested his mining profits to become co-owner in a ferry service across the San Joaquin River, near the present-day Mossdale Landing. During the Gold Rush, the ferry crossing was heavily used, with receipts ranging from $500 to $1,000 a day. This photograph was taken around 1850. (Courtesy of William Seacrest Sr.)

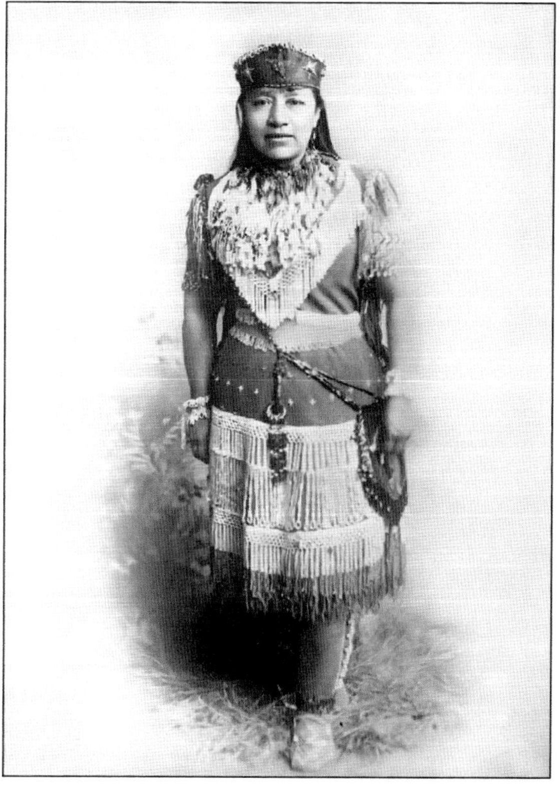

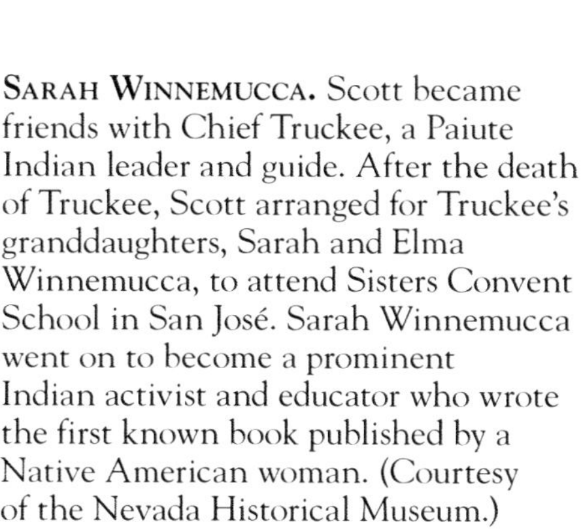

**Sarah Winnemucca.** Scott became friends with Chief Truckee, a Paiute Indian leader and guide. After the death of Truckee, Scott arranged for Truckee's granddaughters, Sarah and Elma Winnemucca, to attend Sisters Convent School in San José. Sarah Winnemucca went on to become a prominent Indian activist and educator who wrote the first known book published by a Native American woman. (Courtesy of the Nevada Historical Museum.)

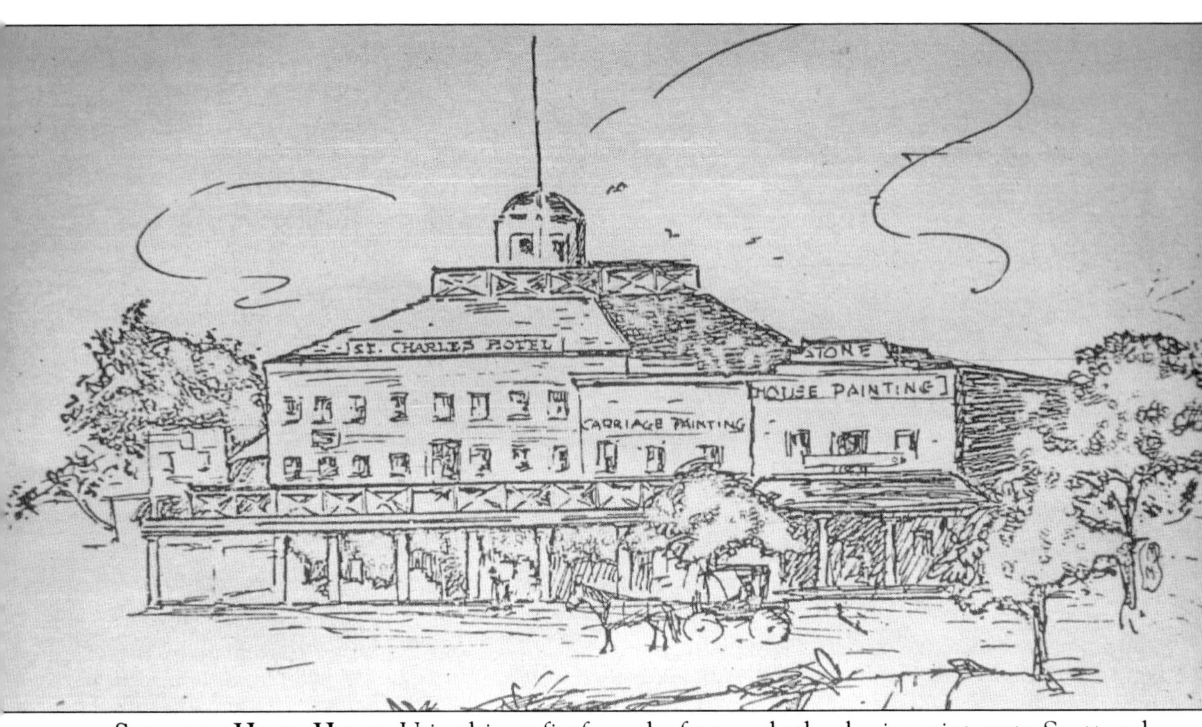


**Stockton House Hotel.** Using his profits from the ferry and other business interests, Scott and his partners built one of the earliest hotels in Stockton. Finished in 1850 at a cost of $87,000, the hotel contained 70 rooms. The first floor had a bar, reading room, dining room, and kitchen. The second story contained the ladies' parlor and bedrooms. The third floor, for men only, had no interior walls and no heat, with only bunks and cots for furnishings. Typical of the time, the third story also had its own stairway for direct access to the street. This hotel was later renamed the St. Charles, which burned to the ground in 1871. In the summer of 1850, Scott used his accumulated wealth to make his biggest purchase yet. Using the installment plan with an initial payment of $5,000, he agreed to pay Joseph Majors $20,000 for the 4,447-acre Rancho San Agustin. In modern-day equivalencies, the 1850s sum of $20,000 would equal $4.5 to $9.5 million. (Courtesy of Charlene Duval.)

**Daniel Scott, c. 1845.** Captain Daniel Scott II, Hiram's father, was a sea captain, farmer, and shipbuilder in Pittston, Maine. His first marriage to Ruth Cumming produced nine children, of which Hiram was the eldest. After his first wife passed away, Daniel II married Nancy Parcher. When news of Hiram's good fortune reached Maine, most of the Scott family eventually sold their farms and businesses and joined him in California. (Courtesy of the Leisz family.)

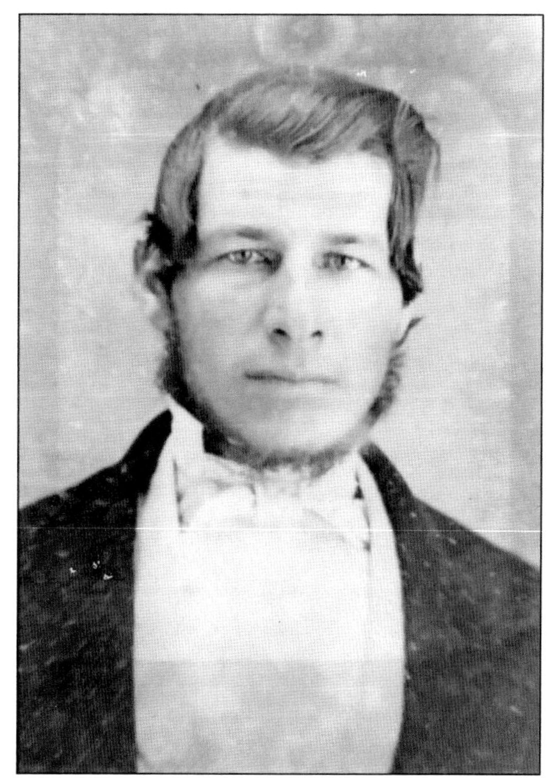

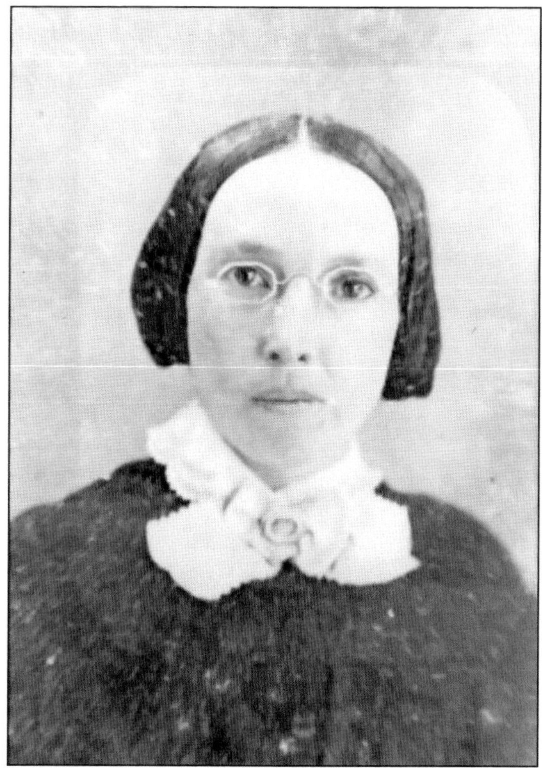

**Nancy Parcher Scott, c. 1845.** George Edwin Scott was the first family member to follow Hiram, and eventually the entire Scott family, except for one married sister, made the long sea journey to California. Daniel served as a Santa Cruz County supervisor in 1857 and died from cancer in 1867. At age 17, Henry Parcher Scott, Nancy and Daniel's youngest son, died in 1870 and was interred next to his father at Evergreen Cemetery. (Courtesy of the Leisz family.)

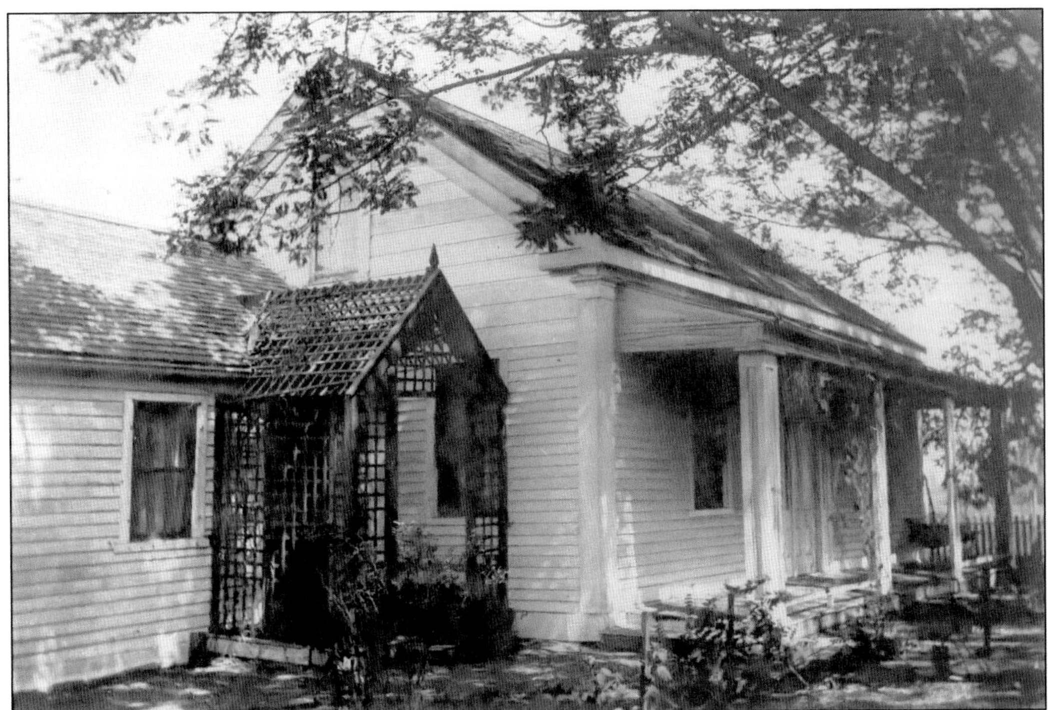

**The Scott House.** In 1853, Hiram began building what is now the Scott House, believed to be the first wood home in Scotts Valley. The Scott men built the New England–style home using hand-hewn lumber and joinery techniques from shipbuilding. Taken in 1912, this is the earliest-known photograph of the Scott House. (Photograph by Ruby Strong, courtesy of SVHS.)

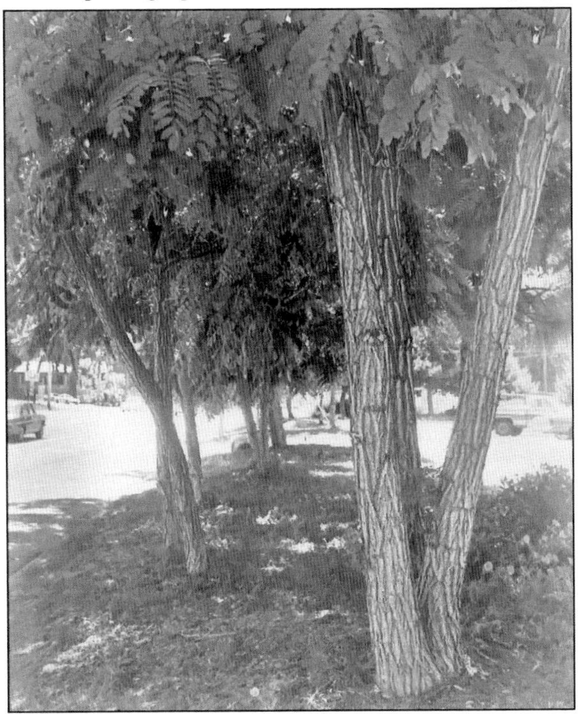

**Scott Locust Trees.** Hiram Scott never permanently resided in the Scott House but built the home for his father's family. Originally located on Scotts Valley Drive, the house was moved to its current location near city hall in 1936 due to the widening of the Los Gatos–Santa Cruz Highway. The locust trees planted by the Scotts can still be seen along Scotts Valley Drive. (Courtesy of the Santa Cruz Museum of Art and History.)

**Agnes Cumming Scott, c. 1859.** Originally from Canada, Agnes Cumming came to California in 1859 to join her sister. Regarded as beautiful and refined, Agnes made her living as a tailor and dressmaker. In 1861, Agnes and Hiram were married in San José and lived for two years on the east side of South Navarra Drive in north Scotts Valley (near the present-day Montessori school). The house burned to the ground in 1924. (Courtesy of the Leisz family.)

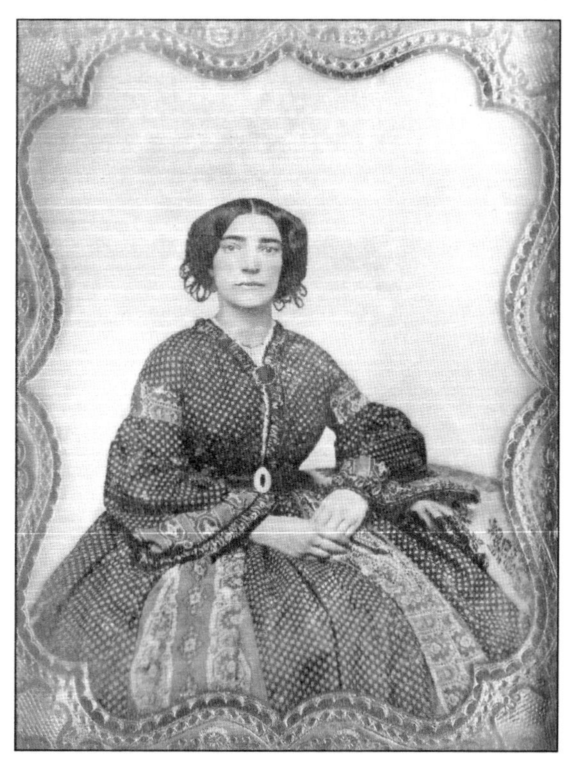

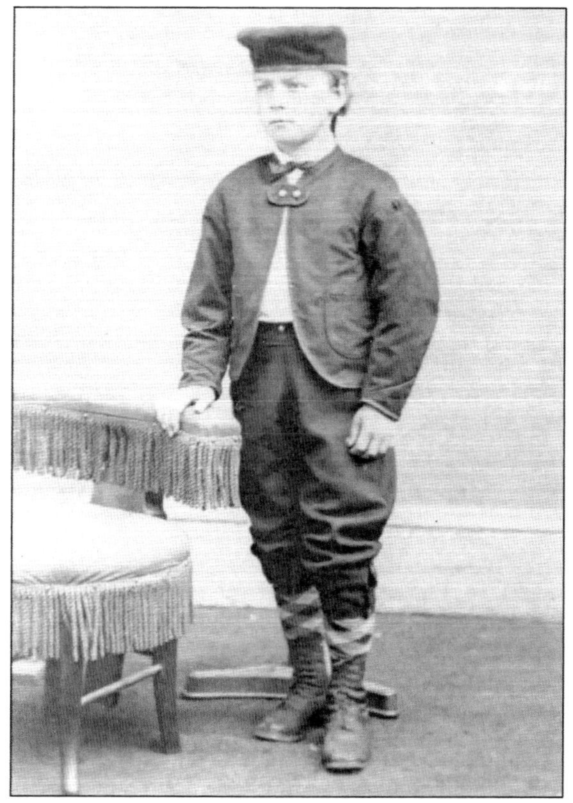

**William Nelson Scott.** While living in Scotts Valley, Agnes and Hiram's eldest child, William "Willie" Nelson, was born in 1862. As an adult, William and his family lived in the company town of Loma Prieta along Aptos Creek, where he worked at the sawmill. Sadly, one son, Homer Scott, also known as "Nibs," drowned after falling into the millpond. (Courtesy of the Leisz family.)

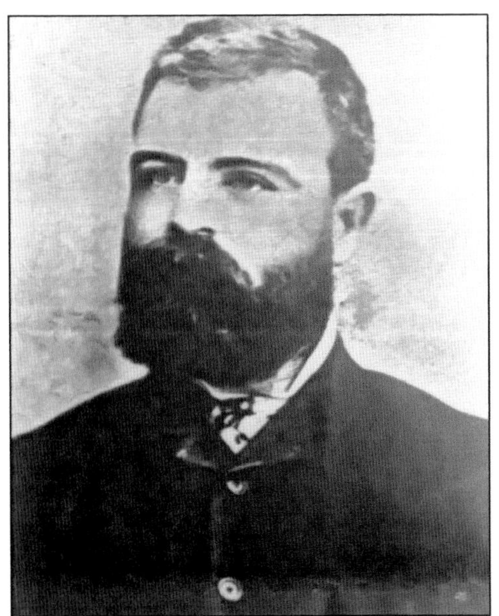

**Mountain Charlie.** In 1858, Scott and Charles McKiernan won a contract to construct a stagecoach road from Scotts Valley to the Summit for $6,000. A doctor reportedly used a metal plate (also reported to be two Mexican silver pesos) to repair a large hole in the skull of Charles Henry "Mountain Charlie" McKiernan, who was severely mauled by a bear. This photograph was taken prior to the bear fight. (Courtesy of the Santa Cruz Museum of Art and History.)

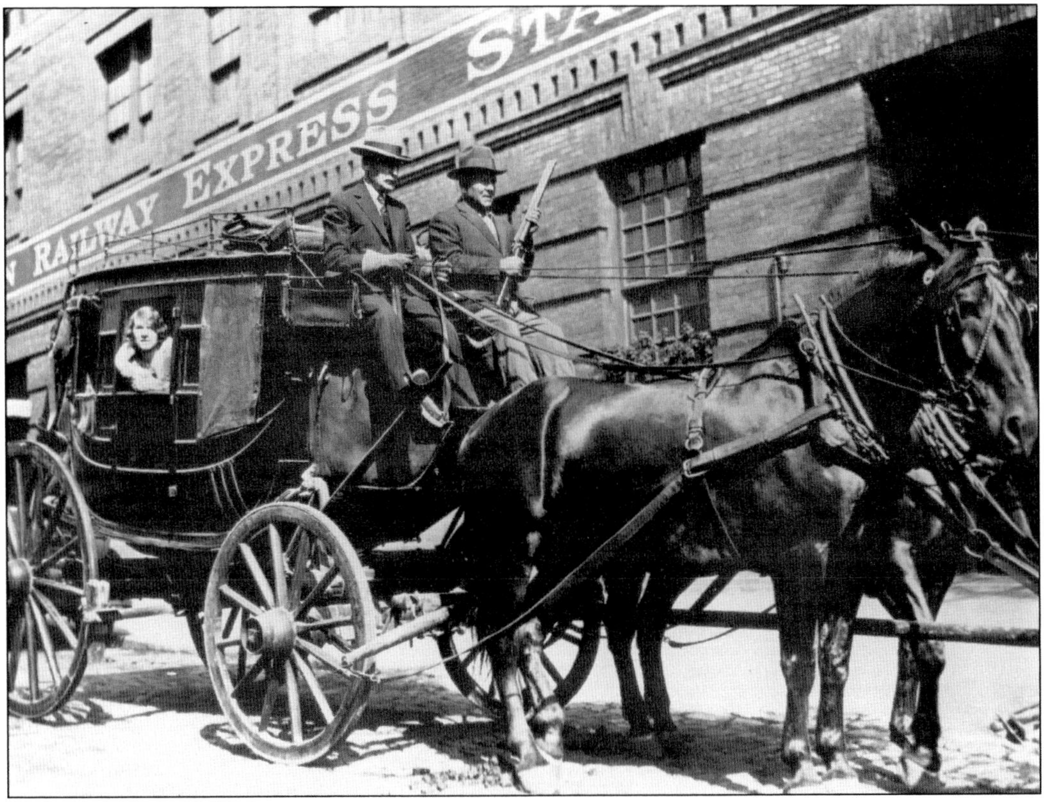

**Stagecoach.** Rediscovered after 50 years in storage, the Los Gatos–Santa Cruz stagecoach can now be seen on display at the Wells Fargo History Museum in San Francisco. Here, George Lewis Colgrove, longtime stagecoach driver, came out of retirement in 1928 to deliver the wagon to the museum. The other two passengers are unidentified. (Courtesy of the Wells Fargo Corporate Archives.)

**ADVERTISEMENT.** In order to raise additional capital to invest in his mining business, Scott sold the major remaining portion of his Scotts Valley property (1,114 acres) to Joseph Errington for $6,750 in 1865. Shown here is the advertisement taken from a local paper dated February 18, 1865. (Author's collection.)

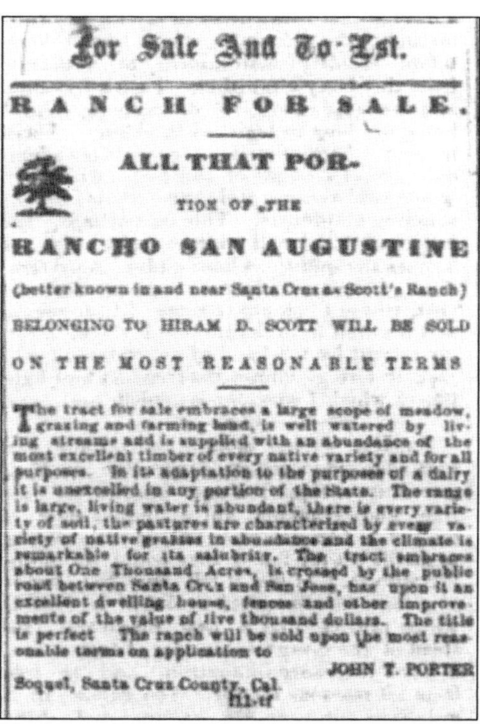

For Sale And To Let.

RANCH FOR SALE.

ALL THAT PORTION OF THE

RANCHO SAN AUGUSTINE

(better known in and near Santa Cruz as Scott's Ranch)

BELONGING TO HIRAM D. SCOTT WILL BE SOLD

ON THE MOST REASONABLE TERMS

The tract for sale embraces a large scope of meadow, grazing and farming land, is well watered by living streams and is supplied with an abundance of the most excellent timber of every native variety and for all purposes. In its adaptation to the purposes of a dairy it is unexcelled in any portion of the State. The range is large, living water is abundant, there is every variety of soil, the pastures are characterized by every variety of native grasses in abundance and the climate is remarkable for its salubrity. The tract embraces about One Thousand Acres, is crossed by the public road between Santa Cruz and San Jose, has upon it an excellent dwelling house, fences and other improvements of the value of five thousand dollars. The title is perfect. The ranch will be sold upon the most reasonable terms on application to

JOHN T. PORTER

Soquel, Santa Cruz County, Cal.

f11-tf

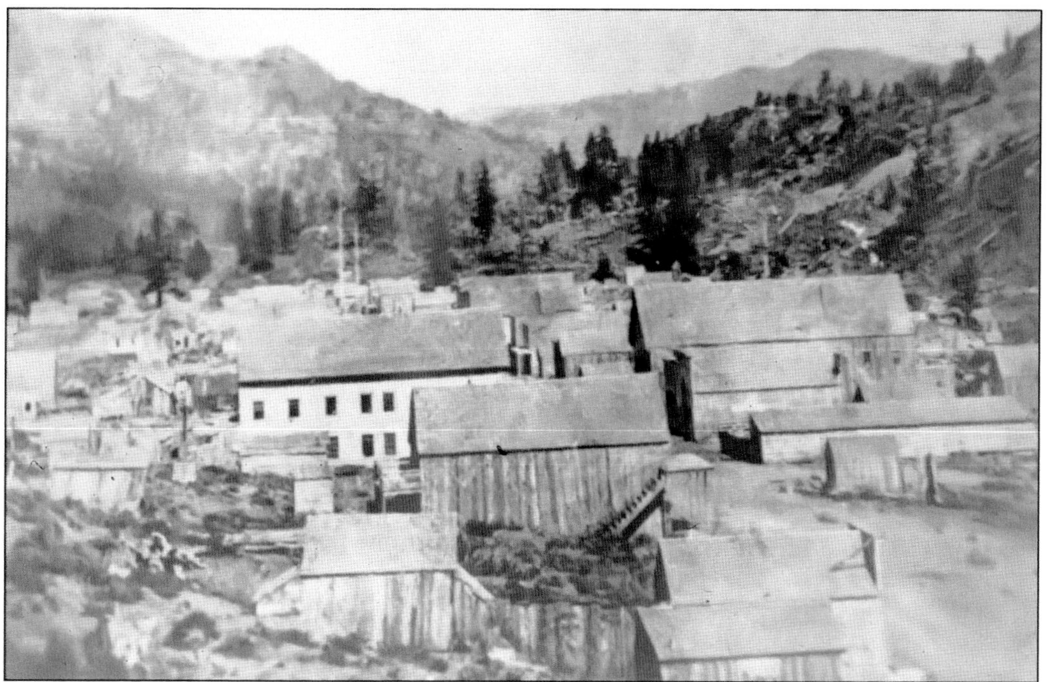

**SILVER MOUNTAIN, 1860S.** Looking to seek another fortune, Scott formed the Eureka Gold and Silver Mining Company at Silver Mountain, Alpine County, (near present-day Ebert's Pass) in 1863. There, he built a new residence for Agnes and Willie, as well as a lodging house. Two daughters, Anna Frances and Nancy Maude, were born at Silver Mountain City. (Courtesy of Charlene Duval.)

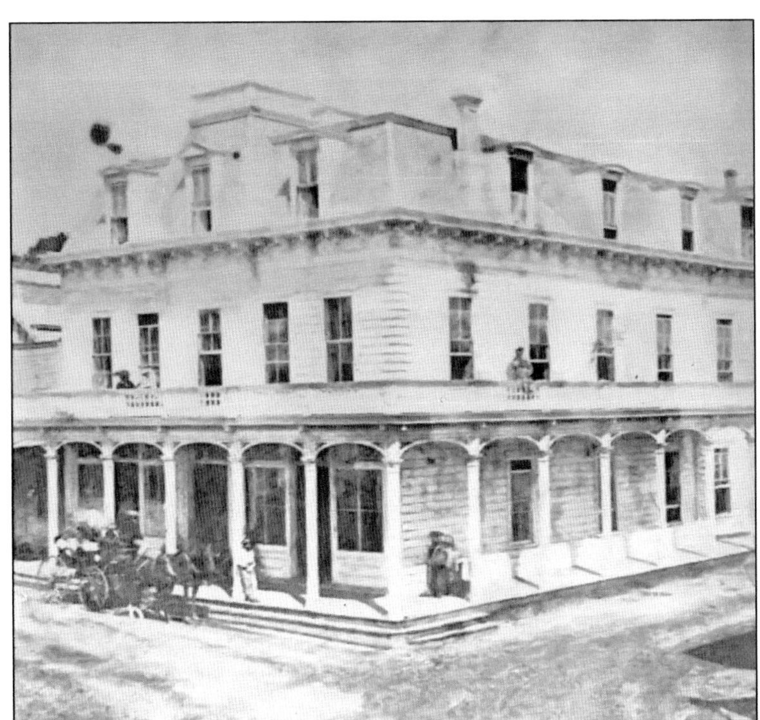

**St. Charles Hotel.** Not finding his fortune in Silver Mountain, Scott and his family returned to Santa Cruz in 1869 and purchased a home. Built of lumber shipped from Maine, the home was one of the oldest in Santa Cruz. Using earnings from mining silver in Nevada, his brother-in-law William Cumming built the St. Charles Hotel at the corner of River and Mission Streets and the Fashion Livery Stable at the corner of Center and Vine Streets. (Courtesy of Charlene Duval.)

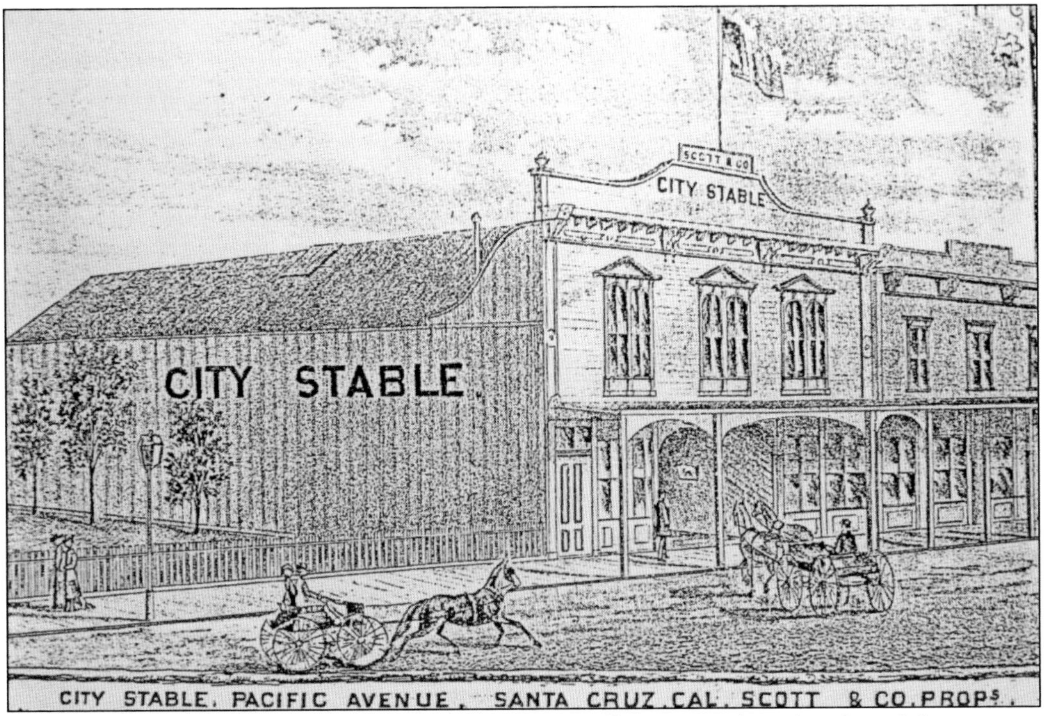

CITY STABLE, PACIFIC AVENUE, SANTA CRUZ CAL. SCOTT & CO. PROPS.

**Scott Livery Stable.** The 1879 *Santa Cruz County Illustrations* describes Scott's business as follows: "Next after a good hotel, the traveler seeks a livery stable. Scott and Co.'s livery has one of the finest fronts on the street of Pacific Avenue, where they are prepared with all sorts of conveyances to please the traveling public." (Author's collection.)

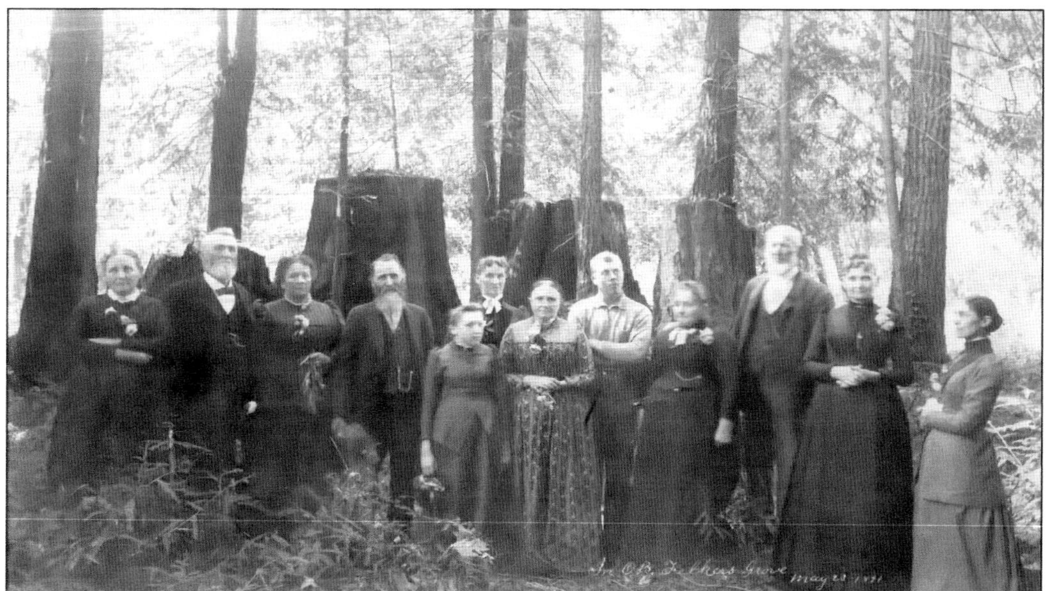

**SCOTT FAMILY PICNIC, C. 1871.** In 1874, the lure of silver in Arizona called to Hiram, but Agnes was unwilling to follow. He deeded the Santa Cruz house to his wife and homesteaded on the southwest side of Phoenix in the Salt River Valley. In 1885, he bought a saloon in Casa Grande, Arizona, renaming it the Fashion Saloon. After being ill for some time, Hiram passed away on March 25, 1886. (Courtesy of SVHS.)

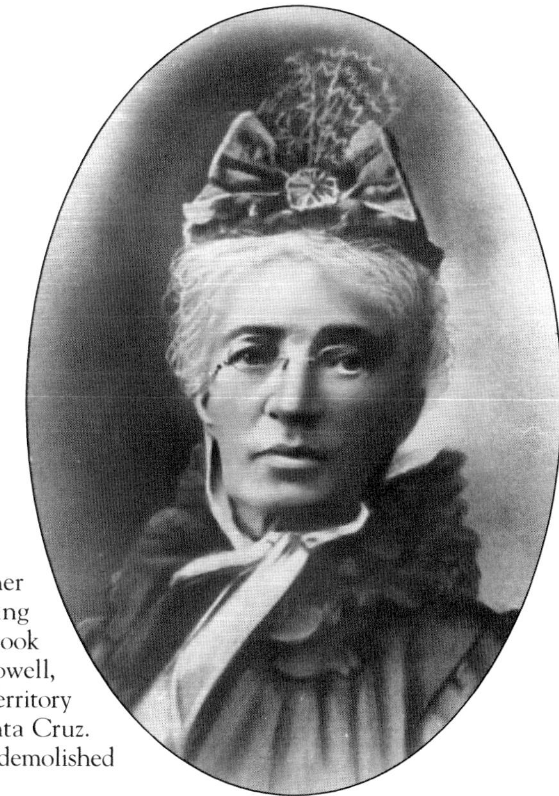

**AGNES SCOTT, C. 1900.** With the death of her husband, Agnes Scott made a living by renting out furnished rooms. The popular children's book *I am Lavina Cumming*, written by Susan Lowell, describes Lavina's journey from the Arizona Territory in 1905 to live with her aunt Agnes in Santa Cruz. Agnes died at the age of 91, and her home was demolished in 1925. (Courtesy of Charlene Duval.)

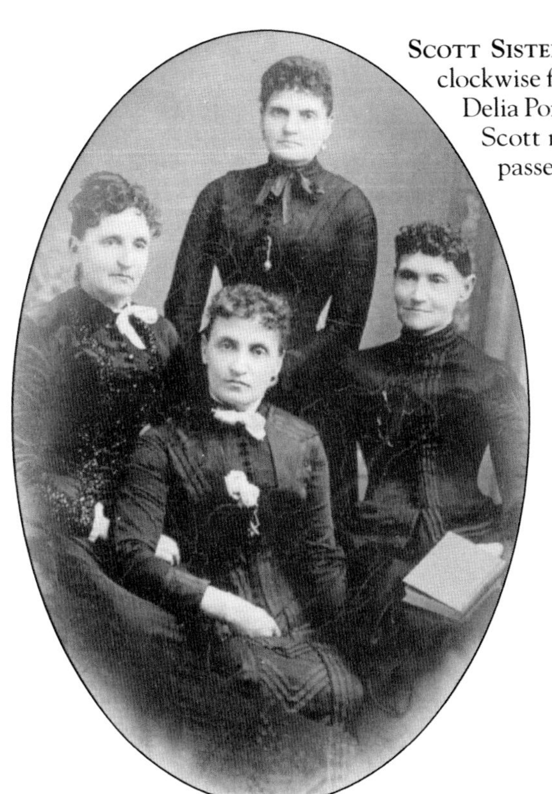

**Scott Sisters.** The four Scott sisters pictured here are, clockwise from top, Carrie Sanborn, Victoria Snow, Ruth Delia Porter, and Sarah Cooper. In 1872, Nancy Parcher Scott made a trip back to Maine to visit family and passed away there. (Courtesy of the Genn family.)

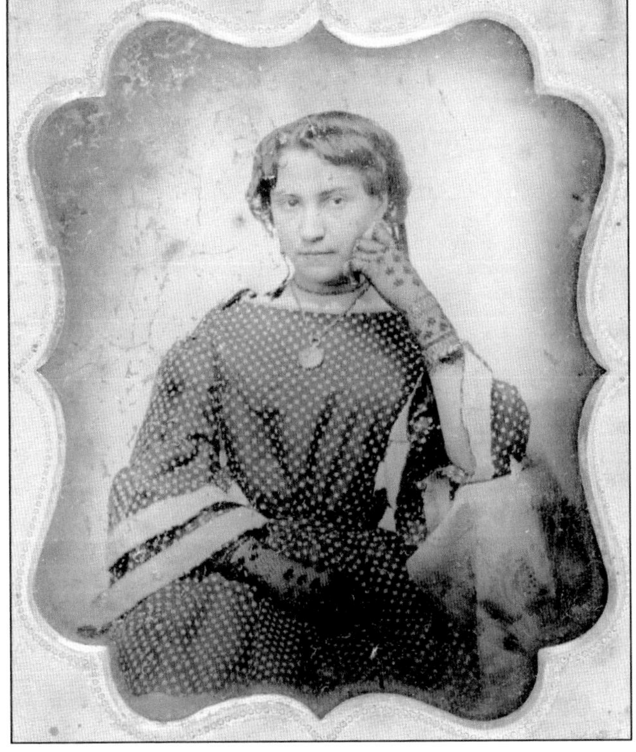

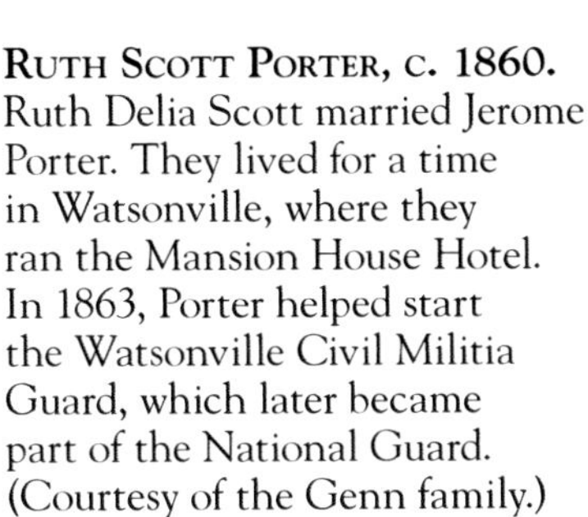

**Ruth Scott Porter, c. 1860.** Ruth Delia Scott married Jerome Porter. They lived for a time in Watsonville, where they ran the Mansion House Hotel. In 1863, Porter helped start the Watsonville Civil Militia Guard, which later became part of the National Guard. (Courtesy of the Genn family.)

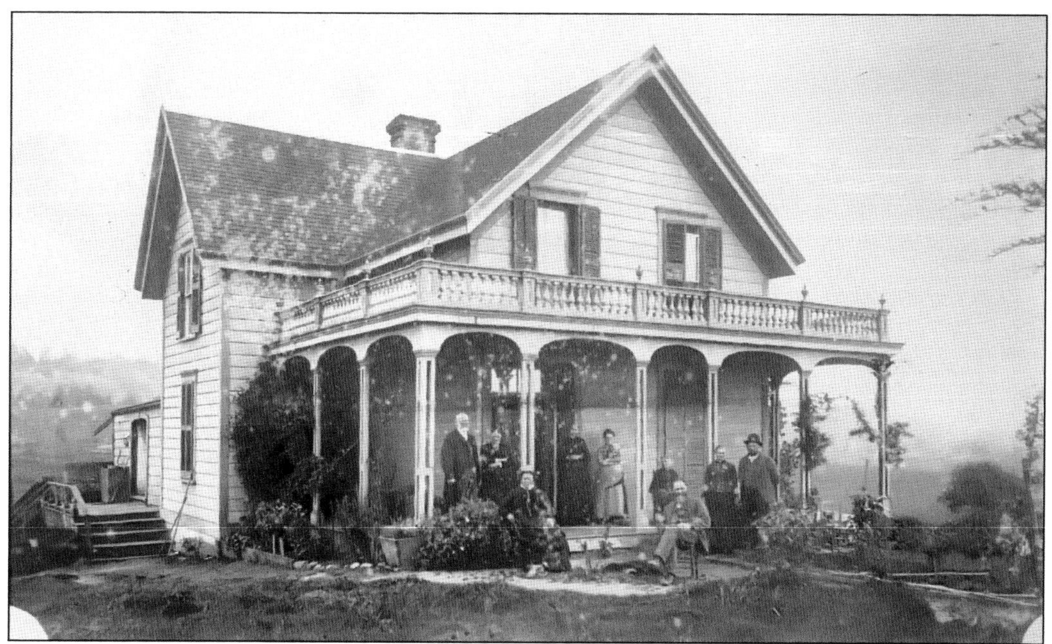

**George Edwin Scott Home, c. 1875.** George Edwin Scott was the only Scott family member to permanently settle in Scotts Valley. In 1859, he purchased a portion of the San Agustin Rancho on the northwest side of the valley (Glenwood High School area) and established a dairy, which remained in operation for many years, passing through several different owners. In 1967, the old Scott home was burned as a practice exercise by the fire department. (Courtesy of SVHS.)

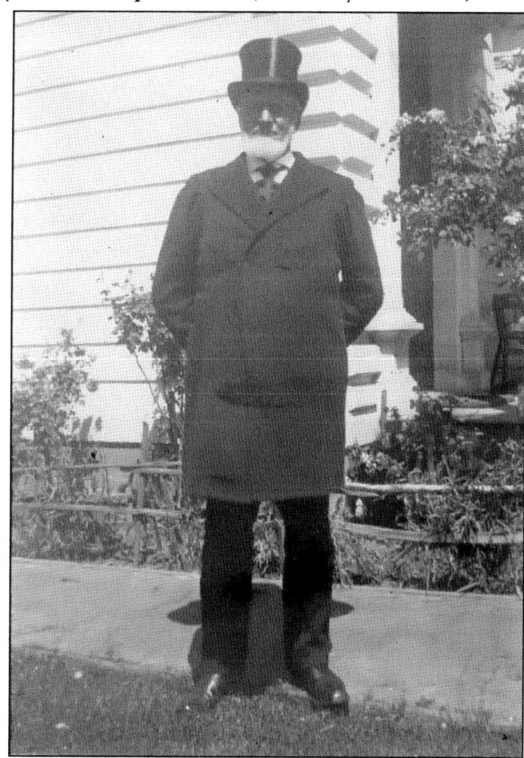

**Joseph Scott.** Hiram's youngest full brother, Joseph Wellington Scott, owned a livery stable, served as chief of police for the city of Santa Cruz from 1884 to 1886, and later co-owned a funeral service. He and his wife, Anna, had two children, Lina and Edna. He died in 1906. (Courtesy of Charlene Duval.)

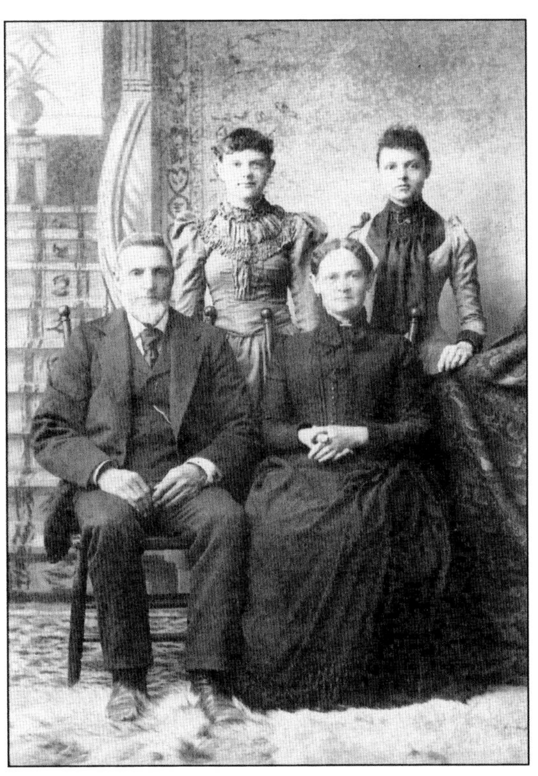

**JOSEPH AND ANNA SCOTT FAMILY, 1891.** Shown seated are Joseph Scott and his wife, Anna. Standing are their two daughters, Lina (left) and Edna. (Courtesy of the Genn family.)

**JOSEPH SCOTT HOUSE, 1902.** The Joseph Scott house was located near present-day Pacific Avenue in Santa Cruz, adjacent to Cinema 9. After her parents and sister died, Edna Scott inherited the house. Efforts were made to save the home, but it was ultimately torn down to make way for a parking lot. (Courtesy of the Genn family.)

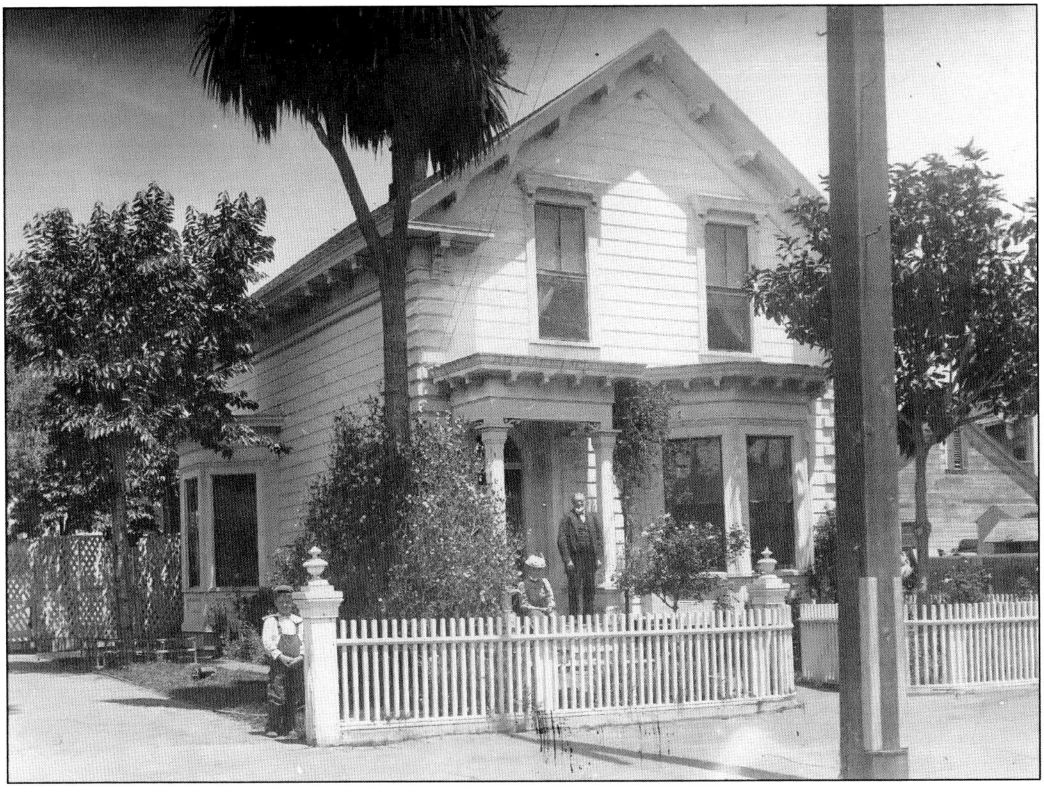

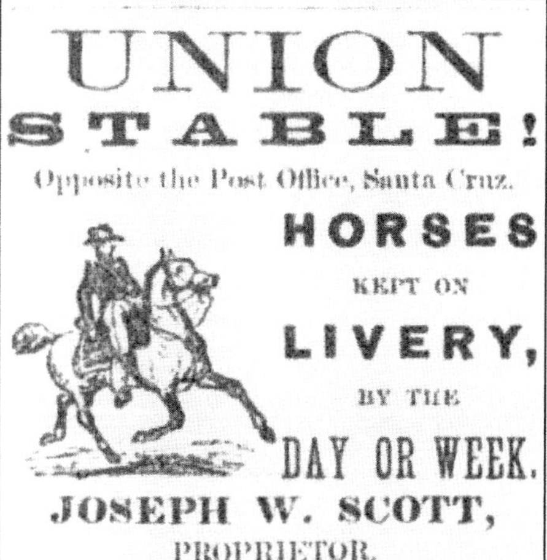


**Union Stables, 1869.** In 1905, Joseph was interviewed about his early days in Scotts Valley and gave this description: "The open lands of the valley were then virgin soil . . . Horses and cattle roamed over the country in a wild state . . . it was not an uncommon sight for those out early in the morning to find a half dozen grizzly bears, feeding from the rank clover. As for quail, they were numberless." (Author's collection.)

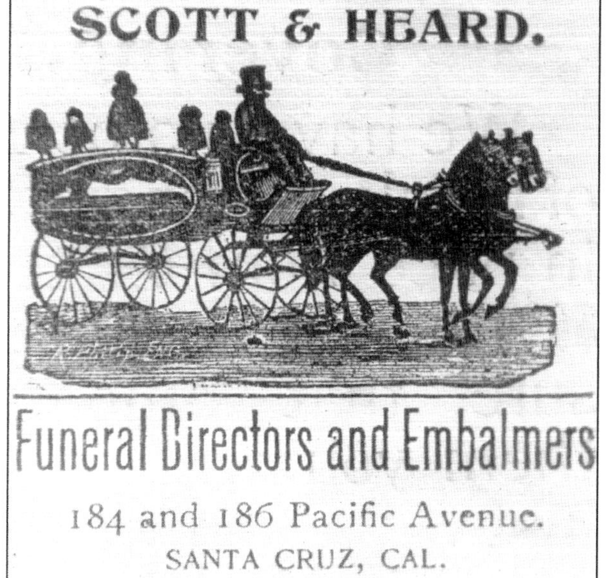


**Scott & Heard.** In addition to operating a livery stable, Joseph Scott owned a funeral parlor in Santa Cruz for many years. (Courtesy of Charlene Duval.)

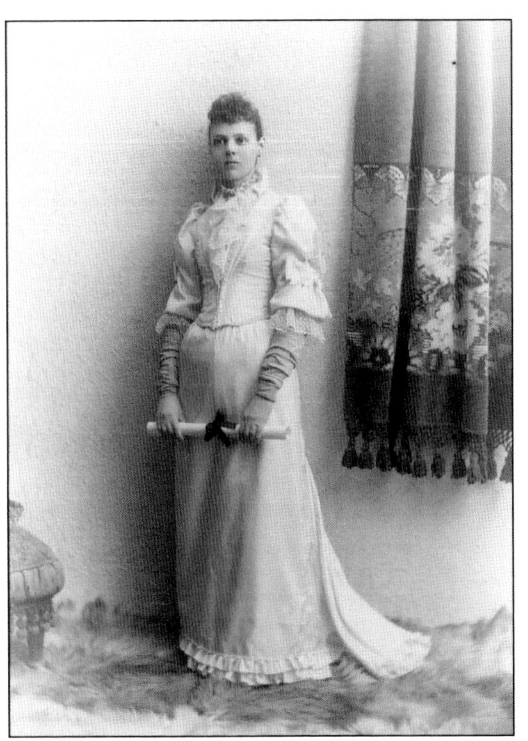

**Edna Scott.** Graduating from San José Normal School (today's San José State University), Edna Scott first taught at the Scotts Valley School, then for many years at the Mission Hill School in Santa Cruz. A newspaper article of the time reports, "This school [Scotts Valley] is under the able management of Miss Edna L. Scott. There is perfect discipline, and a bright clean lot of scholars." (Courtesy of the Genn family.)

**Cowell College Fountain.** In 1966, Cowell College, UC Santa Cruz, commissioned artist Nancy Genn, a descendant of Ruth Delia Scott (sister to Hiram Scott), to create a bronze fountain dedicated to the memory of teacher Edna Scott. The first piece of artwork on campus, the fountain consists of 30 separate sections cast in bronze and then assembled on-site. (Courtesy of Covello & Covello Photography.)

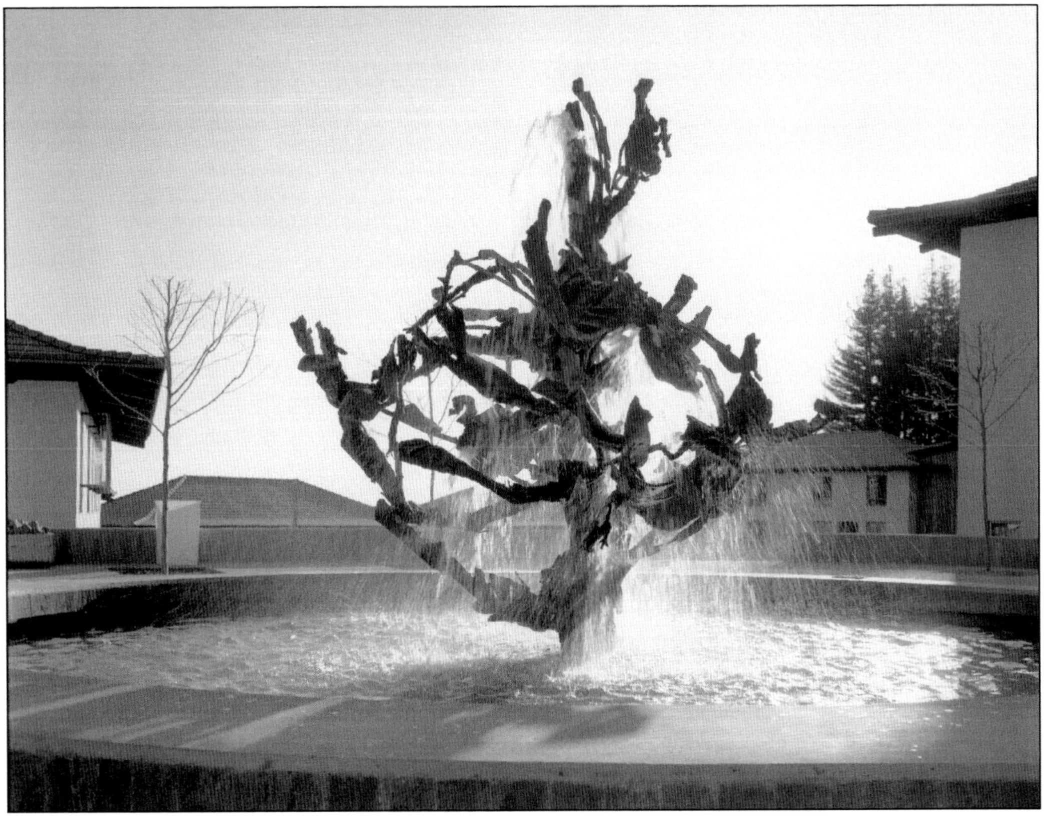

# *Three*

# Early Settlers

By the 1860s, Scott's rancho had been split between Hiram, his father, Daniel, his brother Joseph, his brother George, and three other owners. By 1880, only two of those original owners remained, which included the only remaining Scott family member, George Edwin. Among the 14 other new owners were the Erringtons, the Thomsons, the Lockes, the Kerrs, the Callahans, the Stewarts, and, later, the Hendricks and the Hicks, who built homes, started farms and dairies, and raised families. A *Sentinel* news article from March 12, 1885, describes Scotts Valley as follows: "Virgin soil is being laid bare and tickled with the plow . . . Just as you enter Scotts Valley and this side of the home of Mr. Hendricks, there is a large clearing on the west side of the public road . . . This land is now plowed and ready for the seed, and it delights the agriculturalist's eye, the soil being rich and dark and easily cultivated."

Other early settlers of Scotts Valley included Henry Fell Parsons, a forty-niner from England, and his wife, Emma. Parsons was an undersheriff, deputy surveyor, and county treasurer. In 1897, the Parsons' home was destroyed by fire. It was rebuilt and now is the office of the La Madrona Swim and Racquet Club. Parsons and his neighbor Frederick Waite were the first school trustees for the fledgling school district. Edward Kilfoyle, another early resident, owned much of the present-day Manana Woods area, where he had a dairy and raised chickens. Abraham and Sarah Hendricks owned 348 acres in Scotts Valley and had a farmhouse for many years at the future intersection of Whispering Pines Drive, Scotts Valley Drive, and Mount Hermon Road. The Hendricks, along with their daughter Phoebe Waite and son-in-law Frederick Waite, managed the Alameda House, a hotel and stage stop in Centerville, California, before moving to Scotts Valley, where their home was also used as a stage stop on the Santa Cruz to Los Gatos Stage line.

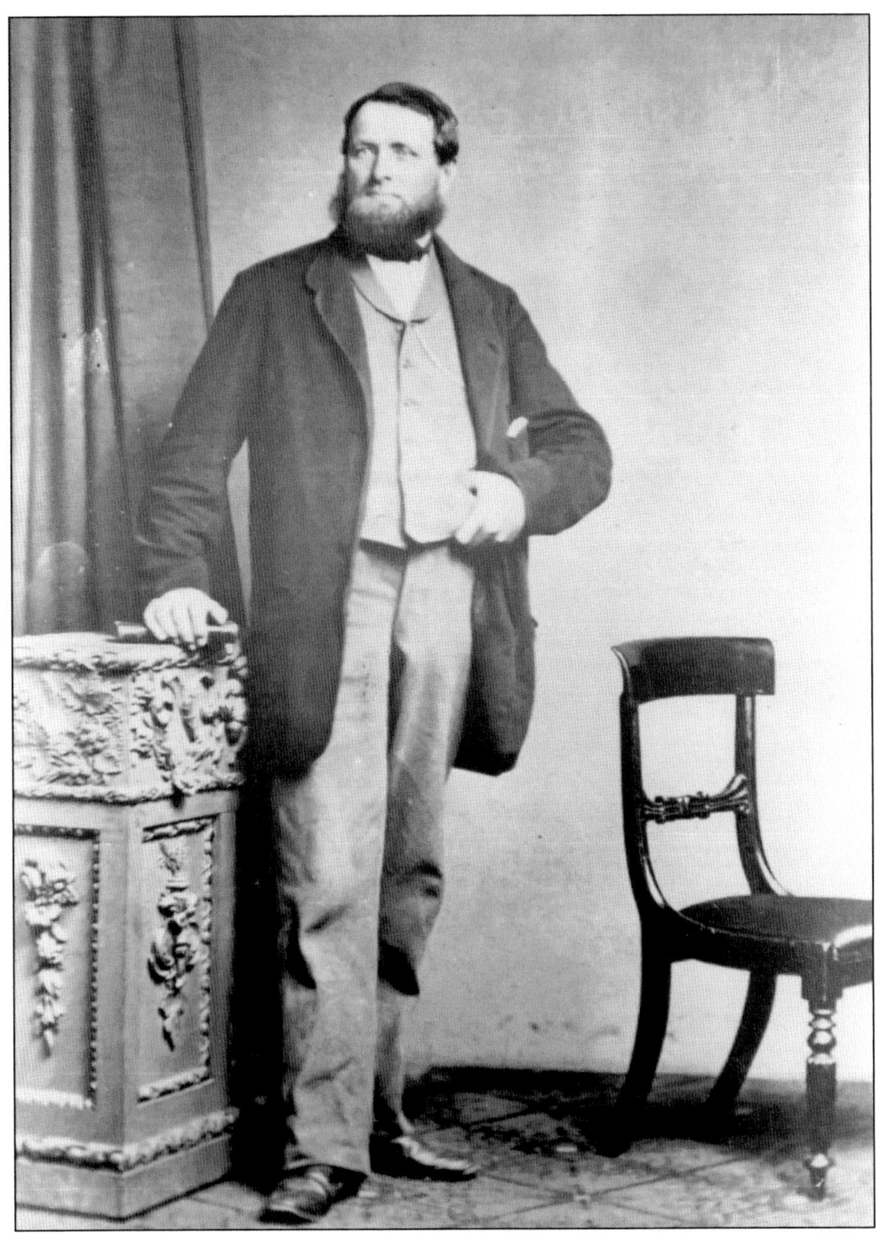

**Joseph Errington.** Anxious to raise capital for his Silver City mining venture, Hiram Scott sold his stock ranch to Joseph and Grace Errington in 1865. In her memoirs, Grace notes, "Mr. Errington then heard of the Scott Ranch so he headed this way and found the place more to his liking. He bought 1,140 acres for $6,750.00. Mr. Scott having refused $10,000 the year before, asking $12,000, but he got the mining craze and so sacrificed the place." Grace also records the following description of the early days on the dairy: "There was plenty to be done on the ranch, building and fixing up for a dairy. We had 40 cows. At first we had no milk room, so took what we afterward used as a parlor and had racks all around. We made an opening into the pantry, which was used for the churning and making the butter. The kitchen had a partition in it. One side I used for my cooking. The other side the men who ran the dairy used for theirs." (Courtesy of SVHS.)

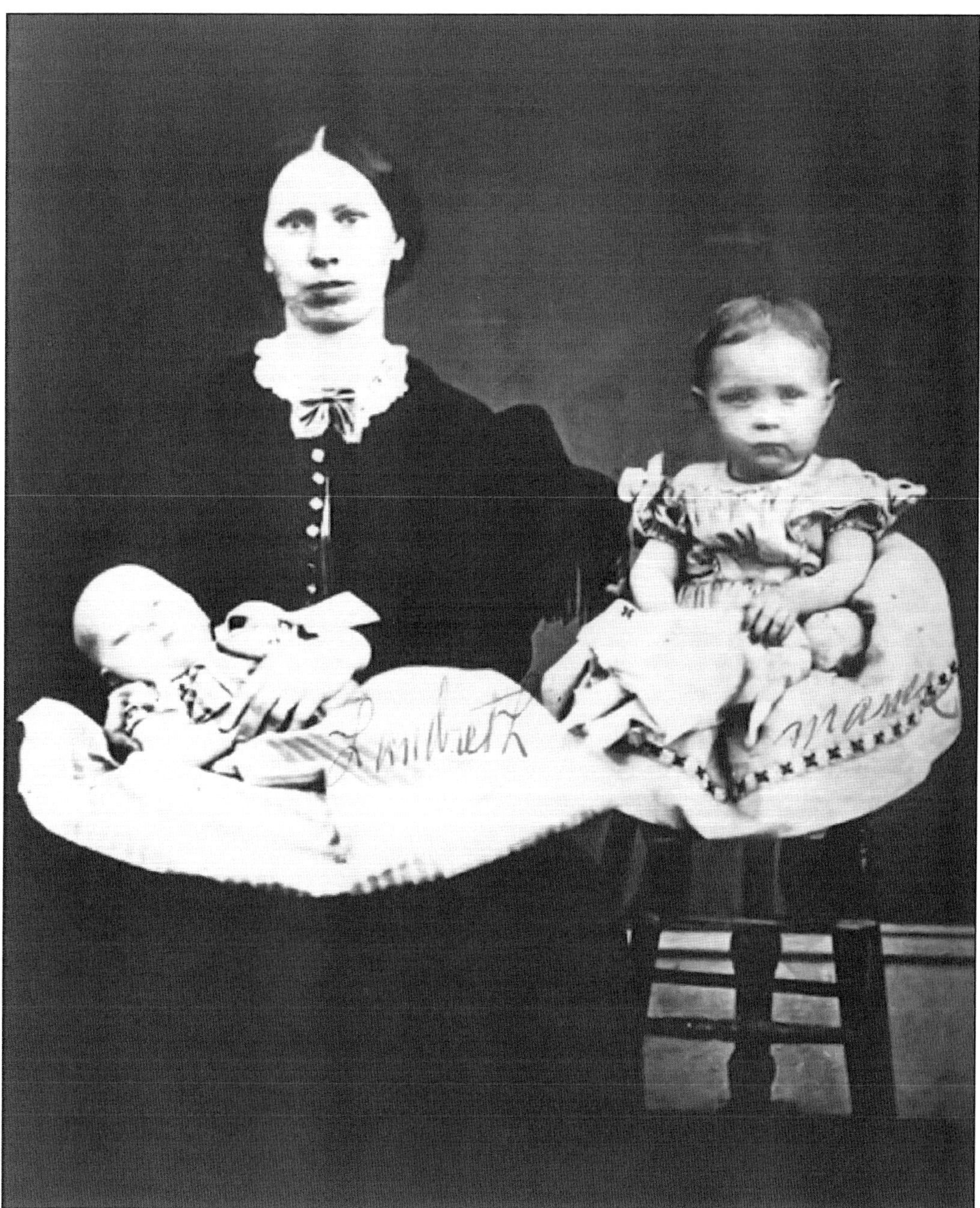

**GRACE ERRINGTON AND CHILDREN.** Grace is shown here with daughter Mary and son Landreth. After Joseph Errington's untimely death in 1869, Grace married Archilles Hicks and, together, they operated the former Errington dairy. Her son Landreth inherited 215 acres from his father and established his own dairy at the north end of town, near the future Santa's Village. The son of Archilles Hicks, Arthur Hicks, inherited 240 acres from his father's estate and also established a dairy. Around 1909, Arthur built a home on Hicks Drive, now Disc Drive, which used redwood logs as a bridge over Carbonera Creek. After the death of her second husband, Grace sold the Live Oak Dairy to the Frapwell brothers in 1907. (Courtesy of SVHS.)

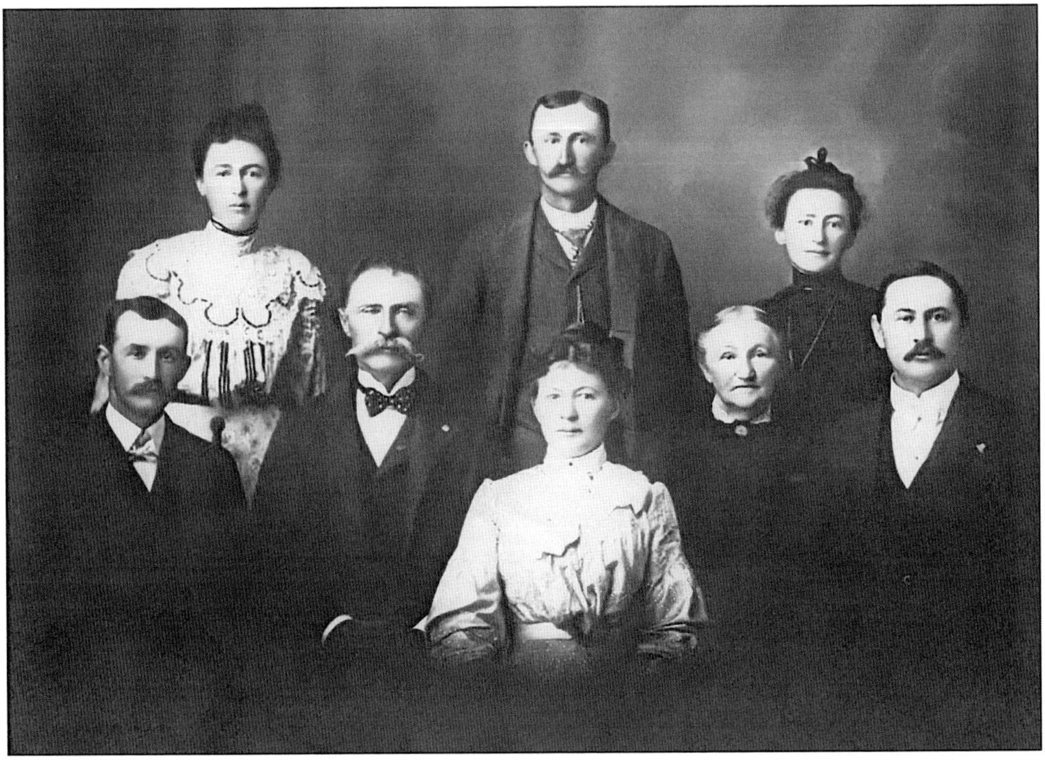

**LARSEN-YOUNG FAMILY, C. 1890.** After Daniel Scott and Nancy Parcher-Scott passed away, a number of different families resided in the Scott House, and the property changed hands many times. From 1872 to 1891, the Larsen-Young family lived in the house. Eric Larsen, a tanner and native of Sweden, married Hannah Pollard. They raised fruit and sold dairy products. (Courtesy of Charlene Duval.)

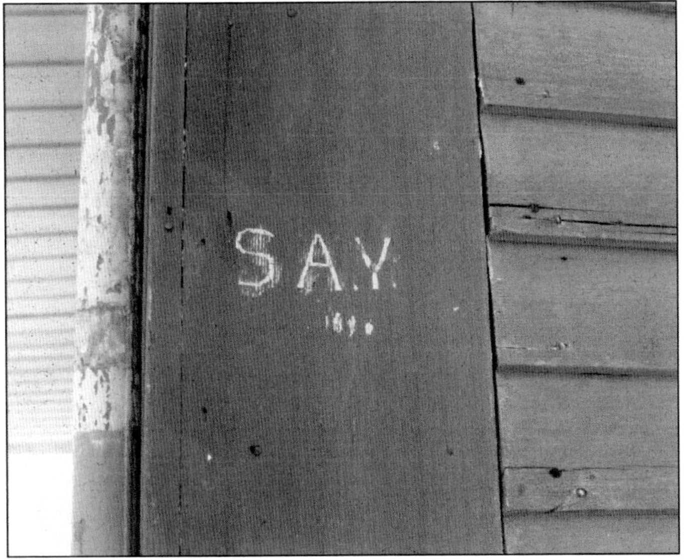


**INITIALS ON SCOTT HOUSE.** Uncovered during renovations and believed to be the handiwork of daughter Sadie from the Young family occupancy, the initials S.A.Y. were found carved into the northeast corner of the house. George and Marcie Claussenius were the longest-term residents of the Scott House and were responsible for the additions to the back of the home. In 1936, it was moved to its present location due to the realignment of the state highway, now Scotts Valley Drive. (Courtesy of Charlene Duval.)

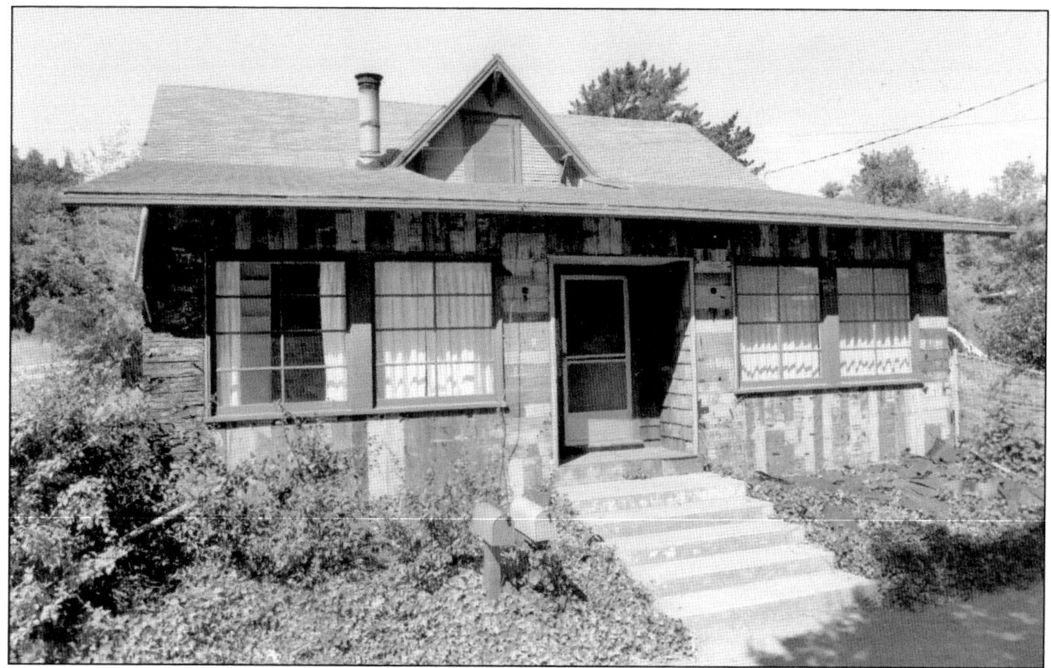

**EVANS HOUSE.** In 1894, Hugh and Mattie Evans purchased 162 acres for $3,616 from Thomas Kilfoyle's estate, located near Branciforte Creek (now La Madrona Drive). Although it had been extensively remodeled, portions of the home were believed to have been over 100 years old. The house was torn down in 1993 to make way for the widening of Mount Hermon Road. This photograph of the home was taken in 1991. (Courtesy of the City of Scotts Valley.)

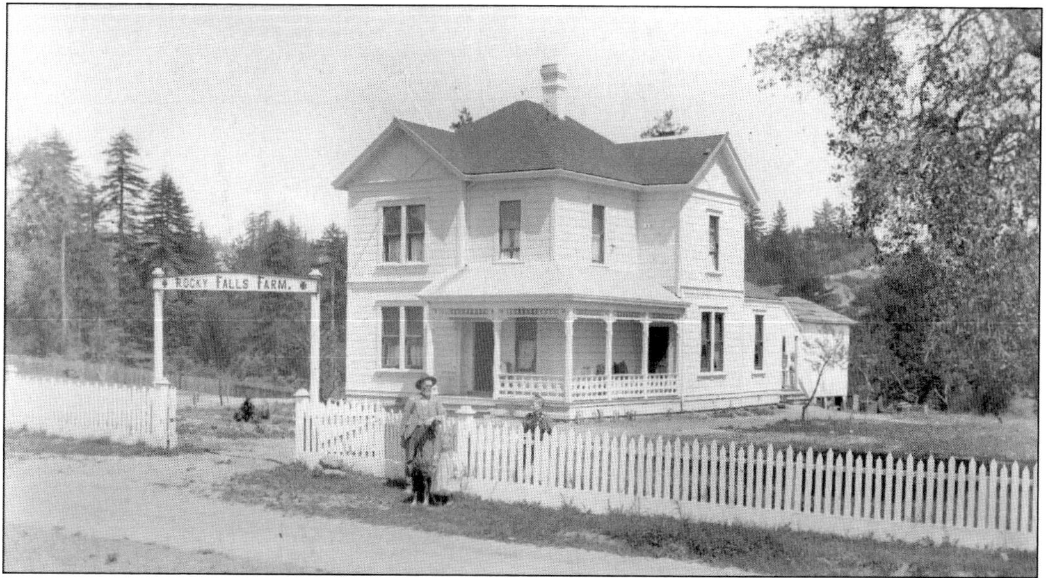


**ROCKY FALLS FARM, 1912.** Daniel Callahan purchased Rocky Falls Farms in 1887 and was noted for his herd of brush-eating white goats. Later owners included the George Shippy family, who ran a dairy, and Fred and Minnie Wellcome, who operated a chicken ranch. After the turn of the century, Dr. A. Scott Bledsoe, noted speaker on the Chautauqua circuit, and his wife, Etta, owned the property. (Courtesy of the Santa Cruz Museum of Art and History.)

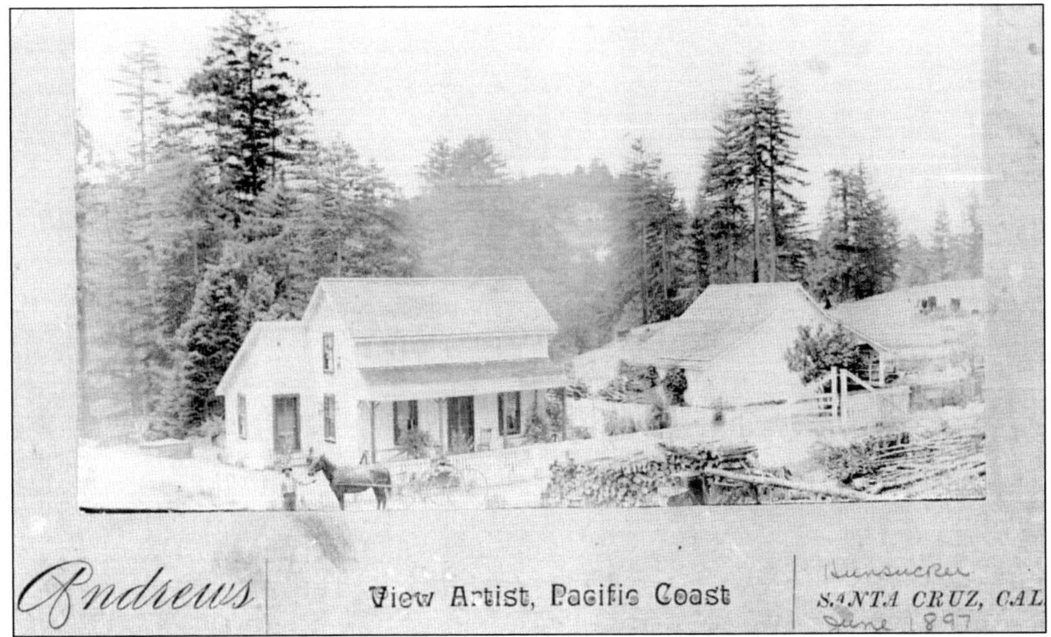


**Hunsacker House and Barn, 1897.** With acreage stretching across Glen Canyon Road, Thomas and Alice Hunsacker farmed their land for many years. Largely due to the efforts of John Mowry, a neighbor on Glen Canyon Road and part-time movie location scout, scenes from the 1932 version of *Rebecca of Sunnybrook Farm* starring Ralph Bellamy and Marian Nixon were filmed on the property, as were scenes for *Way Back Home*, a 1931 movie starring a young Bette Davis. (Courtesy of Linda Finch.)

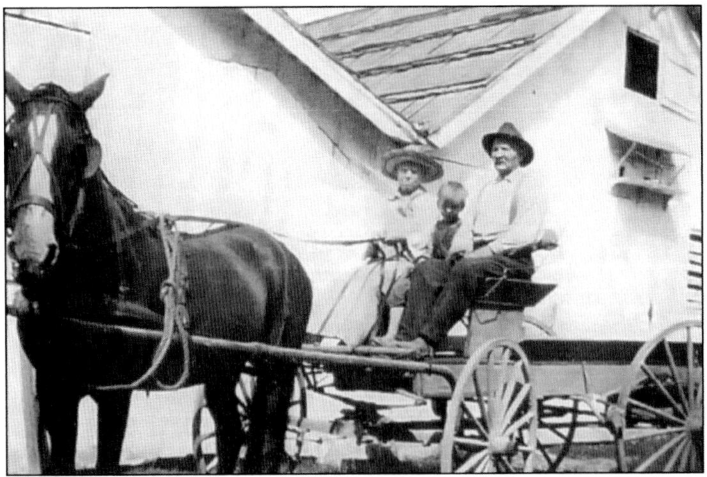

**Thomas and Alice Hunsacker.** This photograph of the Hunsackers was taken in 1924 in front of the still standing barn. Actors Maureen O'Sullivan, Robert Montgomery, and Mickey Rooney were also reported to have shot movie scenes on the farm. Around 1943, Paul and Dorothy Borak purchased the farm and raised foxes and apples. (Courtesy of Linda Finch.)

**DAVID MORRILL LOCKE.** Like Hiram Scott, David Locke was a forty-niner who came to California seeking his fortune. A civil engineer, he quit his job and made the journey west in 1849. Joined by his brother Silas, David tried gold mining but had no luck. Next, the two brothers bought land in San Francisco and made their fortune selling water from their two artesian wells. (Courtesy of Ronnie Trubek.)

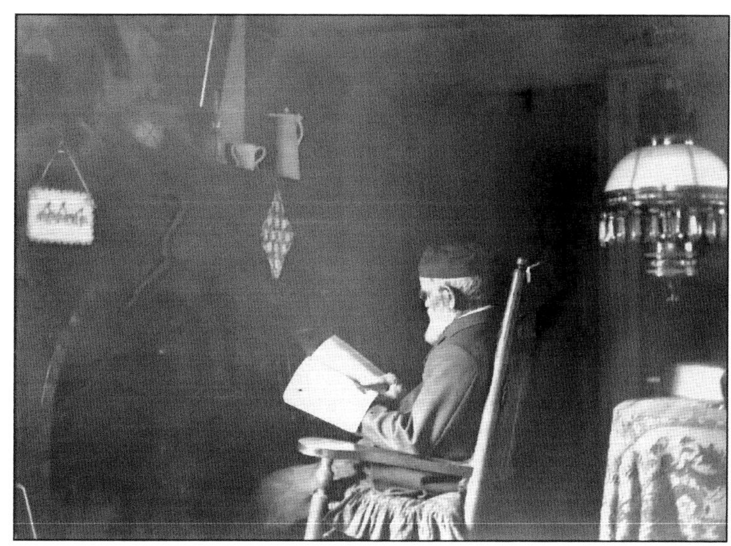

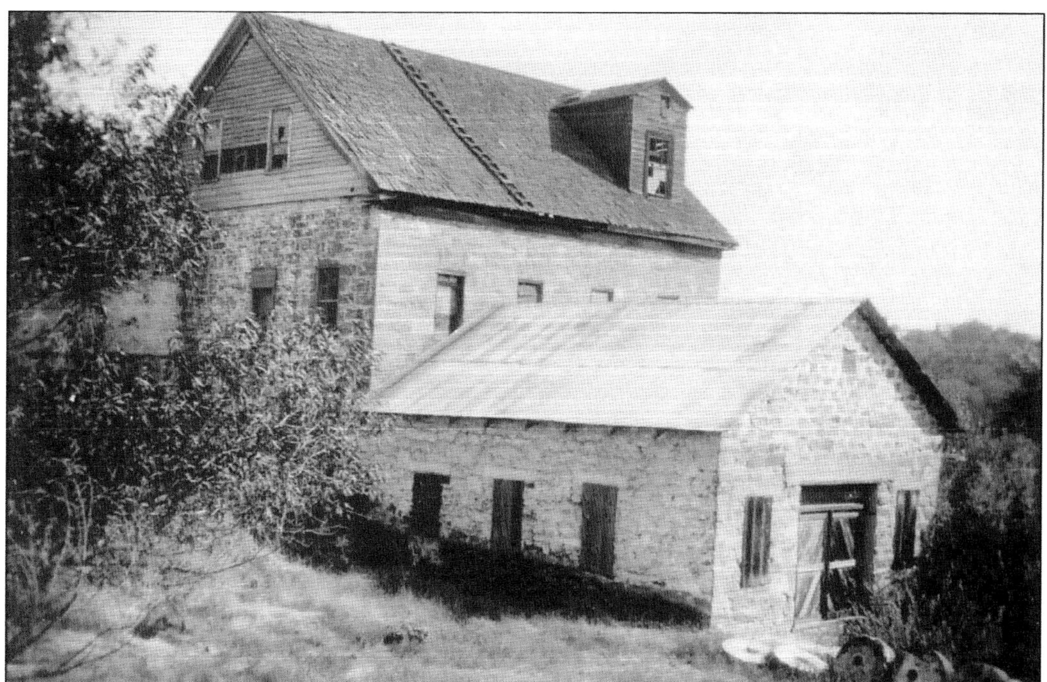

**LOCKE'S MILL.** In 1853, Locke and his wife, Mary, moved to Knight's Ferry on the Stanislaus River. They had two children, Finette "Nettie" and Alexander "Alex." Purchasing materials for $26,000, Locke built a new toll bridge over the Stanislaus. In 1862, a warm, unseasonable rain melted the heavy snows of the High Sierras, causing heavy amounts of runoff. (Courtesy of the Santa Cruz Museum of Art and History.)

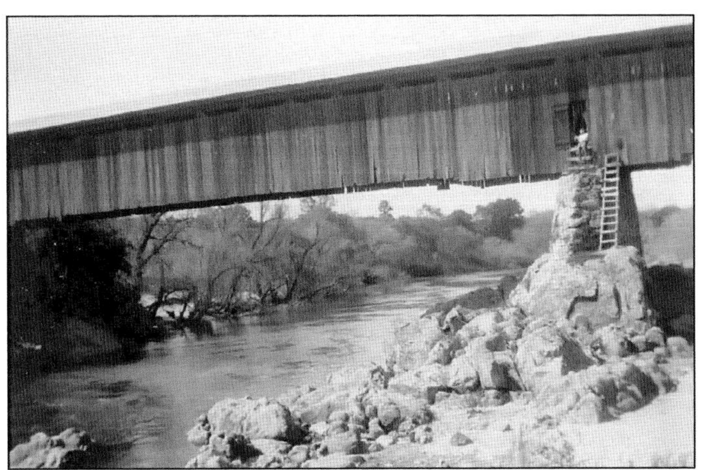

**The Covered Bridge.** Locke's bridge held under the deluge until an upstream span broke loose and smashed most of the waterside buildings to pieces. In just 15 months, Locke rebuilt an even larger span. At 330 feet long, it became the longest covered bridge in California. Locke's bridge still stands today, although only open to foot traffic. (Courtesy of the Santa Cruz Museum of Art and History.)

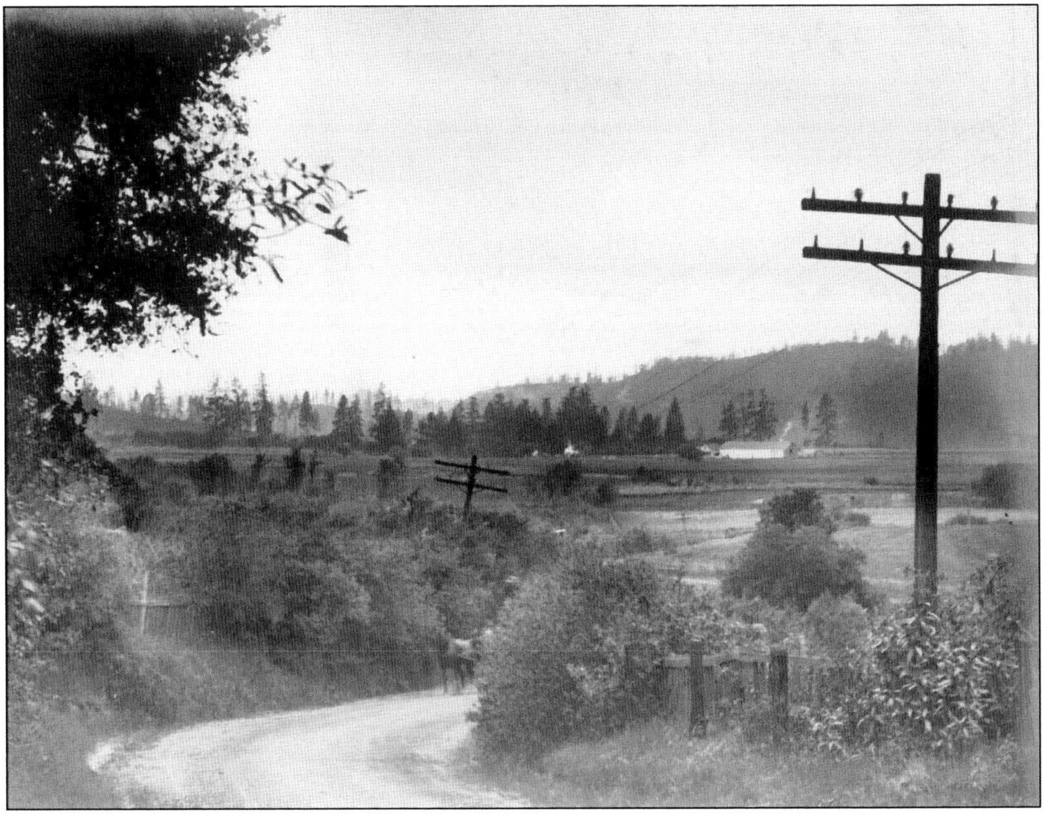

**Scotts Valley Countryside, c. 1900s.** In 1869, the Lockes purchased 1,131 acres from Samuel Dickens in northwest Scotts Valley, with acreage on both sides of today's Mount Hermon Road. Mary Locke became a writer for the *Pacific Rural Press* under the pseudonym Mountain Mary. The Lockes' Springvale Dairy Ranch became renown for its fine butter and herds of Jersey, Holstein, and Aldernay cows. According to the handwritten caption that accompanied this photograph, this is the first glimpse of Springvale from Kilfoyle Hill when returning from town. (Courtesy of Ronnie Trubeck.)

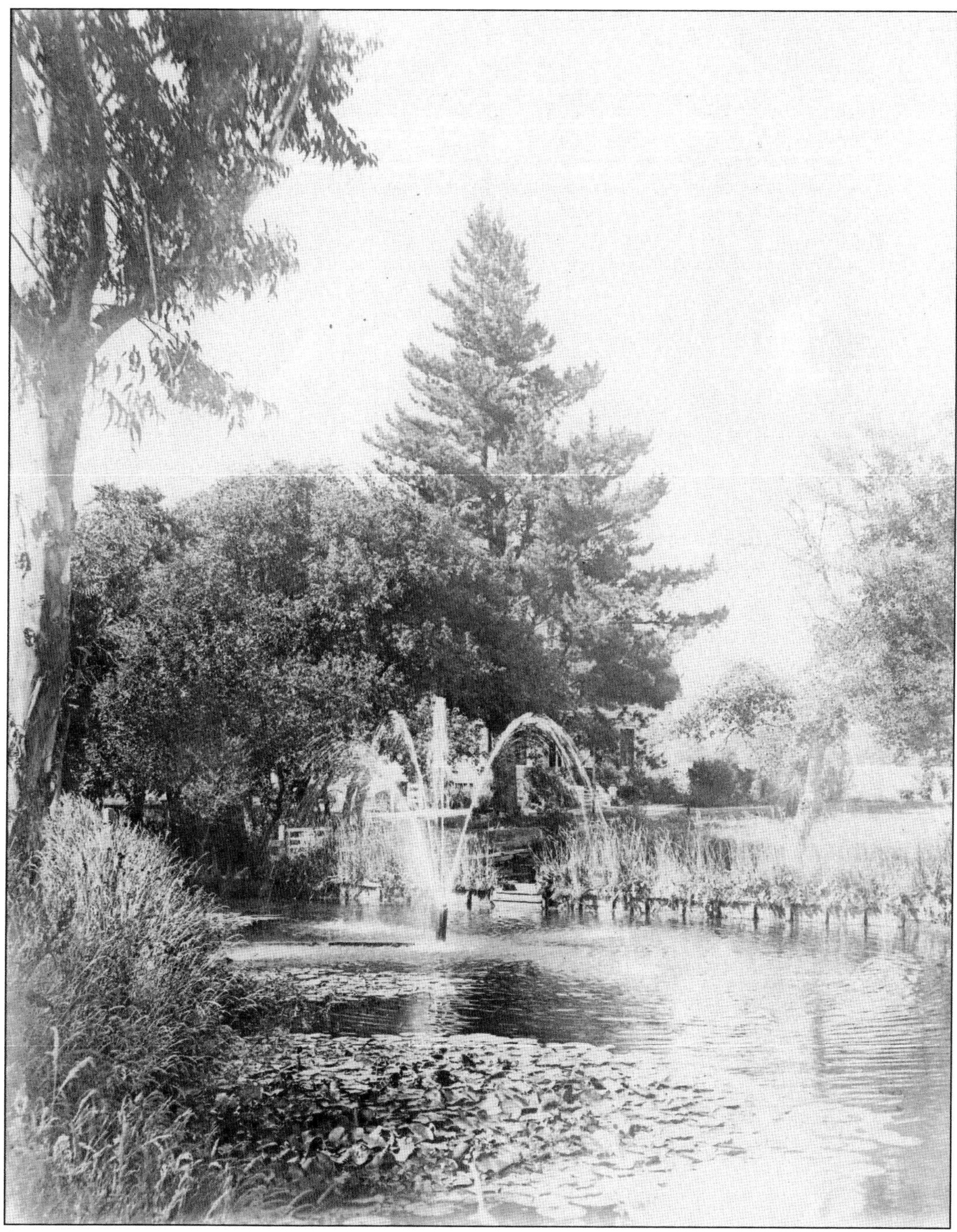

**Springvale Pond.** In 1881, Mary Locke passed away while visiting her children enrolled at the University of California, Berkeley. In tribute, the *Santa Cruz Sentinel* published a large front-page article containing excerpts from her newspaper writings from Scotts Valley. (Courtesy of the Santa Cruz Museum of Art and History.)

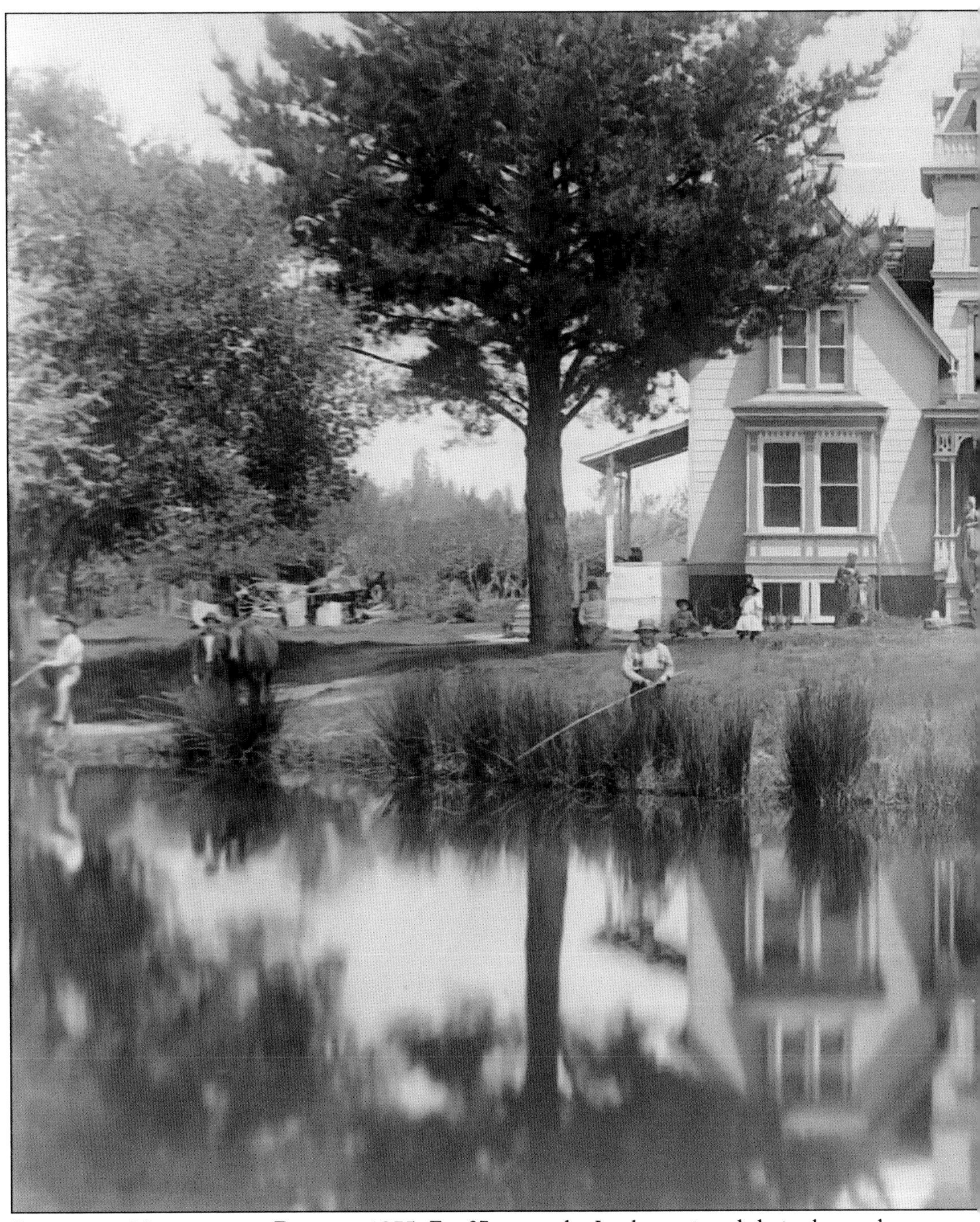

**Springvale Mansion and Pond, c. 1875.** For 37 years, the Lockes enjoyed their elegant home and grounds located on Mount Hermon Road near the future Lockwood Lane. Various newspaper accounts at the time tell of the family's participation in local education, agricultural and political

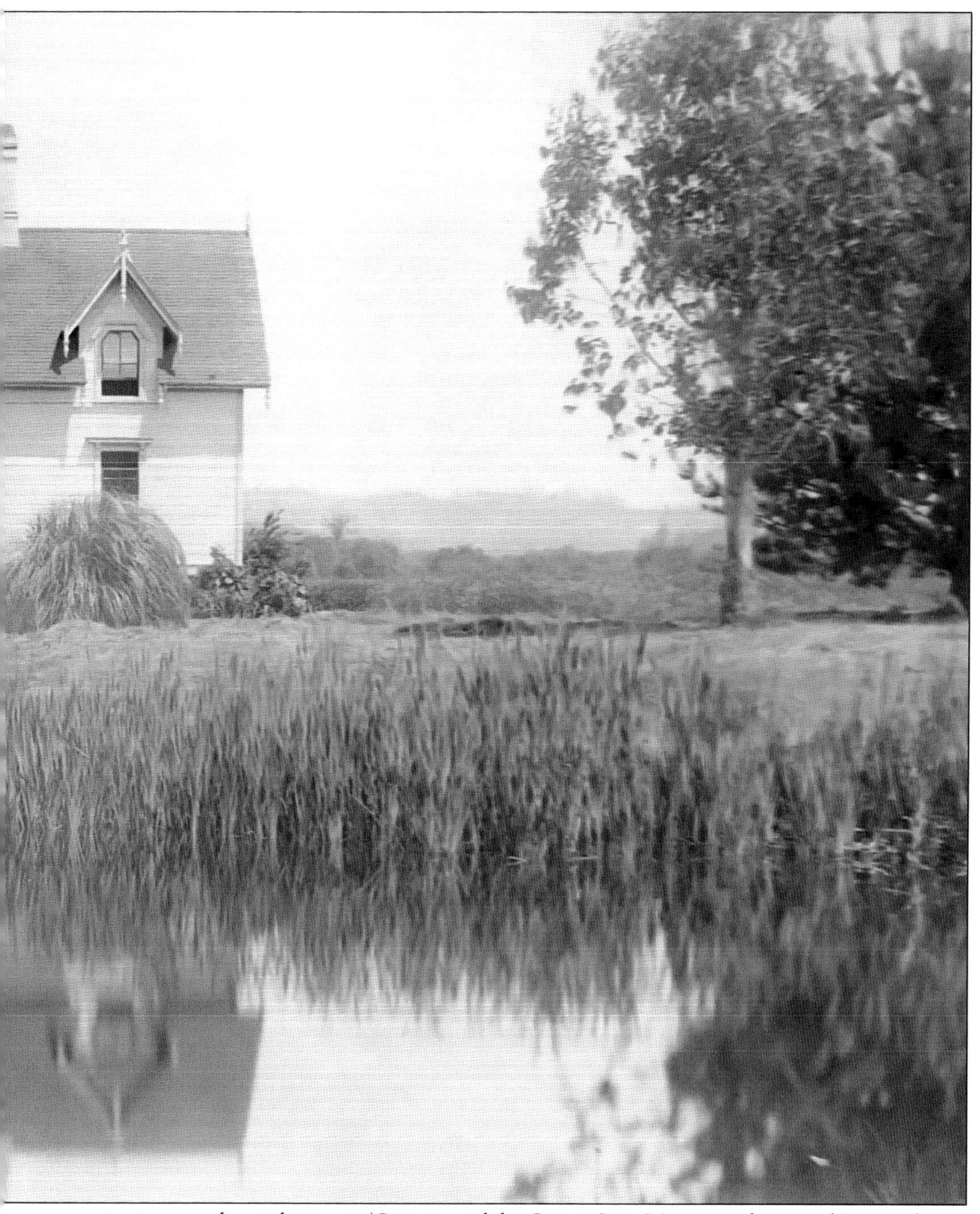

organizations, and social events. (Courtesy of the Santa Cruz Museum of Art and History.)

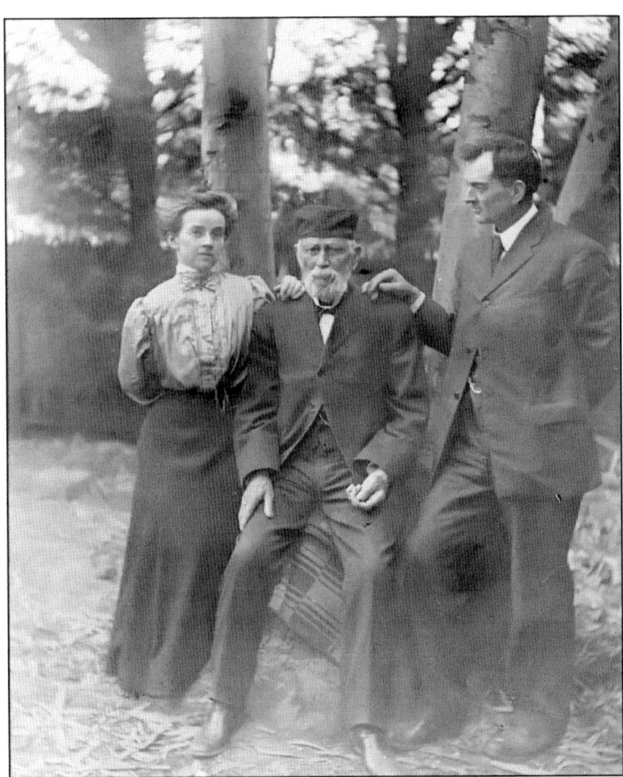

**D.M. Locke and Children, 1907.** Following in her mother's footsteps, Nettie became a correspondent for the *Santa Cruz Surf* newspaper. Her brother Alex farmed in Scotts Valley but also owned a house in Berkeley. (Courtesy of the Santa Cruz Museum of Art and History.)

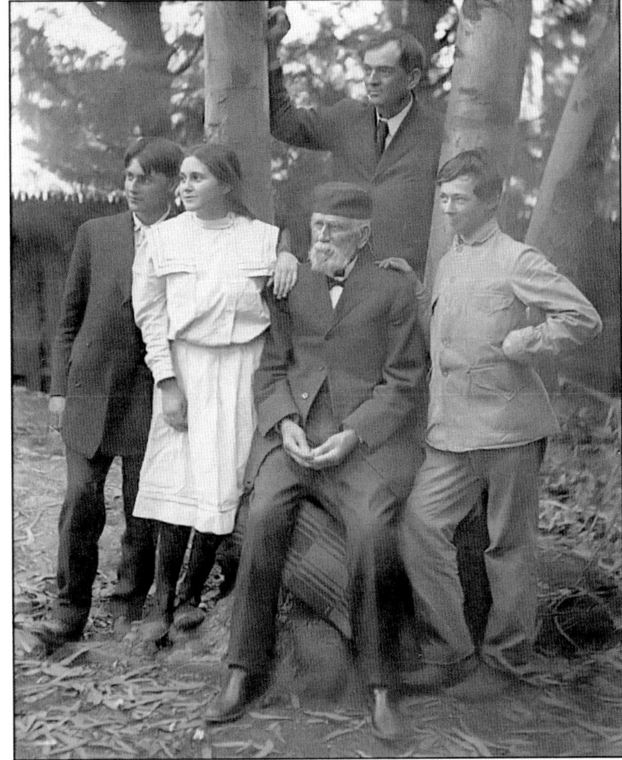

**Three Generations of Lockes, 1907.** Alexander Locke is shown at the top. From left to right are his son Alexander Jr. (or "Roland"), daughter Sarah, David Locke, and Alexander's son Eric. (Courtesy of the Santa Cruz Museum of Art and History.)

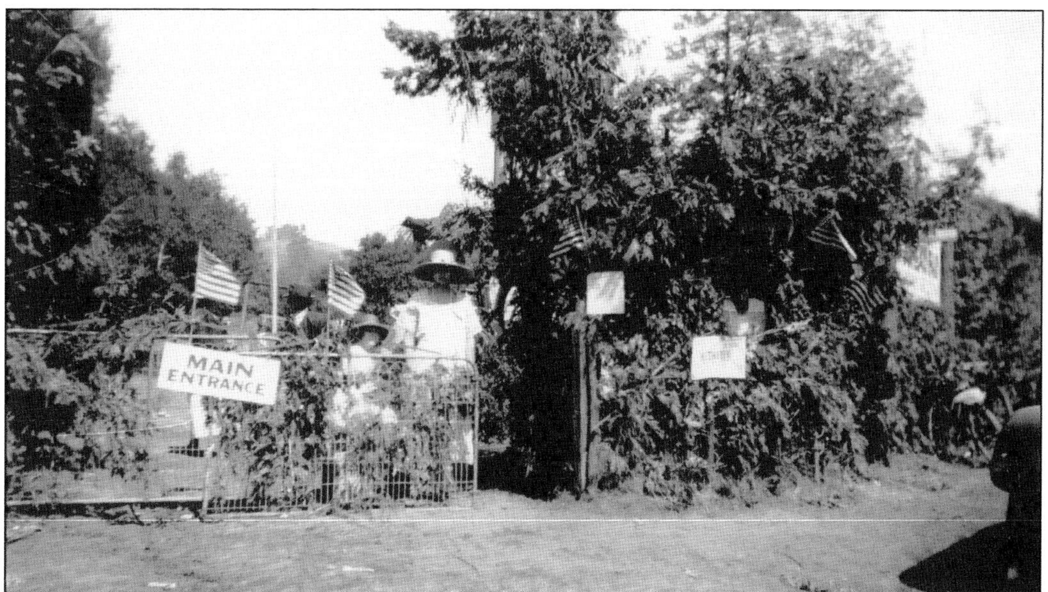


**COUNTY FAIR, 1918.** Although writing on the back identifies this photograph as "the first Santa Cruz County Fair at Scotts Valley School," it may have been an exhibition put on by the Scotts Valley Farm Bureau to raise money for the Scotts Valley School and to showcase local products. (Courtesy of SVHS.)

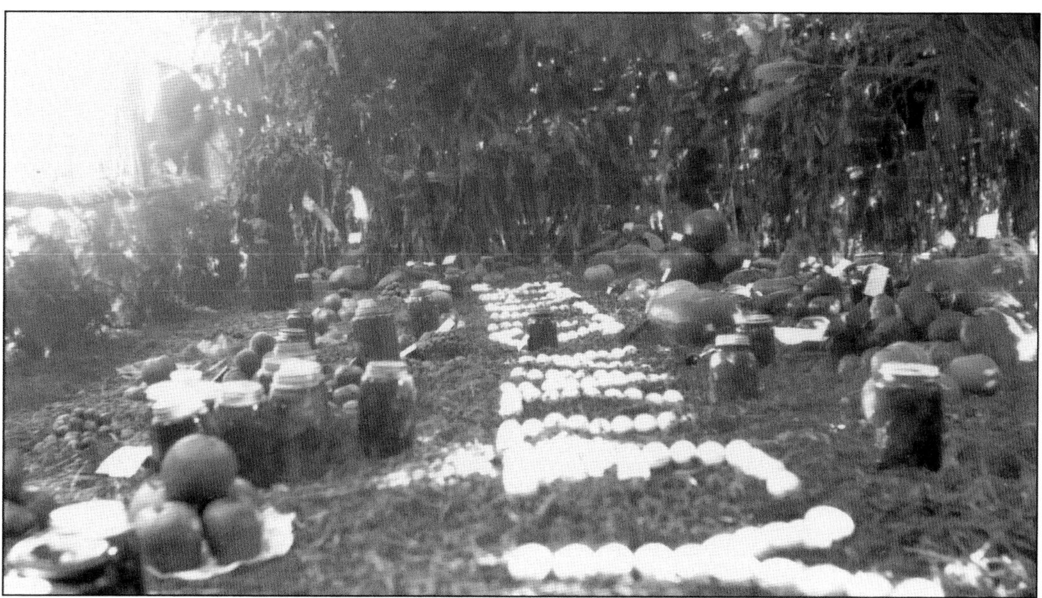

**FAIR EXHIBIT, 1918.** An exhibit of preserved products and fresh fruits and vegetables is seen at the fair. The rocks spell out "Scotts Valley." (Courtesy of SVHS.)

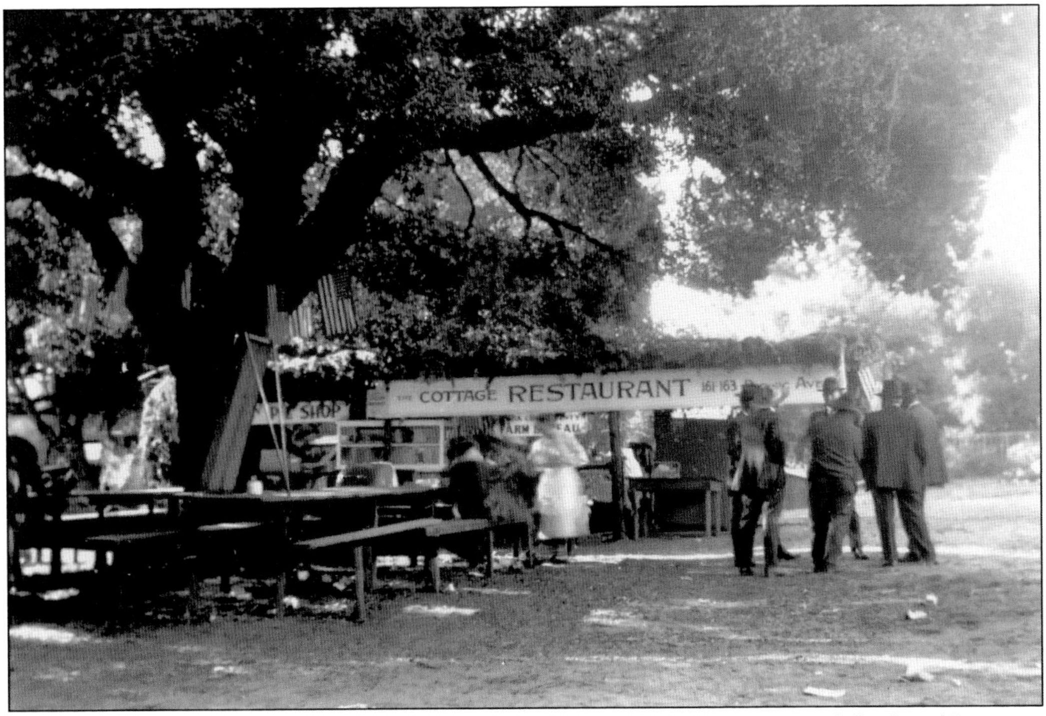

**Refreshment Area, 1918.** This photograph depicts the refreshment area of the fair. (Courtesy of SVHS.)

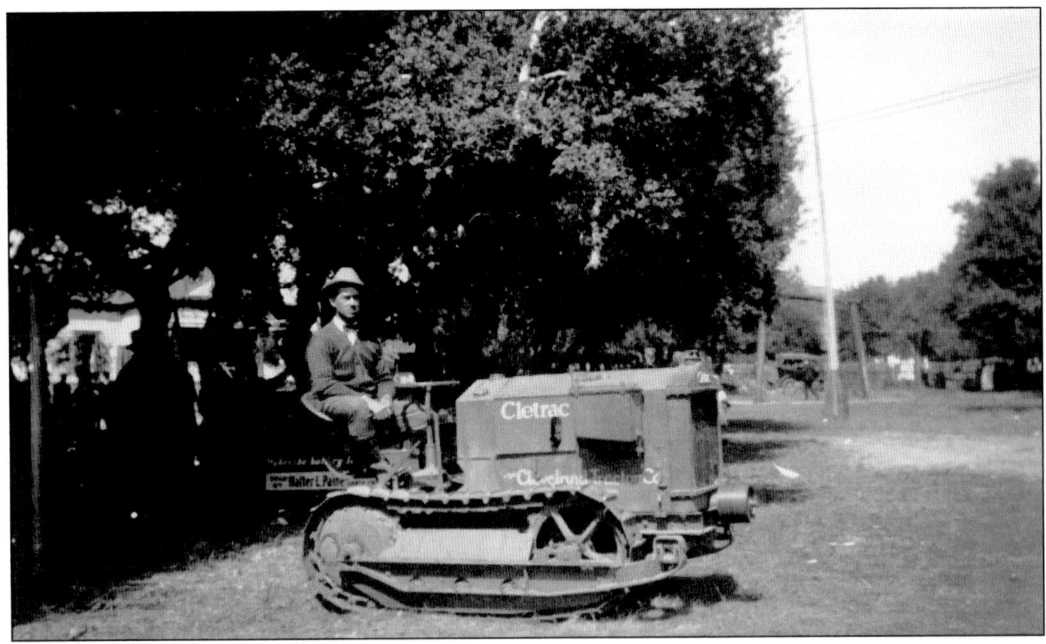


**Tractor Display, 1918.** The Cletrac, manufactured by the Cleveland Motor Plow Company, was a crawler-type tractor for general farm use. (Courtesy of SVHS.)

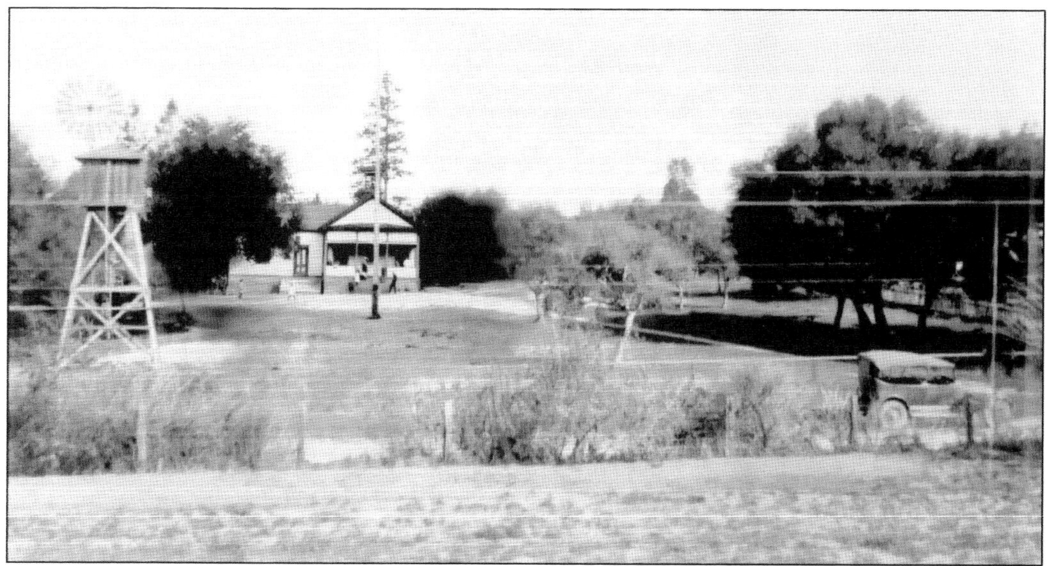

**Scotts Valley School, c. 1918.** The first school in Scotts Valley was likely held in a privately owned one-room shed. Residents recognized the need for a local school and formed the Scotts Valley School District in 1865. The district was not able to raise enough funds to build a school until 1872, when David Locke donated four acres for the school and $150 for the building. The school was completed with private donations. (Courtesy of SVHS.)

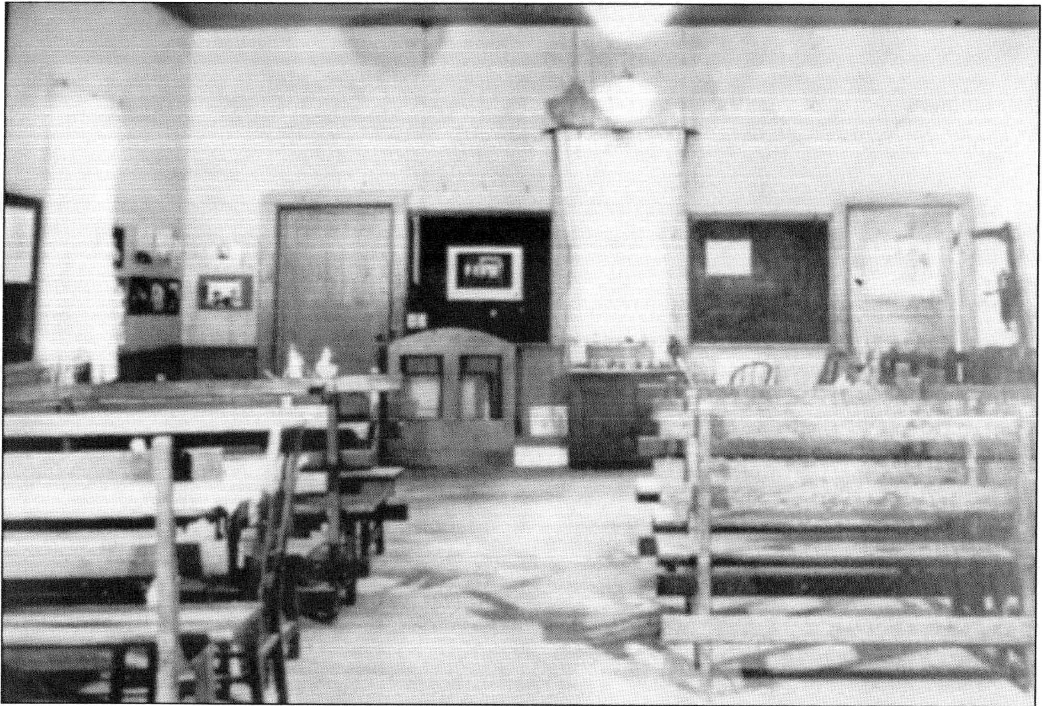

**Scotts Valley Classroom, 1915.** The Scotts Valley School quickly became the community center of the area. Newspaper articles from the time tell of many meetings, dances, and other social events held at the school. In 1892, a small addition provided blackboards, bookcases, and charts. (Courtesy of Charlene Duval.)

Benefit Entertainment and Dance

At Scotts Valley School-house

FRIDAY EVENING, APRIL 16th, 1897.

To raise funds for improvement of school-house.

GOOD PROGRAM including some of the best Santa Cruz talent. First-class music for dancing. Refreshments.

Admission, 50c per couple.

SCHOOL BENEFIT. Although it was not a wealthy community, Scotts Valley residents appeared to be committed school supporters, much like in the modern day. This announcement is from an 1897 newspaper. (Author's collection.)

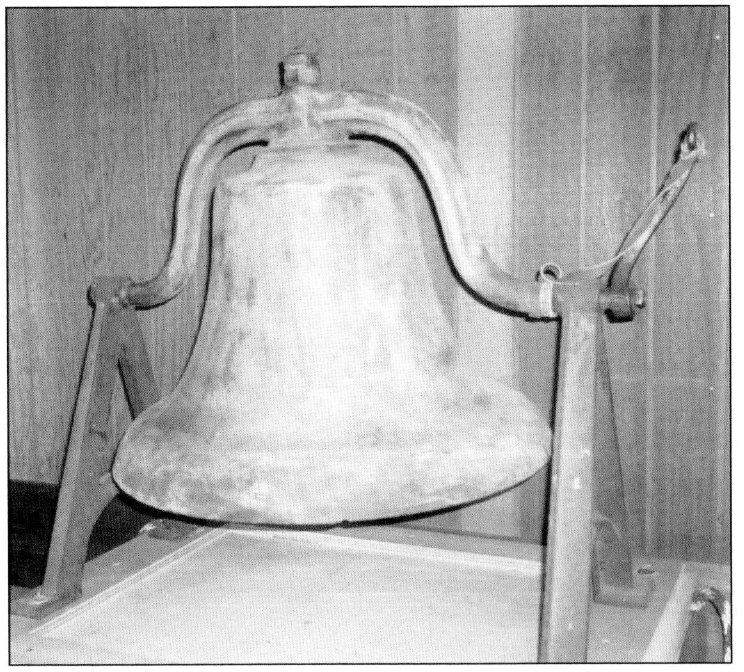

SCHOOL BELL. In 1891, a large bell weighing 250 pounds was added to the school. The bell rang loud enough to be heard throughout the valley, striking at 8:30, 8:55, and finally at 9:00 a.m. to signal the start of the school day. The old school bell can be seen today in the chambers of the Scotts Valley City Council. (Courtesy of SVHS.)

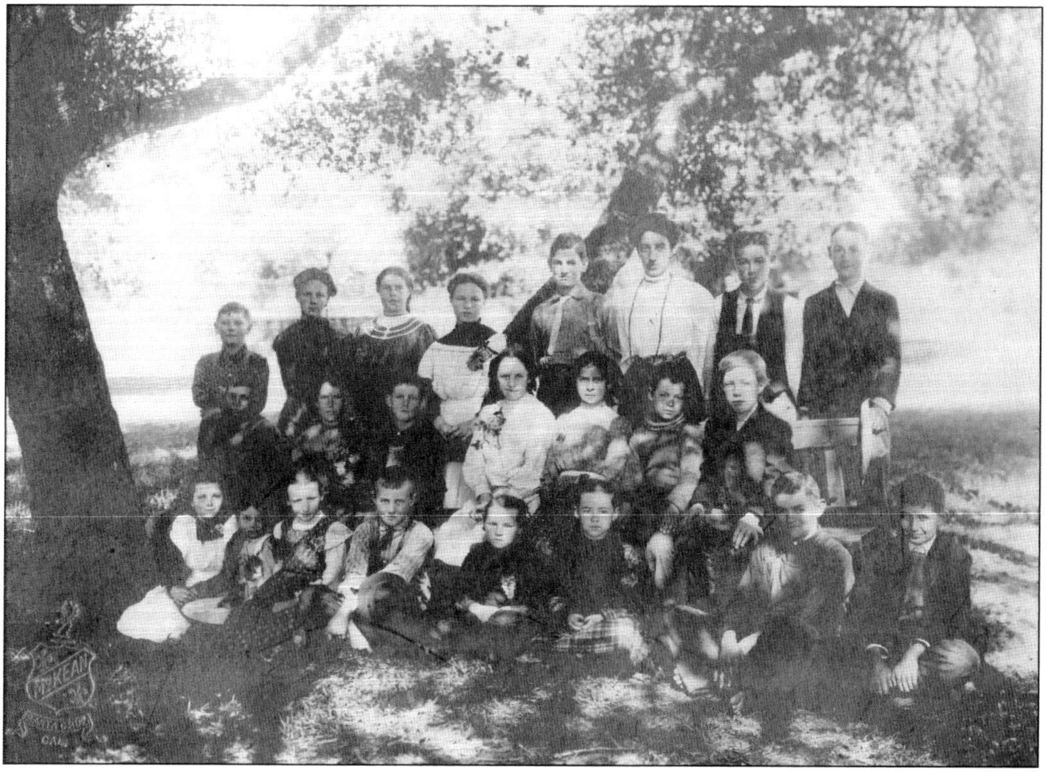

CLASS PHOTOGRAPH, C. 1915. Pictured here are students of the Scotts Valley School. (Courtesy of Terry Reynolds.)

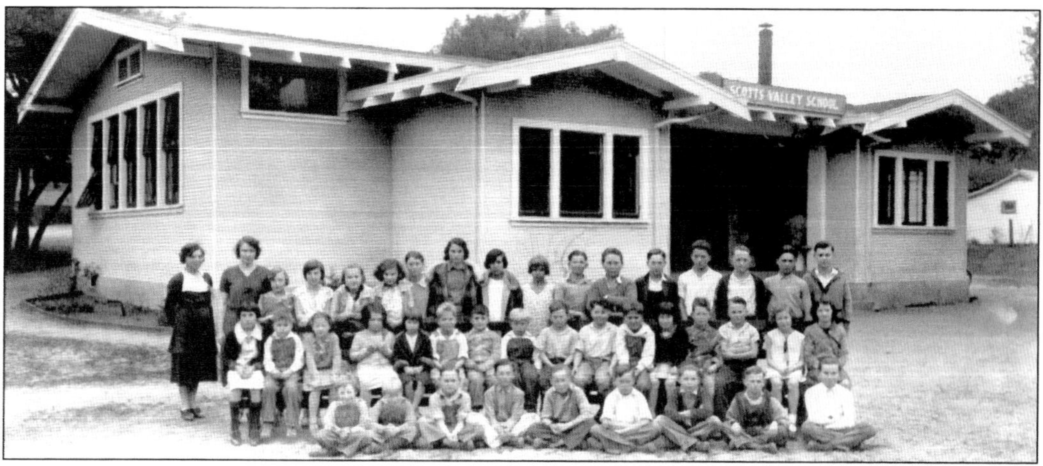


**SCHOOL PHOTOGRAPH, C. 1925.** Financed with a $7,000 school bond, a larger two-room Craftsman-style schoolhouse was constructed in front of the old school building in 1925. By 1940, the school had already outgrown this space and required further expansion. (Courtesy of SVHS.)

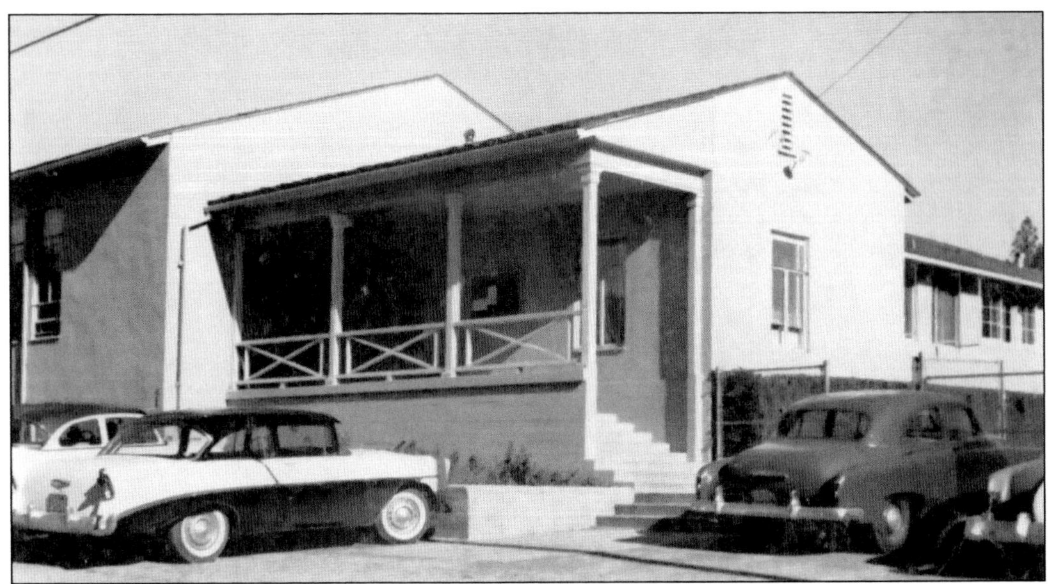

**Third Scotts Valley School.** The third Scotts Valley School was one of the last WPA projects in the United States. The existing school incorporates the original 1941 building as the school office, library, and front classrooms. During the 1940s, rising student population led to classes being held off campus. In 1948, the lower wing of the school was built. (Courtesy of the Scotts Valley School District.)

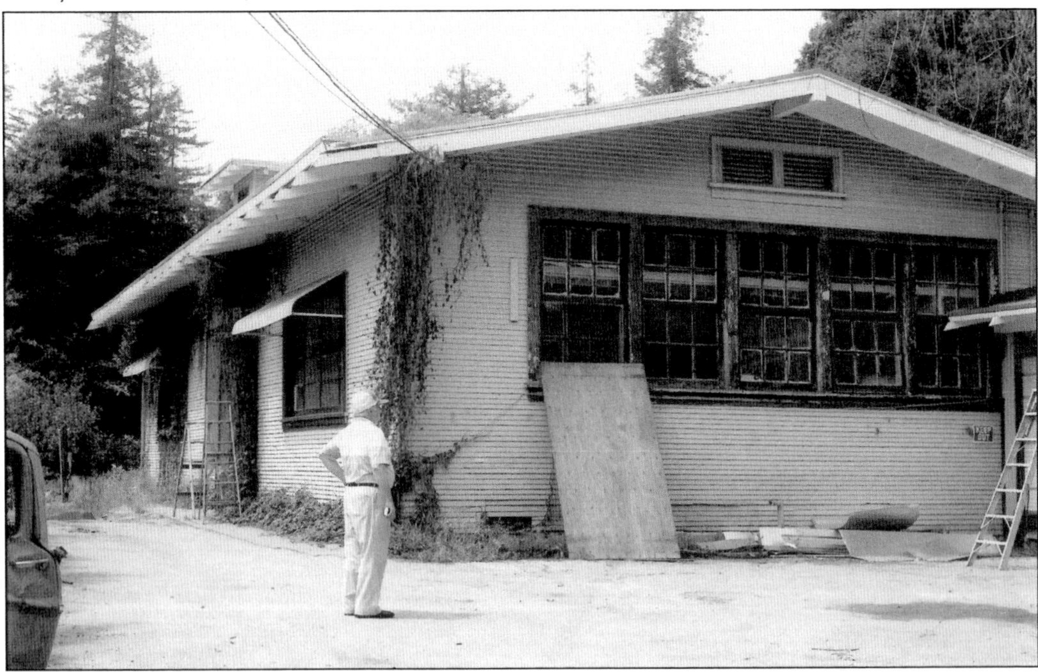

**Second School.** In 1941, the first school was torn down, and the second school was sold and moved to Glen Canyon Road, where it saw new use as a lamp shade factory owned by Helen Mowry. Her husband, John Mowry, served as a school district trustee, blackout warden, and volunteer fireman. Scotts Valley's volunteer fire truck was kept at the ready next to the old schoolhouse. (Courtesy of Julie Fetter.)

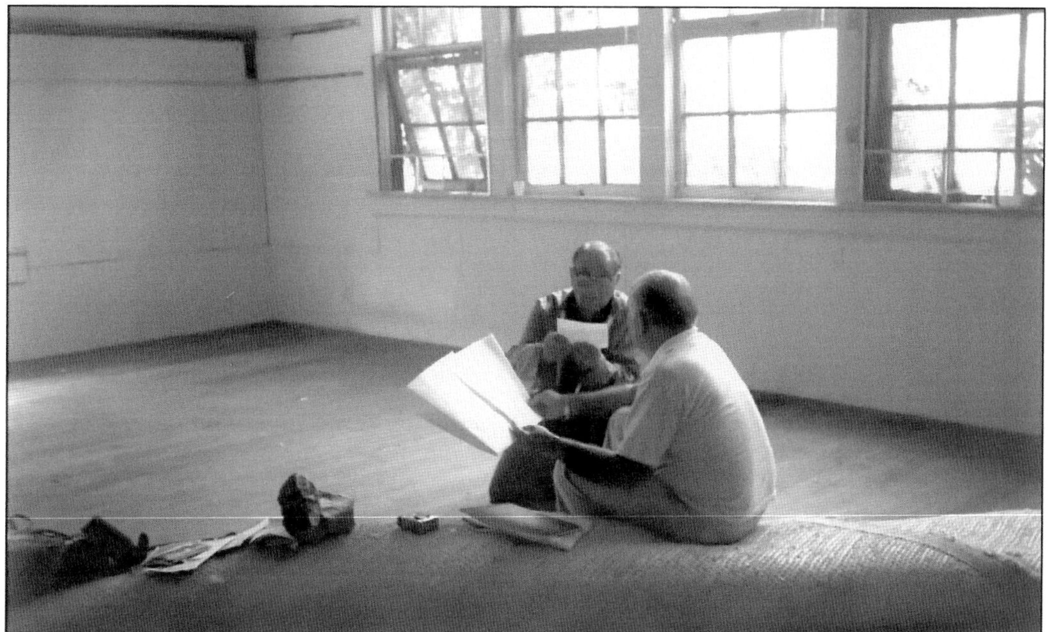

**Inside the Schoolhouse.** In 1989, city approval was given to demolish the second schoolhouse. An attempt was made to move the structure, but there were no applicants. A reunion and open house was held one last time at the old schoolhouse. (Courtesy of Julie Fetter.)

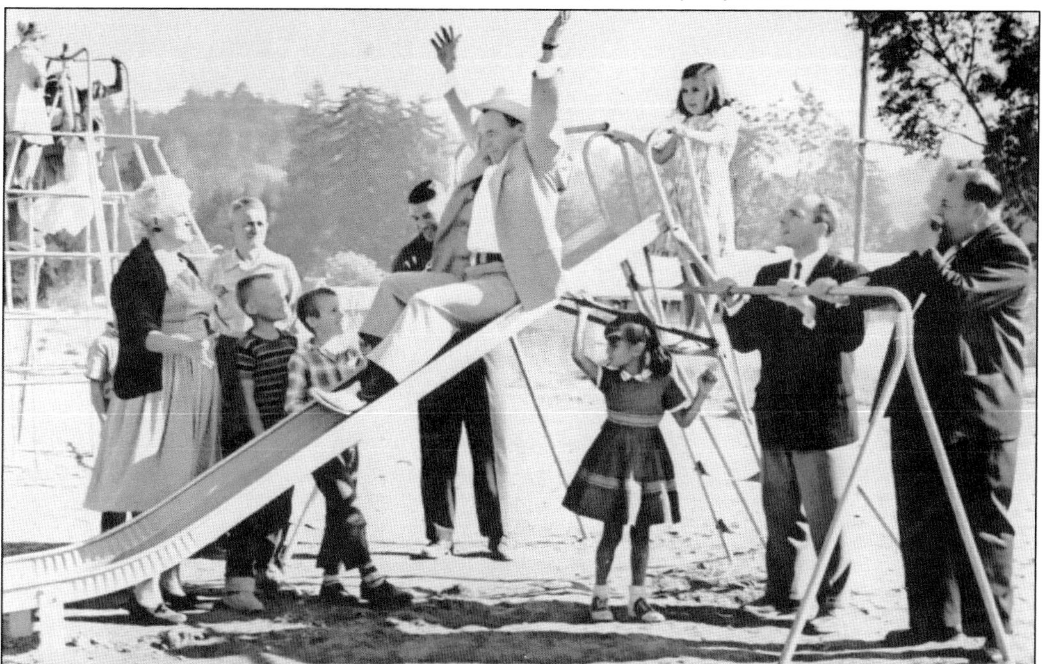

**Don Santos.** Vine Hill Elementary originally opened with two classrooms in 1960, and six additional classrooms were added in 1962. This photograph, taken in 1962, shows Mayor Don Santos enjoying a ride down the new Vine Hill School playground slide. Brooknoll School, Scotts Valley's other elementary school, was constructed in 1964. (Courtesy of the Scotts Valley School District.)

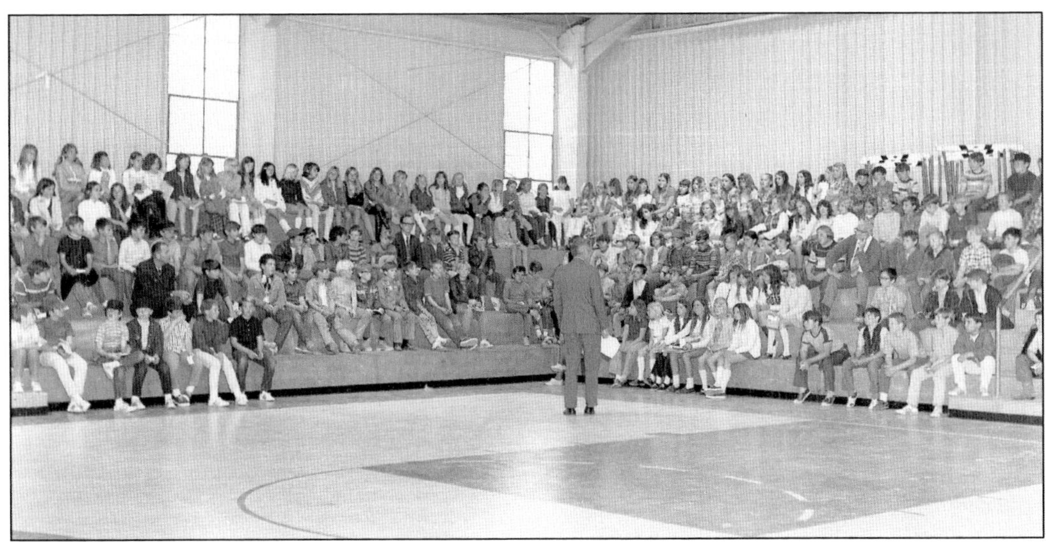

**Assembly.** This c. 1970 photograph shows an assembly at the Scotts Valley Middle School, held in the school's multipurpose gymnasium/auditorium. In 2014, Scotts Valley voters approved a $35 million bond measure to rebuild the aging middle school. (Courtesy of Colleen Wagner.)

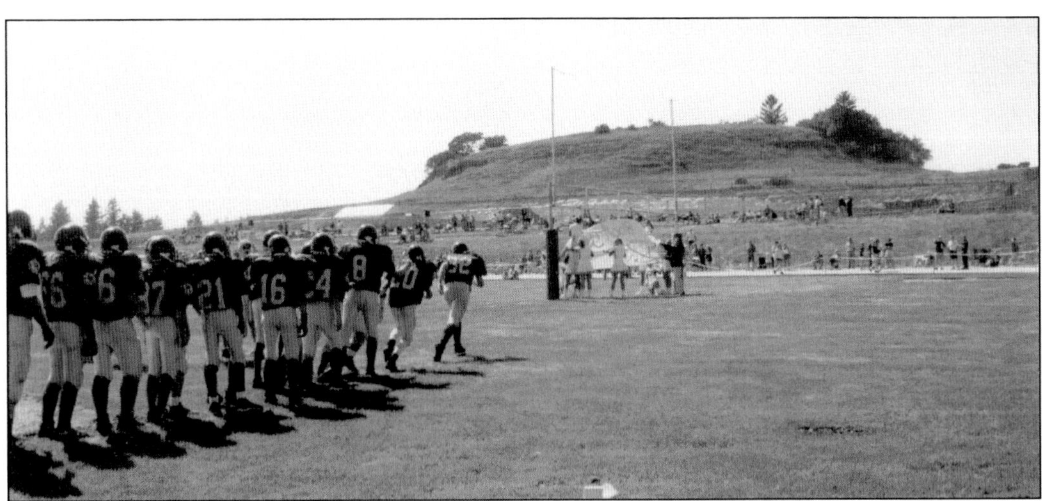

**Falcon Football.** Scotts Valley's first high school opened to students on September 8, 1999, welcoming 330 freshman and sophomore students. After a year in temporary classrooms, the students then moved into permanent faculties. Scotts Valley's first high school football team is pictured in 1999. (Courtesy of Julie Fetter.)

# *Four*

# The Dairies

By the 1900s, Scotts Valley had grown into a typical small farming community of the time. Dairy products such as milk, butter, and cheese were primarily raised for resale; however, farmers also produced fruits and vegetables, poultry and eggs, grapes for wine, and cut wood for shingles, lumber, and firewood. Most dairy farms also raised hogs. At that time, there was no market for skim milk, so it was mixed with barley and vegetables, formed into gruel, and fed to the hogs. There was no denying that working a farm or a dairy was hard work, day in and day out.

When asked about growing up on the Live Oak Dairy in a 1991 newspaper interview, Elvis Frapwell, age 84, gave his unfavorable opinion of milking cows: "Seven days a week, twice a day . . . On Sundays, an hour earlier, getting up at 4:00 a.m., sitting down to the same old cow tail, beating your head against it. The routine . . . Your hands go to sleep at night." His sister Elda had a more positive memory of her childhood spent on the 750-acre family dairy: "The hills, we could just rove over . . . We had special haunts we liked, places where the wildflowers grew . . . the harebells . . . and the white woodland violets." Although Elvis Frapwell disliked working with cows and refused his father's offer of setting him up with his own dairy, he recalled many happy times in Scotts Valley, including the time he caught 50 trout in Carbonera Creek.

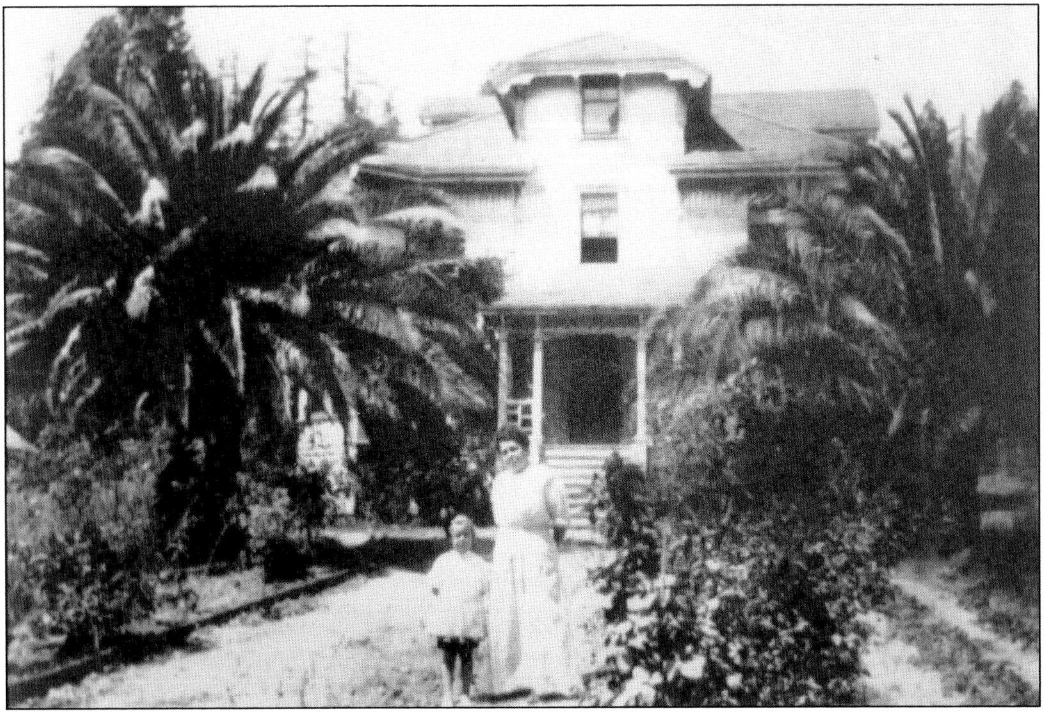

THOMSON MANSION. In 1892, William and Ellen Thomson constructed a three-story, 22-room Victorian mansion on their 400-acre property in Scotts Valley that stretched across both sides of what was then Glenwood–Santa Cruz Road. This c. 1910 photograph depicts Eva Frapwell and an unidentified child in front of the home. (Courtesy of Eric Taylor.)

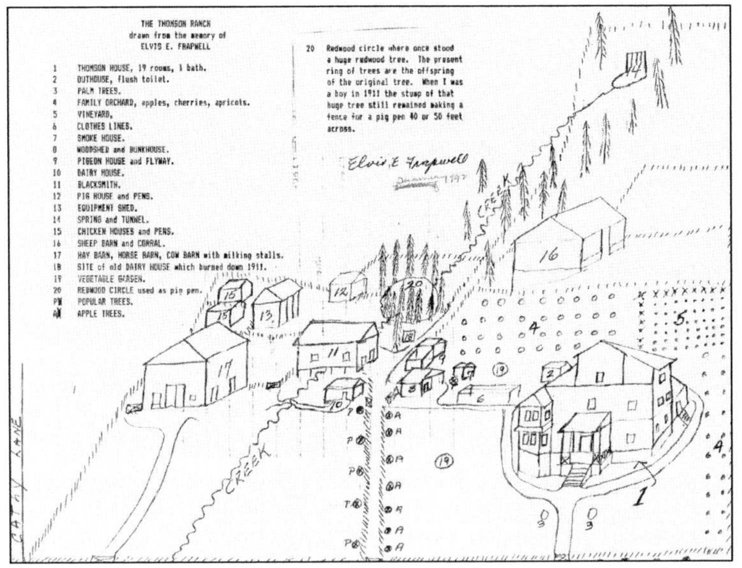


MAP OF PROPERTY. Known as Edgewood Farm, the home had 11 bedrooms, two carved redwood burl and tile fireplaces, and large bay windows with stained-glass inserts. A generating plant provided the gas for the lights in the house, supplemented by kerosene lamps. The only heat sources were the two fireplaces and the kitchen stove. This map was drawn from the memory of Elvis Frapwell. (Courtesy of SVHS.)

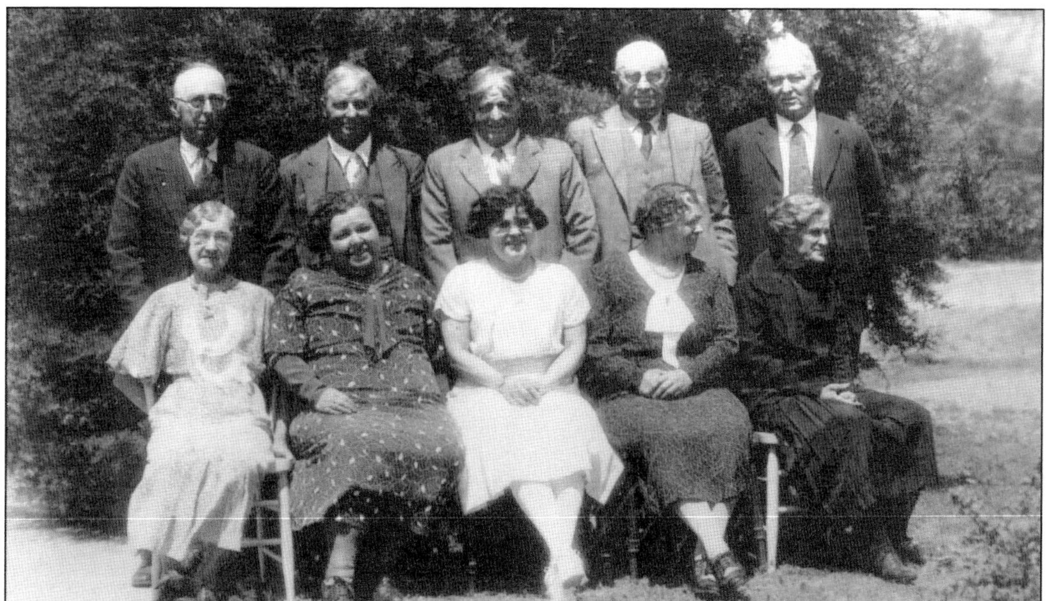

**FRAPWELL BROTHERS AND WIVES.** c. 1920. In 1911, John, George, and Edward Frapwell, paying $40,000 in all, purchased two separate parcels of land totaling 750 acres from Ellen Thomson and Grace Errington Hicks. The Frapwell family moved into the Thomson mansion and managed the Scotts Valley ranch and dairy, which became known as the Live Oak Dairy. Pictured above are the five Frapwell brothers and their wives. (Courtesy of SVHS.)

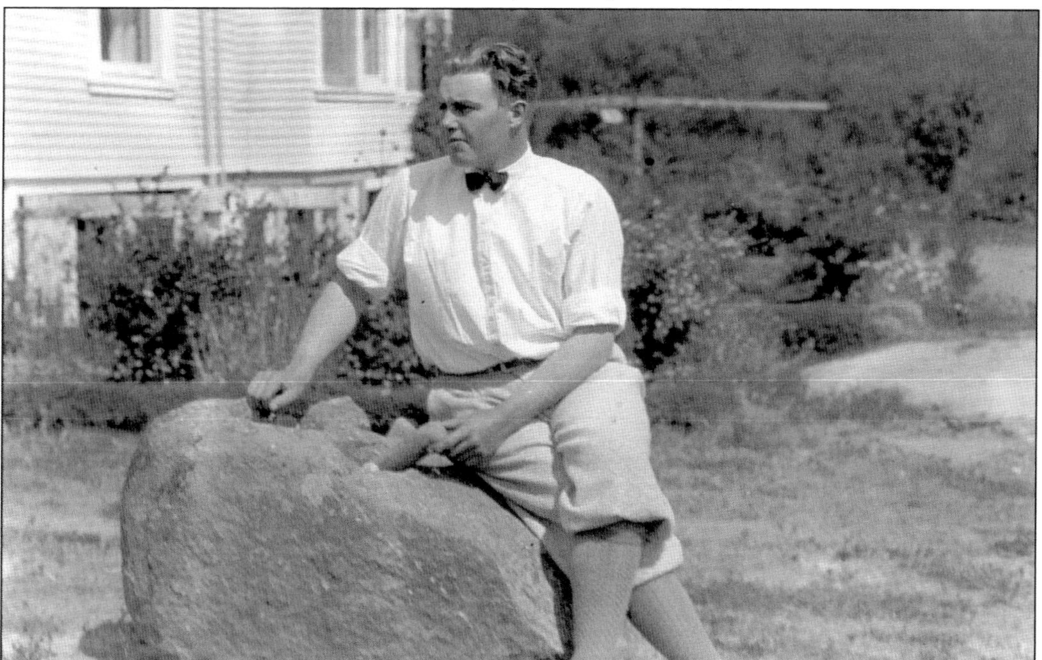

**ELVIS FRAPWELL.** Elvis Frapwell, pictured here on an Indian grinding rock, was Edward and Eva Frapwell's youngest child. His interest in photography and love for Scotts Valley resulted in many rare photographs of this time. Elvis stated the rock shown in this photograph, taken in 1923, came from a nearby old Indian village located on the east side of Carbonera Creek. (Courtesy of SVHS.)

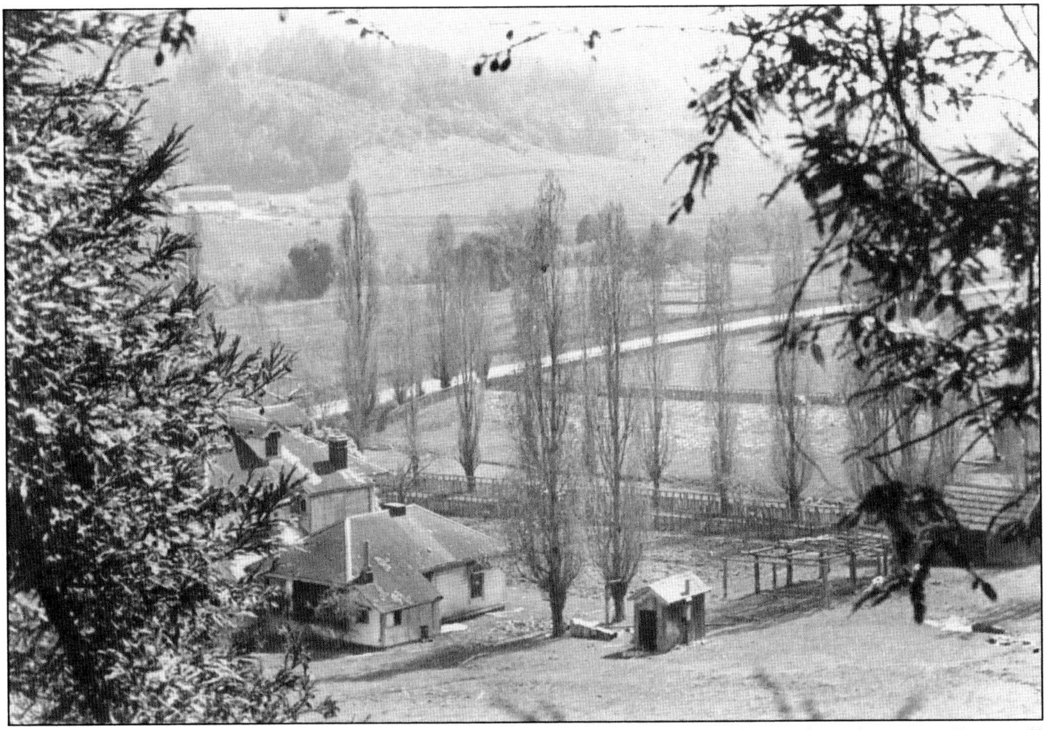

VALLEY SCENE. Looking east to the valley, this view was taken from above the Thomson-Frapwell house. The Hicks Dairy Barn can be seen in the distance to the left. In 1933, the Frapwell brothers deeded an easement to the California State Division of Highways, and in 1936, the prior Scotts Valley dirt lane became the three-lane Los Gatos–Santa Cruz Highway, now Scotts Valley Drive. This photograph was taken by Elvis Frapwell in 1927. (Courtesy of SVHS.)

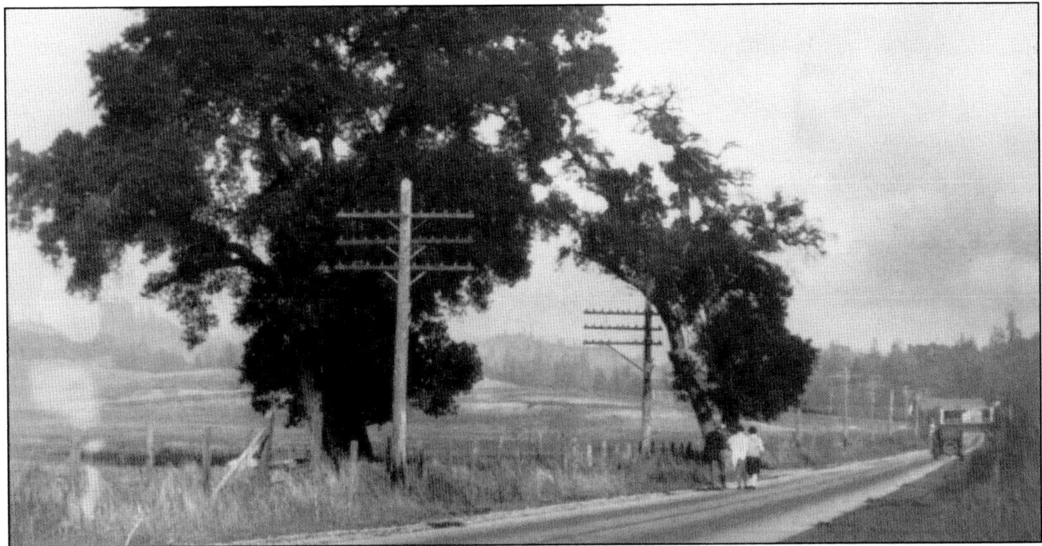

ALONG THE ROAD. Here is another view of what was then Glenwood–Santa Cruz Road, believed to have been taken just north of the old sandpit on the edge of the Thomson-Frapwell homesite. The original road through the middle of Scotts Valley was a crooked, unpaved farm path. It was not paved until after World War I. (Courtesy of SVHS.)

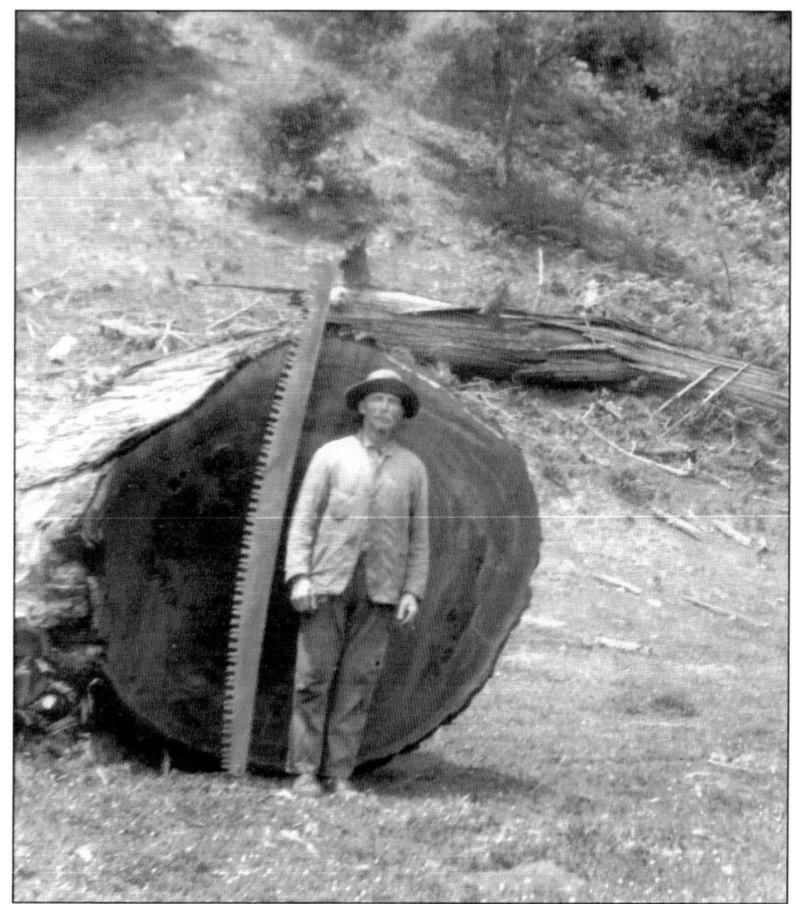

**Fallen Redwood.** The Frapwells cut wood for fence posts and other lumber on the heavily forested 250 acres of their ranch. Photographed by Elvis Frapwell in 1918, this image depicts a hired woodcutter, his saw, and an enormous fallen redwood tree. (Courtesy of SVHS.)

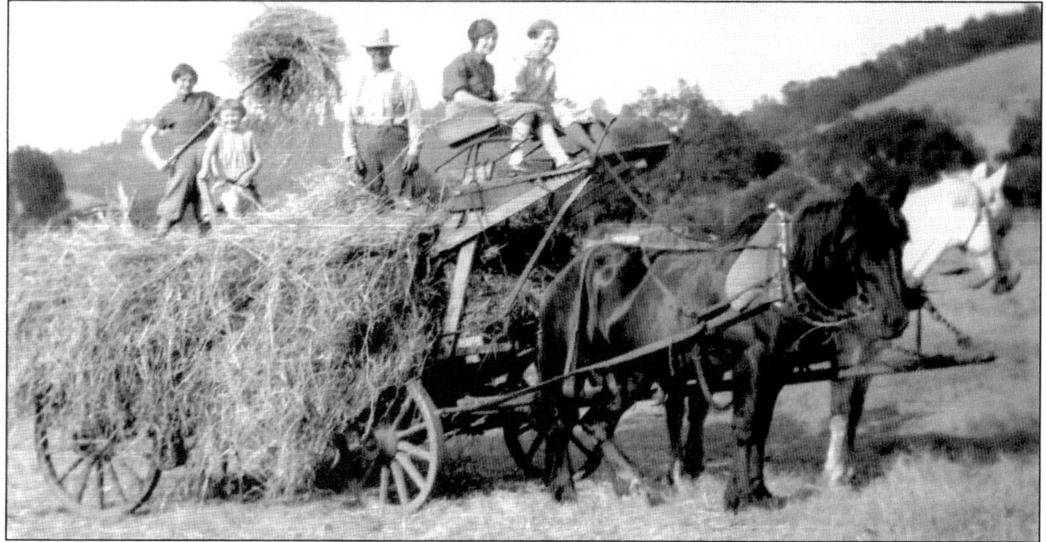

**Hay Wagon.** Elvis Frapwell captured this image of four young visitors to the ranch helping Edward Frapwell harvest hay in 1920. Edward was a school trustee, a member of the Santa Cruz County Farm Bureau, and an organizer of a county-wide farm fair. (Courtesy of SVHS.)

# DON'T BE MISLED.

If you wish to obtain the best **Butter** for table or cooking, try the

**ELITE AND SCOTTS VALLEY BUTTER,**

FOR SALE BY

**Williamson & Garrett**

**WHOLESALE and RETAIL GROCERIES. PROVISIONS. FRUITS. ETC.**

SANTA CRUZ, CAL.

**SCOTTS VALLEY BUTTER.** Taken from an 1887 newspaper, this advertisement attests to the high quality of Scotts Valley cream and milk. Raw milk from Holstein cows at the Live Oak Dairy was taken to Santa Cruz, bottled in the basement of George Frapwell's home at 444 Ocean Street, and then sold door-to-door. (Author's collection.)

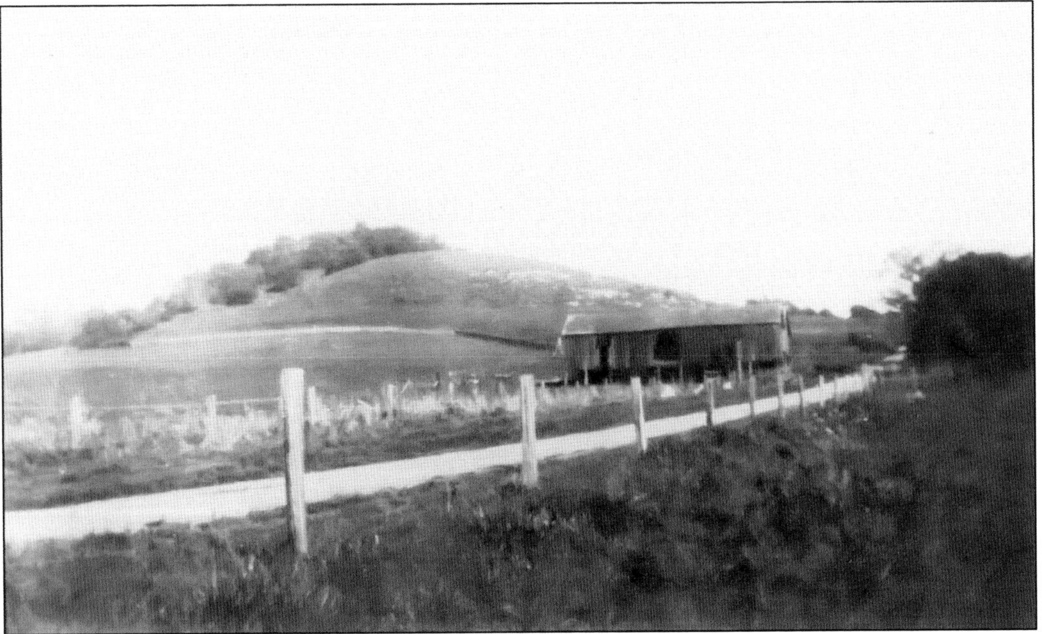

**GRANITE CREEK ROAD.** Now a busy two-lane feeder street, Granite Creek Road did not connect with what was then Los Gatos Highway until 1921. Going to school required opening gates and crossing various pastures. This photograph was taken around 1910. (Courtesy of SVHS.)

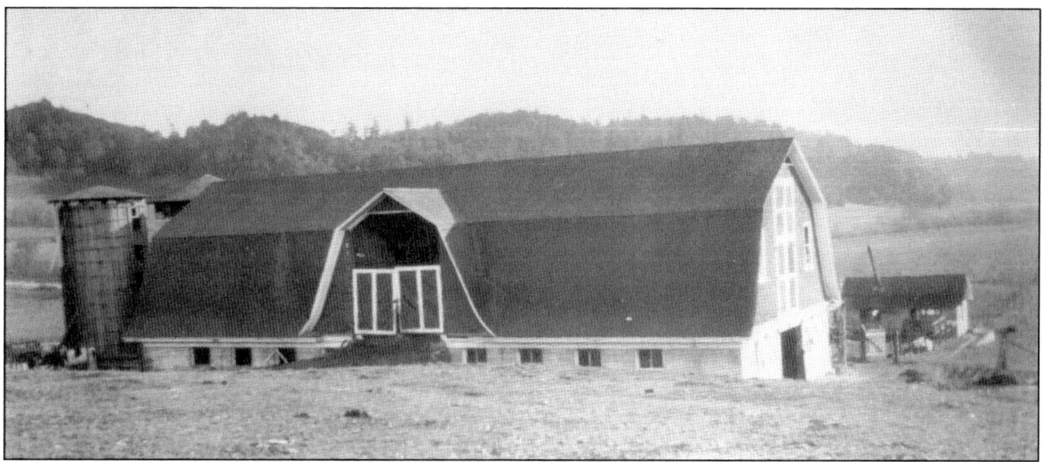

**Frapwell Barn.** Due to inadequate drainage around the old Hicks barn, the Frapwells decided a new barn should be built. They hired noted local architect Edward Van Cleek, who also designed the first casino for the Santa Cruz Beach Boardwalk. In 1914, construction was completed on a large two-story, Dutch-style barn with a gambrel roof. (Courtesy of Catherine Seapy.)

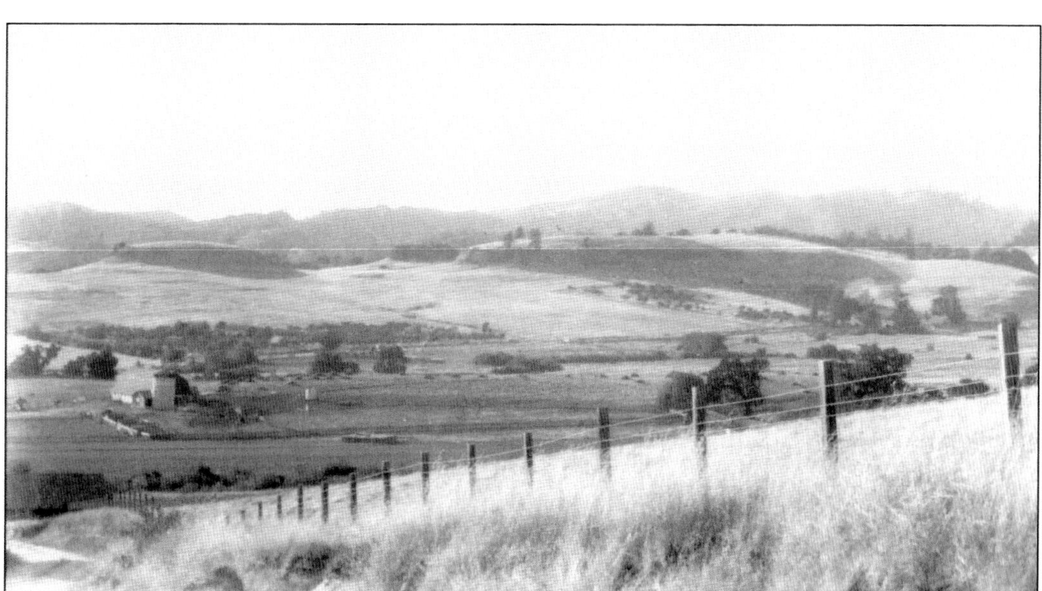

**Western Valley View.** Here is the Frapwell barn as seen in a view looking west from the eastern hillsides. Cupcake Hill is to the left of the photograph. (Courtesy of SVHS.)

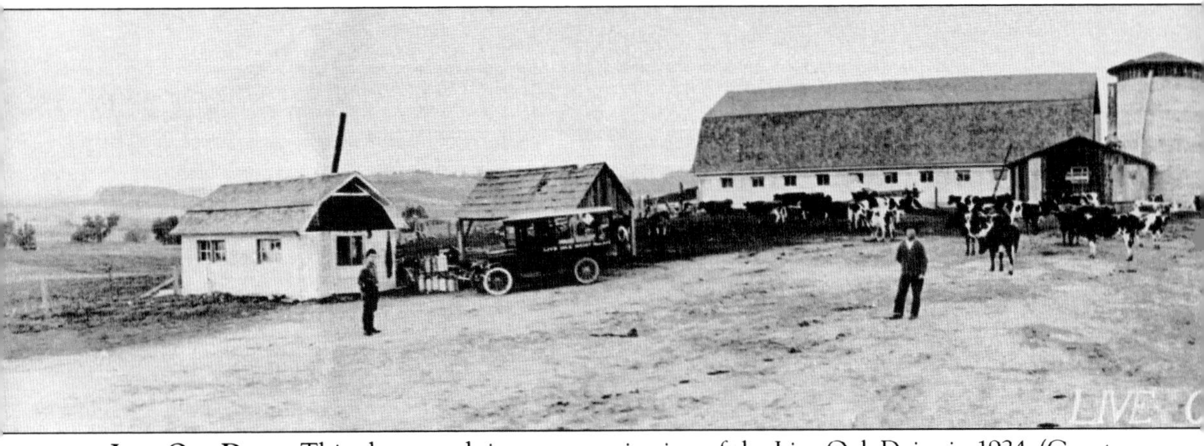


**Live Oak Dairy.** This photograph is a panoramic view of the Live Oak Dairy in 1924. (Courtesy

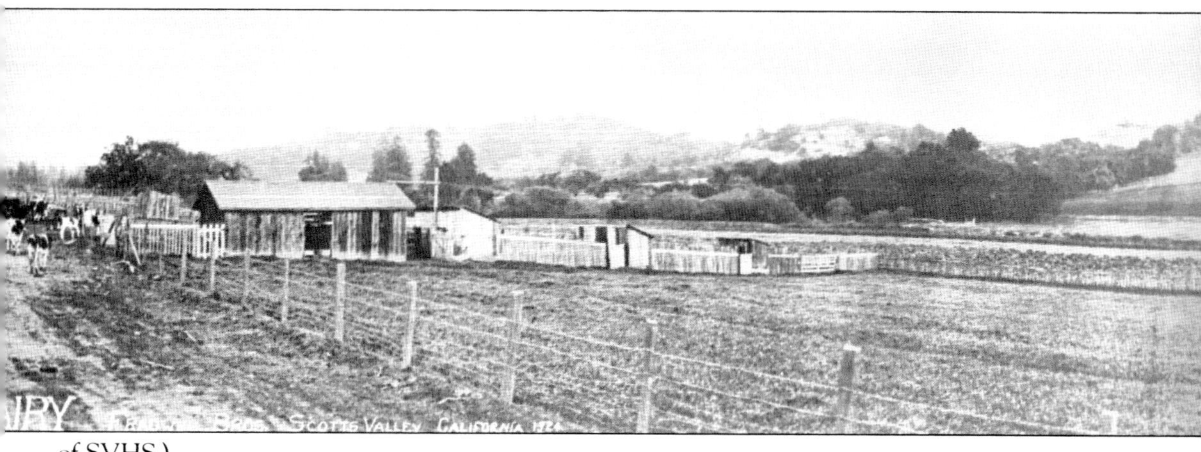


of SVHS.)

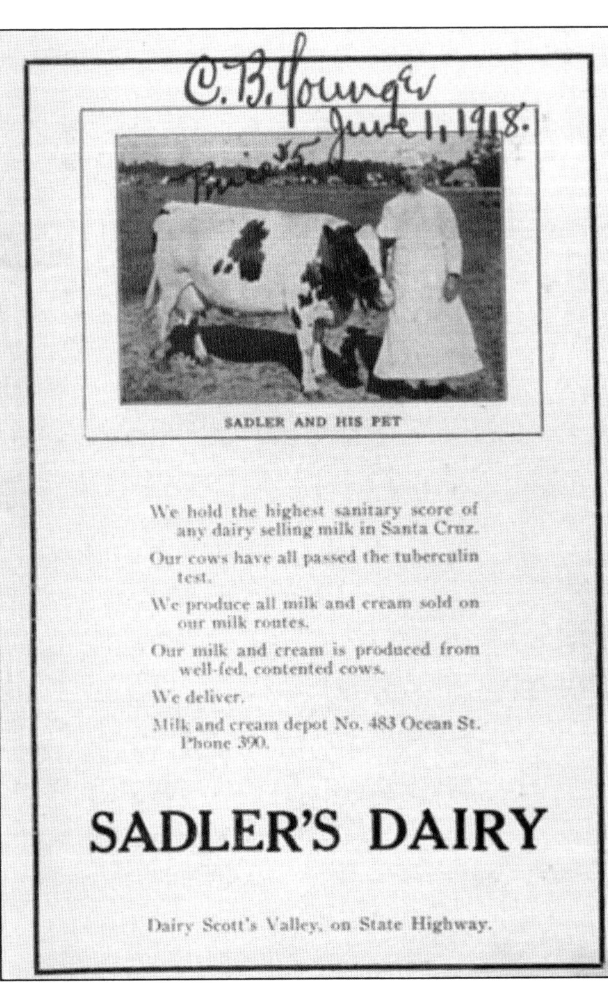


**SADLER'S DAIRY.** For a short period of time, from 1920 to 1922, the Frapwells rented out their farm to Sadler's Dairy, which also sold milk and cream door-to-door. The advertisement shown here is from a 1918–1919 Santa Cruz County directory. (Author's collection.)

**DAIRY TOKENS.** Used during the days of home milk delivery, dairy tokens could be exchanged for advance payment or bottle deposit. (Author's collection.)

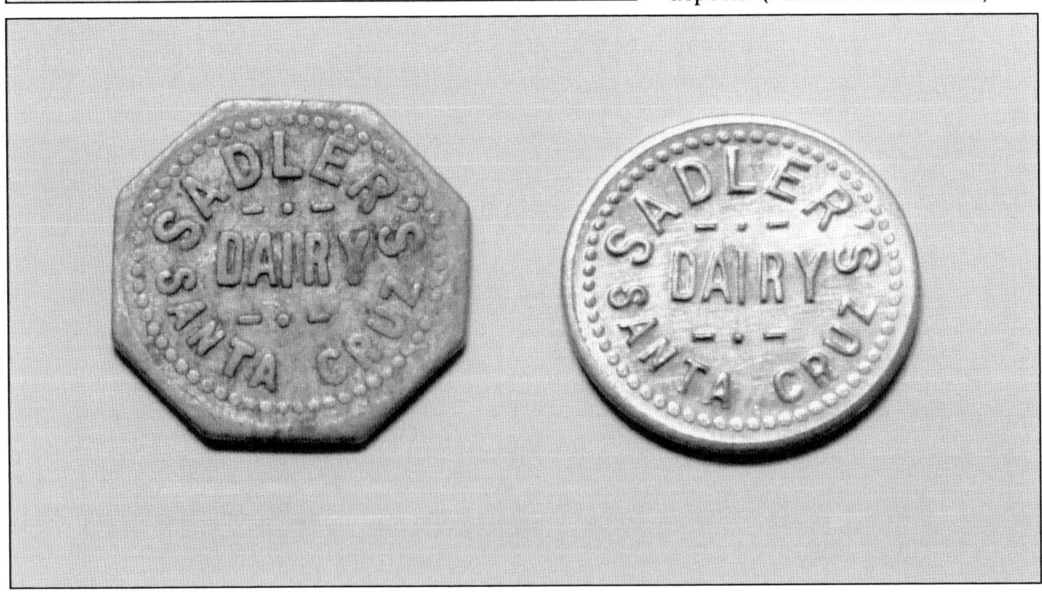

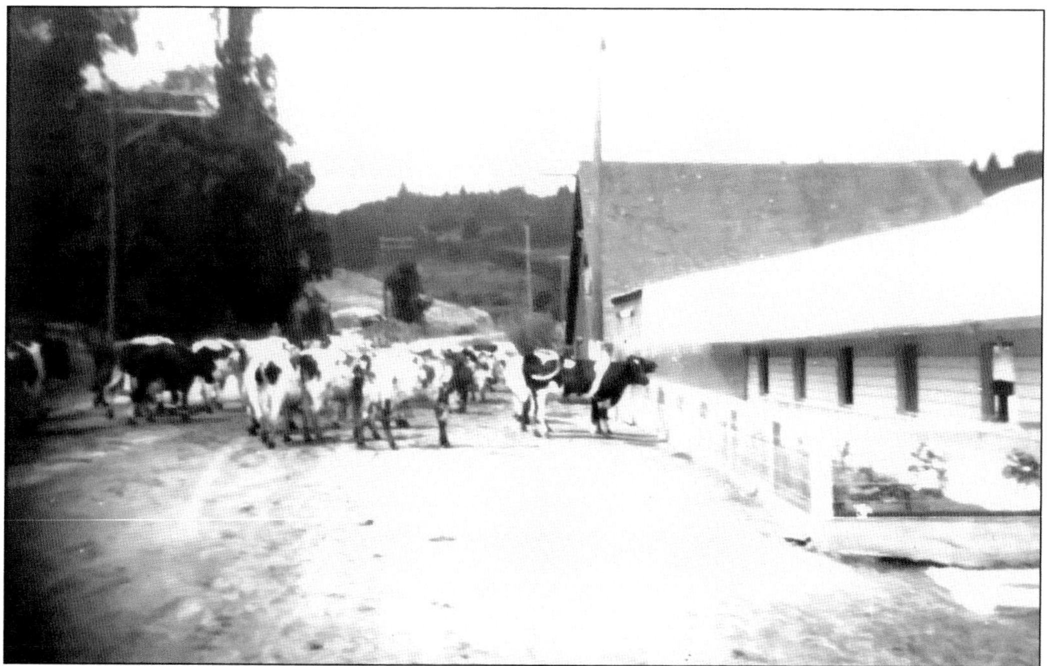

**SANTOS BARN.** George Edwin Scott's granddaughter Edith and her husband, Arthur Harington, inherited the property and continued operation of the G.E. Scott ranch. In 1945, Don Santos purchased the ranch and dairy and operated the business until his retirement in 1957. This 1945 photograph shows the Los Gatos–Santa Cruz Highway as it went through the middle of dairy, with the creamery building to the right. (Courtesy of Catherine Seapy.)

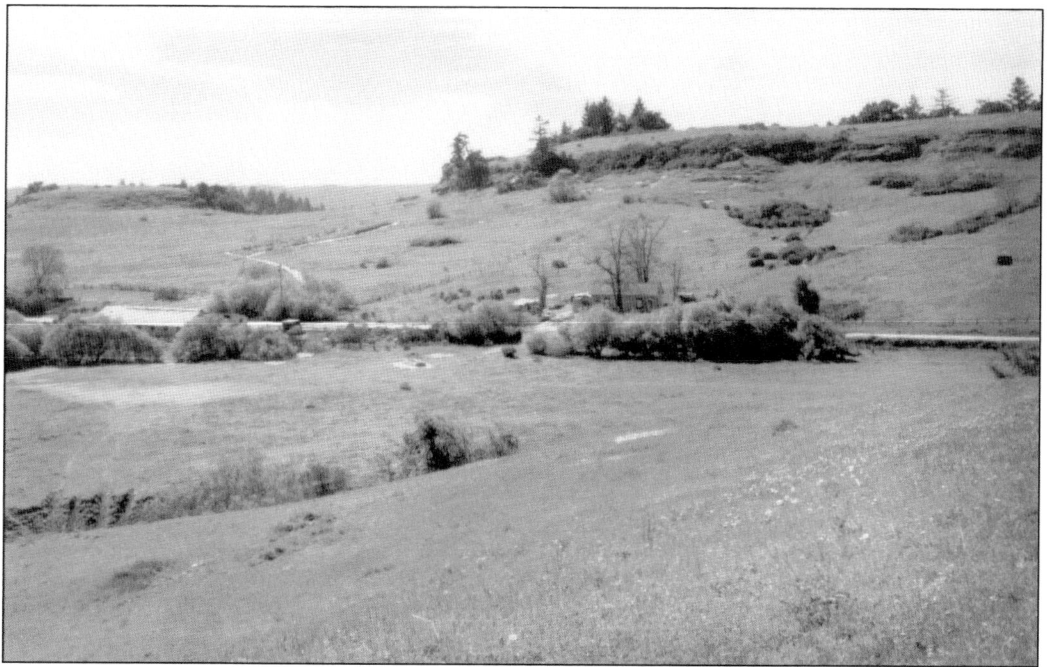

**SANTOS RANCH, C. 2000.** This photograph depicts the remains of the Santos Dairy. The future high school site and Cupcake Hill are located to the left of the photograph. (Courtesy of SVHS.)

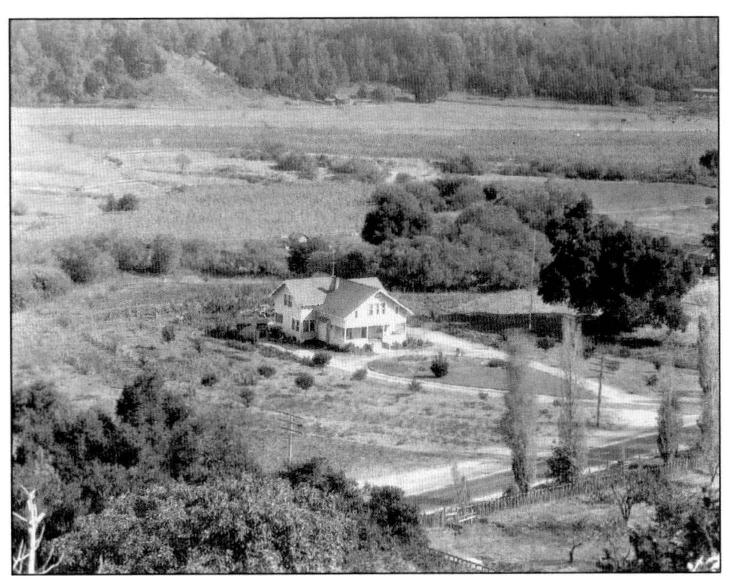

**Second Frapwell Home.** As the Thomson-Frapwell house grew to be too much work for the Frapwells to maintain, they commissioned Edward Van Cleek to design a second home. After briefly living in a temporary home, the family moved into their new home across the street from the mansion. This photograph was taken by Elvis Frapwell in 1923. Currently, the property is home to Scotts Valley Sprinkler, as well as a private residence. (Courtesy of SVHS.)

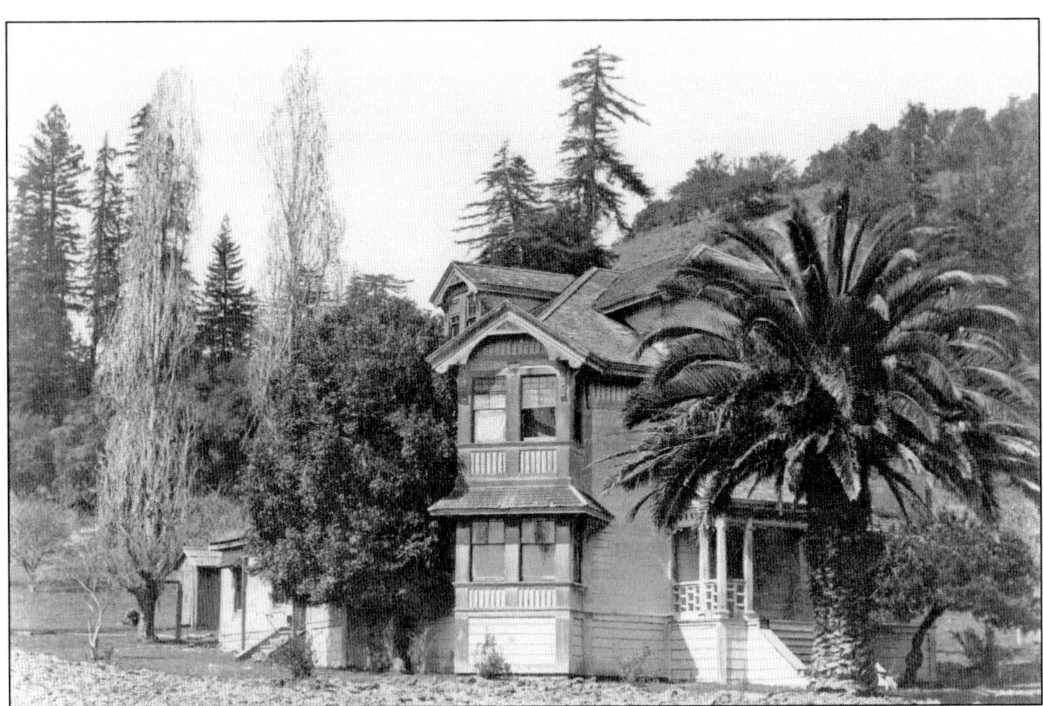

**Thomson-Frapwell Home.** After the Frapwells moved across the street, the old Thomson home went through a variety of uses, including rental property, boardinghouse, and storage. Unfortunately, the distinguished old home was torn down in 1969, just before it was to receive National Historic Landmark status. This photograph was taken by Elvis Frapwell in 1927. (Courtesy of SVHS.)

**The Barn.** In 1946, the Frapwell brothers sold their remaining 500 acres of the Live Oak Dairy for $50,000. A new owner purchased the barn and began subdividing the large property. In 1948, the Scotts Valley Community Club purchased the barn for $1,000. The milking stalls downstairs were removed, and a kitchen and large dining hall with a 200-person seating capacity were added. (Courtesy of the Scotts Valley School District.)

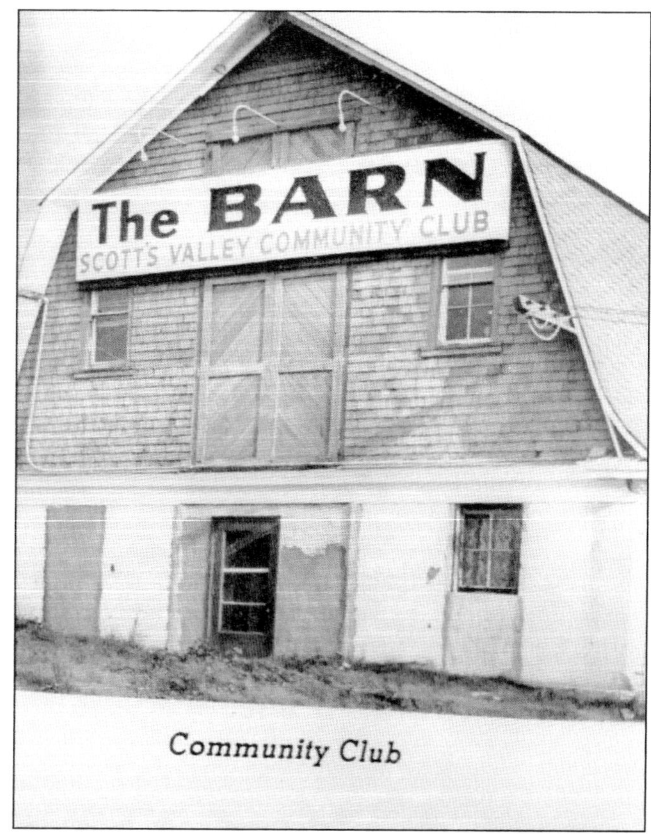


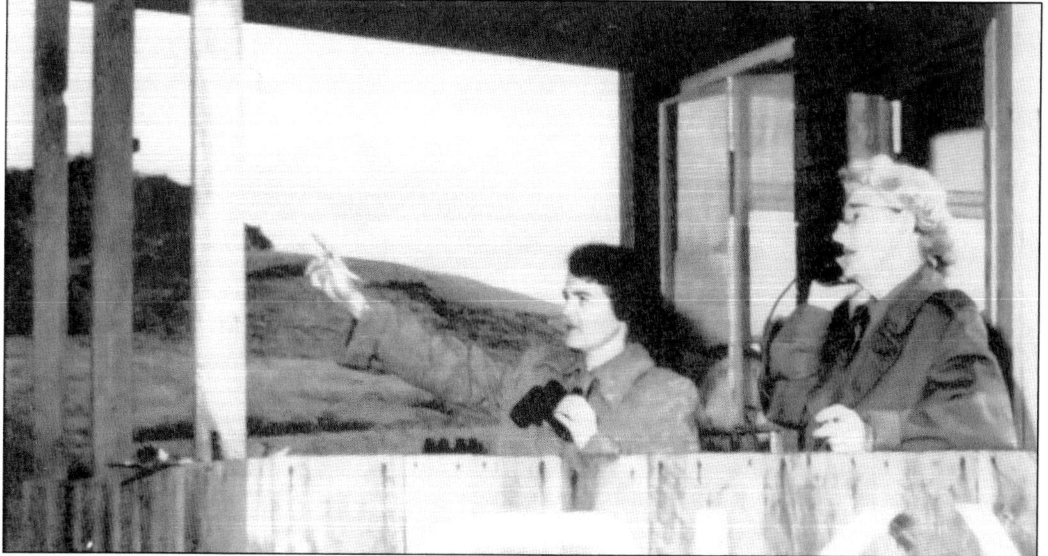

**Operation Skywatch.** Due to the threat of attack from Soviet planes during the Cold War, a Ground Observer Corps was formed in Scotts Valley in the spring of 1950. At a site located on a knoll behind the barn, volunteers trained in aircraft recognition scanned the skies 24 hours a day. As radar and missile technology advanced, the Skywatch programs were terminated around 1960. (Courtesy of the Scotts Valley School District.)

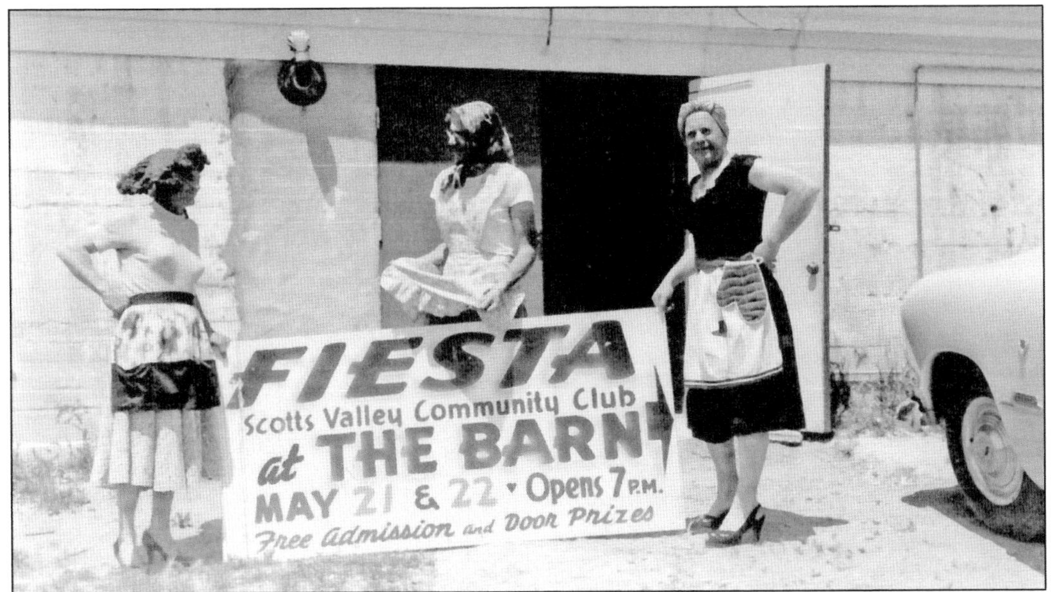


**FIESTA.** Three city fathers, one believed to be Bill Graham, dressed up as women to publicize the upcoming fiesta fundraiser at the Barn. The building served as a community center for dances, spaghetti dinners, rummage sales, annual fiestas, Easter egg hunts, annual Christmas parties, basketball games, and various community fundraisers. (Photograph by Ruby Strong, courtesy of Terry Reynolds.)

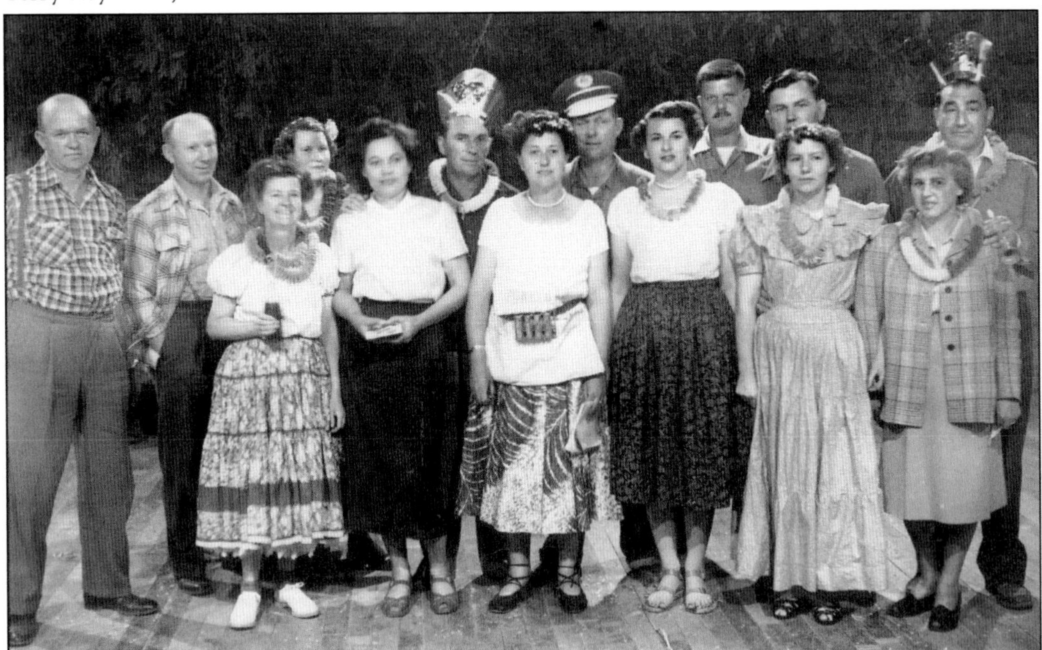

**LUAU.** Organizers and volunteers of a luau held at the Barn are pictured in 1955. From left to right are Mr. and Mrs. Marlin, Mr. and Mrs. Judd, Mr. and Mrs. Roberson, Mr. and Mrs. Temon, Mr. and Mrs. Taylor, Mr. and Mrs. Henderson, and Mr. and Mrs. Erba. After about 10 years as a community center, the Barn was sold to the Boy Scouts and then to the Scotts Valley Volunteer Fire Department, in addition to its stint as an antique shop. (Courtesy of Eric Taylor.)

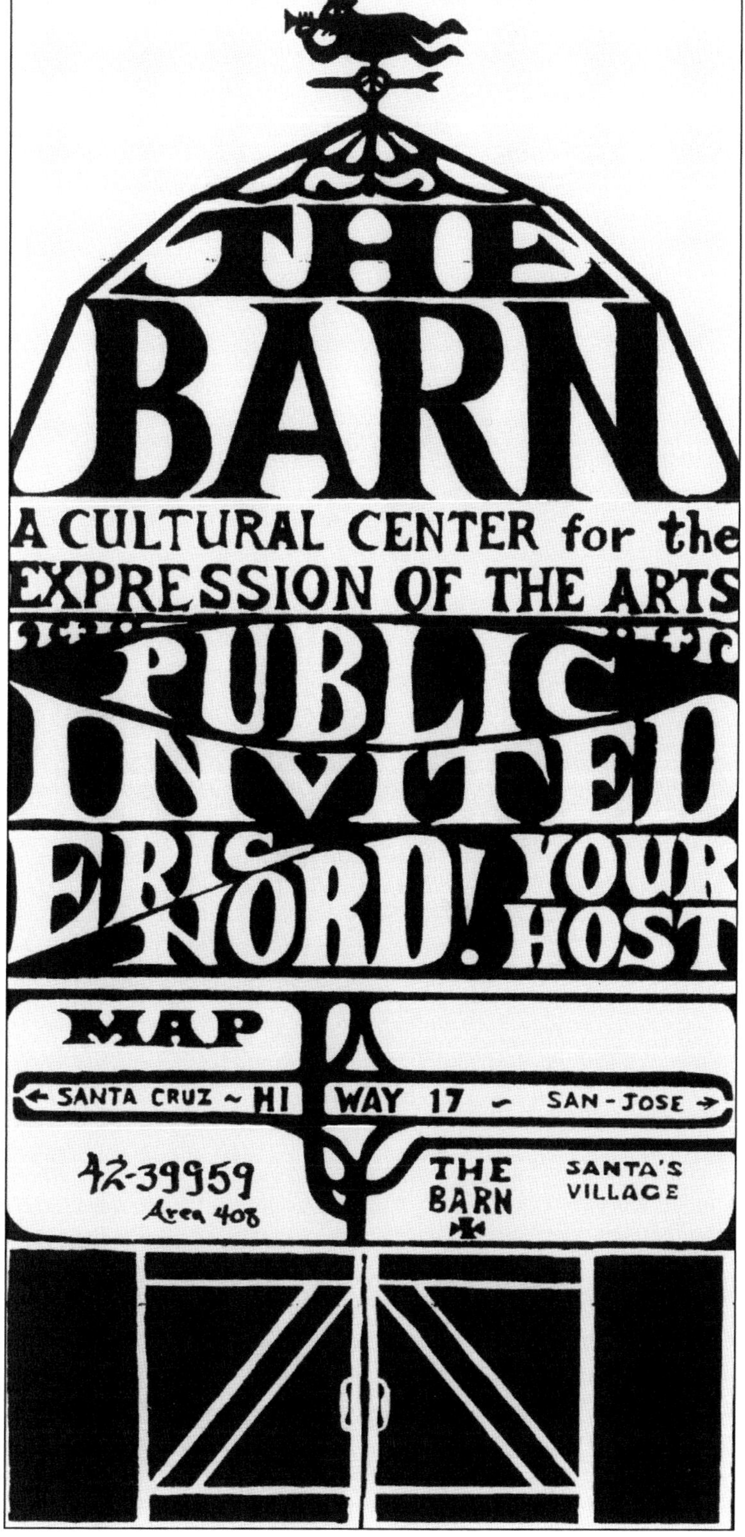


**Barn Poster.** In 1964, Eric "Big Daddy" Nord leased the Barn and opened a coffee shop. Nord, founder of the well-known San Francisco comedy club the Hungry i, had a varied career as a Beat Generation poet, musician, actor, business owner, and hipster. Nord leased the Barn to Dr. Leon Tabory, a clinical psychologist. Although he had been refused a permit for live music, Tabory held dances, concerts, and art shows, complete with colorful wall murals and a psychedelic light show. On weekends, the surrounding residents complained the loud rock music could be heard at least three-quarters of a mile away. Documented performers of that time include Big Brother and the Holding Company with Janis Joplin, Country Joe McDonald and the Fish, Captain Beefheart and His Magic Band, and the New Delhi River Band. Other noted visitors were authors Tom Wolfe and Ken Kesey. The colorful, psychedelic painted bus owned by Kesey and his band of "Merry Pranksters" must have been a sore point with the Scotts Valley Police, as it was ticketed for illegal parking at the Barn. (Courtesy of SVHS.)

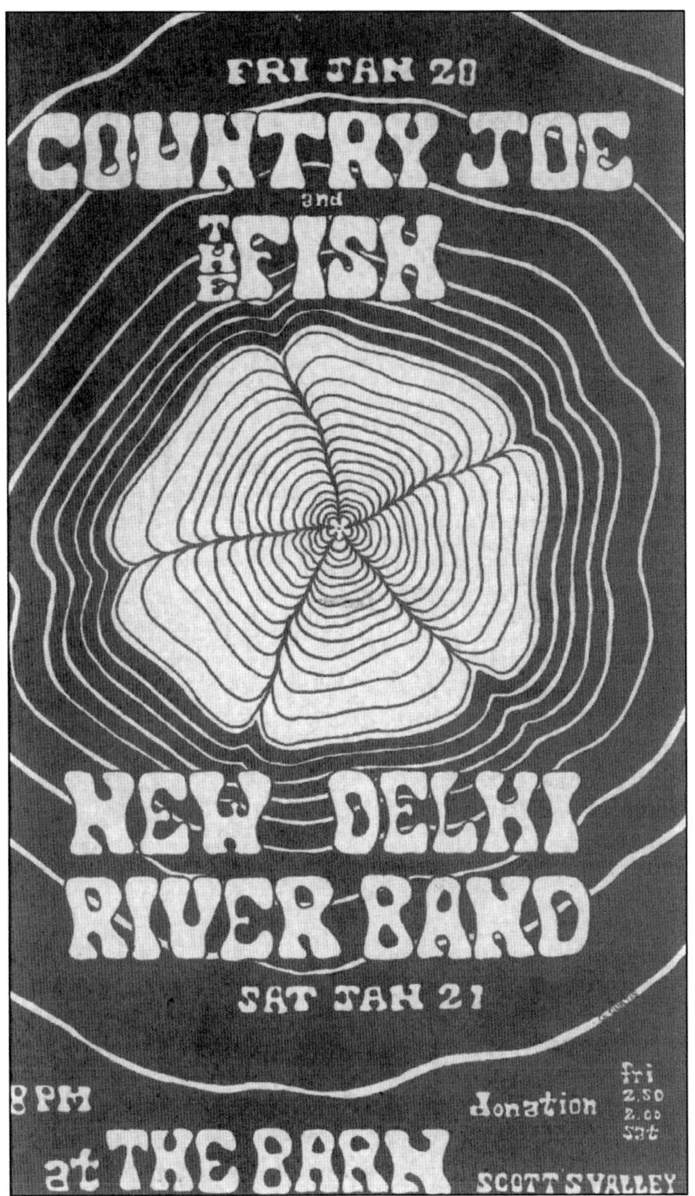


**Rock Poster.** An extended court battle ensued between Tabory and the City of Scotts Valley over the rock club operation, with Tabory filing lawsuits against Mayor Bill Graham, then succeeding mayor Friend Stone, and finally Paul and Flora Corr, local owners of the *Scotts Valley News*. Around this time, newspaper headlines proclaimed, "Hippies Stir Up a Storm" and "Go Go Dance Girl Taken From Barn After Bad 'LSD Trip' Reaction." In a 1968 court hearing, Tabory claimed his operation was not subject to city regulations, as the rock bands, light shows, and dances were not entertainment but "sensitivity workshops." The presiding judge was not convinced and shut down the nightclub for good. Purchased by David and Claire Hodgin, the Barn became part of a newly built 15-acre recreational park called Holiday Host Travel Park. The owners used the Barn for park activities but also allowed community use for meetings, wedding receptions, square dances, luncheons, and church services. In 1979, the Hodgins started the Holiday Barn Dinner Theater. Productions included *Godspell*, *My Fair Lady*, and *South Pacific*. (Author's collection.)

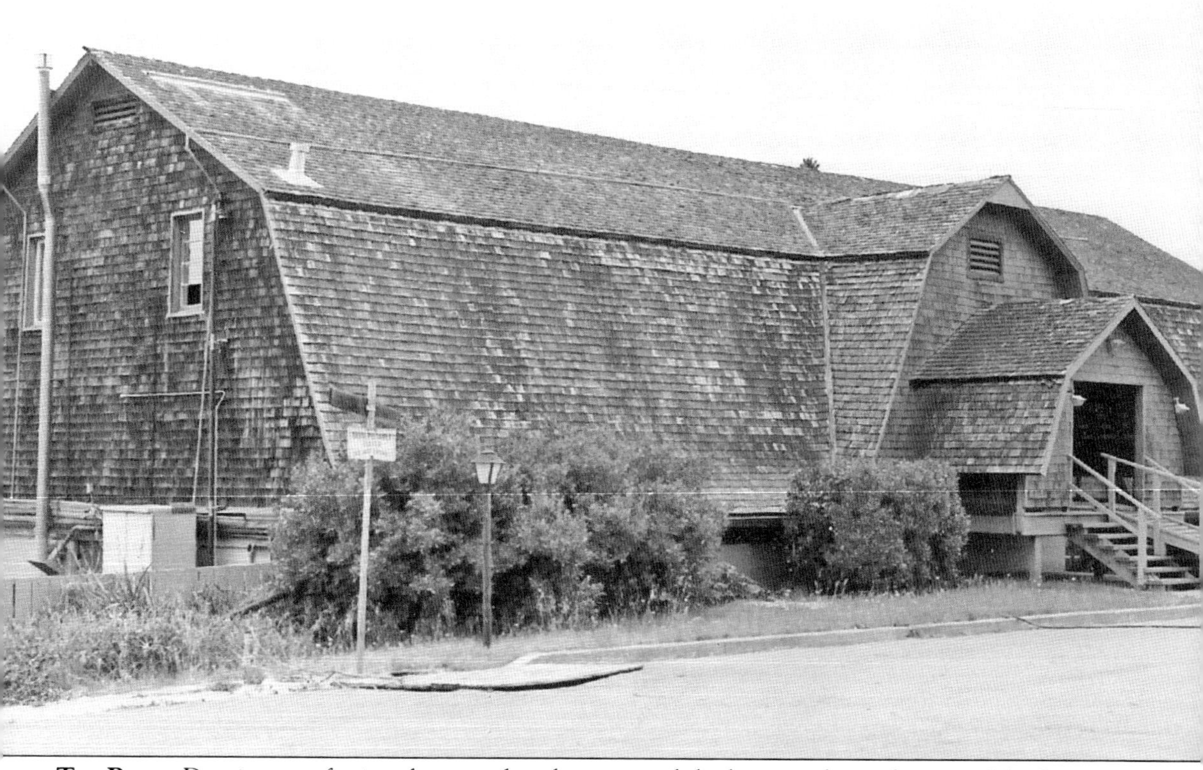

**The Barn.** Despite a professional report that documented the historical significance of the Barn and an application for nomination of the Barn as a historical landmark from the Scotts Valley Historical Society, the Scotts Valley Cultural Resource Preservation Commission voted 4-1 not to hold a public hearing on the matter and next voted 4-1 to allow the applicant, Borland International, to demolish the structure. Although the decision to demolish the Barn was appealed to the city council, the Barn was razed on August 3, 1991, ironically the city's 25th anniversary of incorporation. An estimated 250 people attended one last gala party to bid farewell to the well-loved structure. (Courtesy of Charlene Duval.)

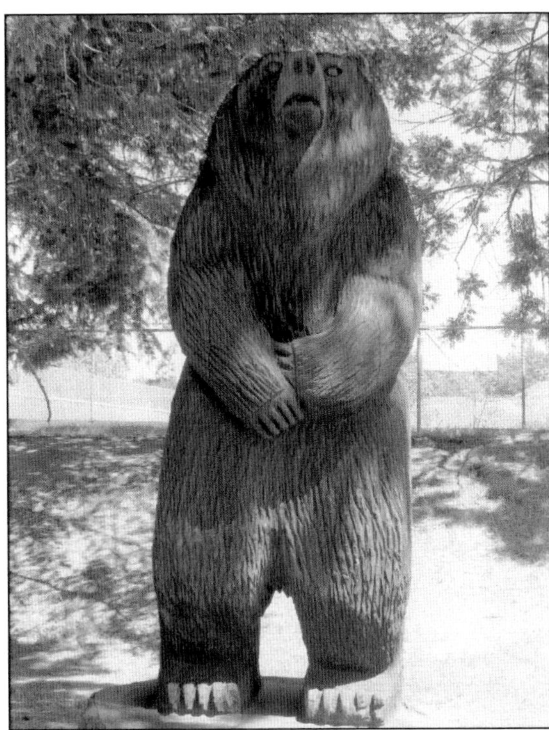

**Vine Hill School Mascot.** California grizzly bears have long been a source of interest, and visitors to this area still ask if there are any in Scotts Valley. Pictured on both the state flag and the state seal, the California grizzly represents massive size, strength, and beauty. Many accounts from early settlers reported numerous grizzly bears, which were attracted to the abundant game and wildlife in the area. (Photograph by the author.)

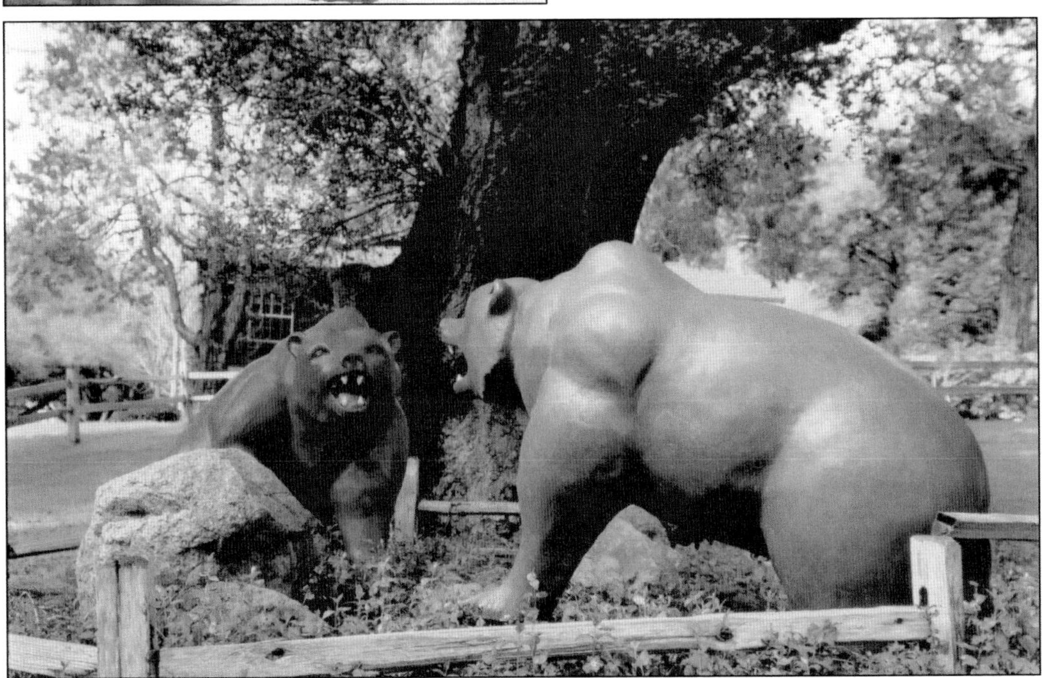

**Lost World Bears.** Once numbering in the thousands, the California grizzly bear was hunted to extinction in the 1920s. Reportedly, the last remaining grizzly bear in Santa Cruz County was shot and killed on Bonny Doon Ridge in 1889. Temporarily removed, these bear statues from the former Lost World park were donated to the city by the Thompson family and stand guard at the entrance to Scotts Valley City Hall. (Photograph by the author.)

# *Five*

# Roadside Attractions

Situated in a pleasant green valley between the Santa Cruz Mountains and the Pacific Ocean, Scotts Valley has long been a resting place for the weary traveler. On a journey done mostly on foot and horseback by the native Indians and missionaries, Scotts Valley provided a respite from the difficult trip over the high mountains and through the deep ravines. When Hiram Scott and Charles McKiernan built the toll road to the Summit, Scotts Valley again became a rest stop where stagecoach horses were added or removed depending on the direction of travel. The establishment of the railroad brought visitors to the numerous tourist resorts to enjoy the cool weather and towering redwood trees. The greatest impact on Scotts Valley began in 1915 when the state highway was routed along the former farming tracks. Financed by a newly assessed 2¢ per gallon gas tax, the narrow dirt lanes were expanded to a two-lane concrete road in 1921.

Despite the upgraded road, automobile congestion on the highway did not improve. According to a newspaper article in the *Santa Cruz Evening News* on June 1, 1931, "Traffic in the valley was unusually heavy. Cars taking the Mount Hermon to Camp Evers cut-off were lined up for more than two hours last evening waiting turns to get on the Los Gatos Highway. Many returned to the San Lorenzo valley and waited until late at night." Once officially part of Highway 5 and known as the Stockton-Oakland-Santa Cruz Highway, the new four-lane highway, completed in 1943, was renamed Highway 17. However, the new highway now bypassed Scotts Valley and its many tourist-oriented businesses.

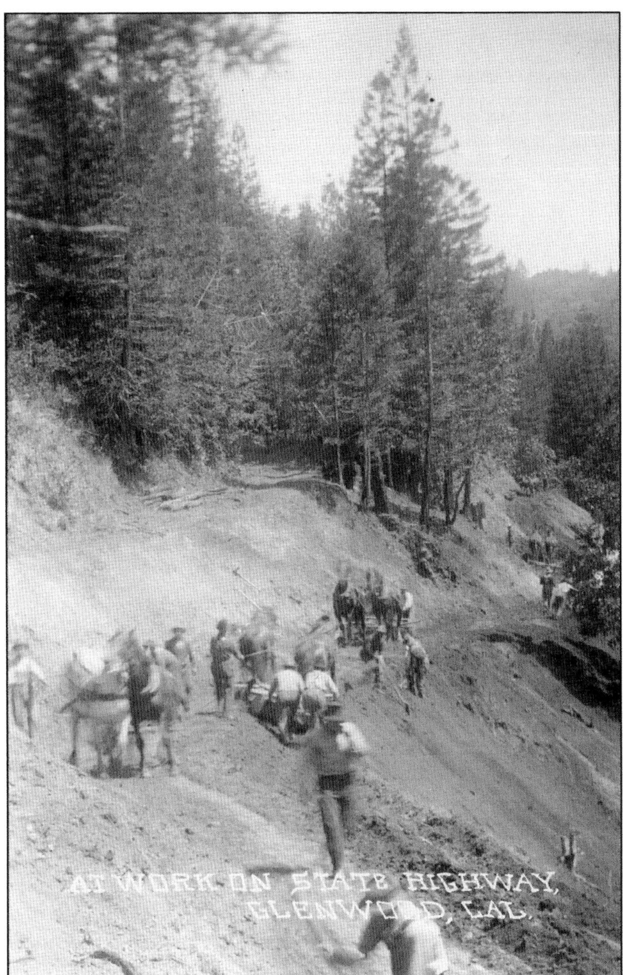


**BUILDING THE HIGHWAY.** The passage of an $18 million state road bond in 1911 required every county center to be linked with adequate roadways. The road coming over the mountains between Los Gatos and Santa Cruz was chosen for upgrading. Construction began in 1912 after a study had determined the best route was through the area of Glenwood. (Courtesy of Ronnie Trubeck.)

**EARLY BEACH TRAFFIC.** Today's much safer Highway 17 is unrecognizable from the 1930s- and 1940s-era two-lane roadway with stretches through Scotts Valley that included a "suicide" passing lane in the center. (Courtesy of Ronnie Trubeck.)

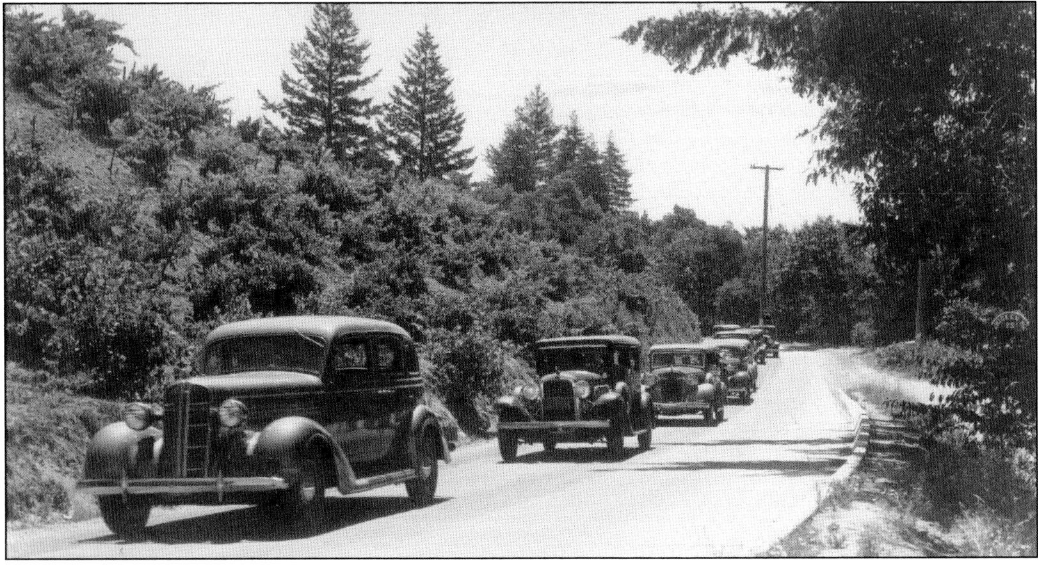

**FREEWAY CONSTRUCTION.** This aerial photograph depicts the building of the Mount Hermon interchange off Highway 17 in 1959. A $1.2 million project completed in 1961, the new three-mile stretch upgraded the road to full freeway status. Several businesses and homes were removed to allow for the construction on the new freeway exit. (Courtesy of Covello & Covello Photography.)

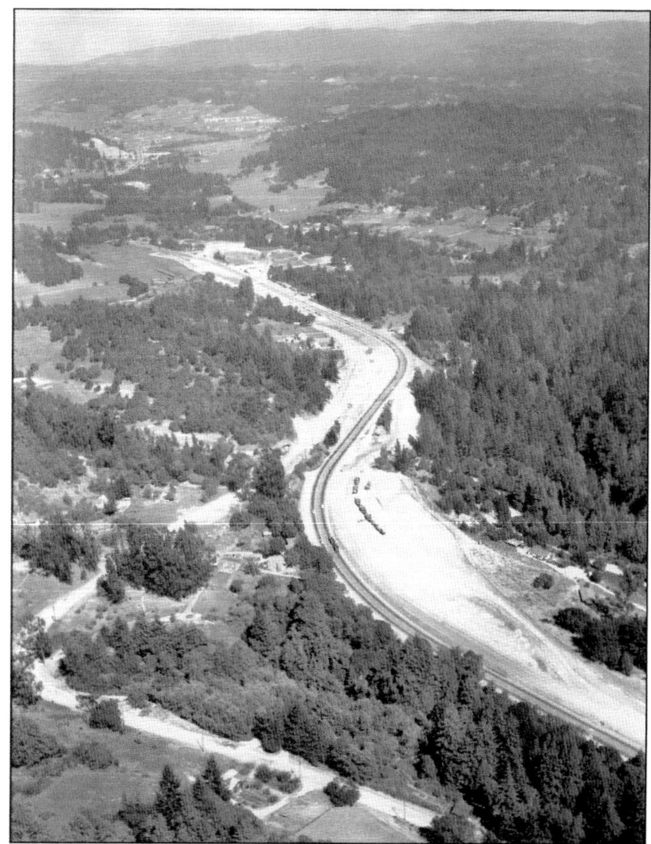

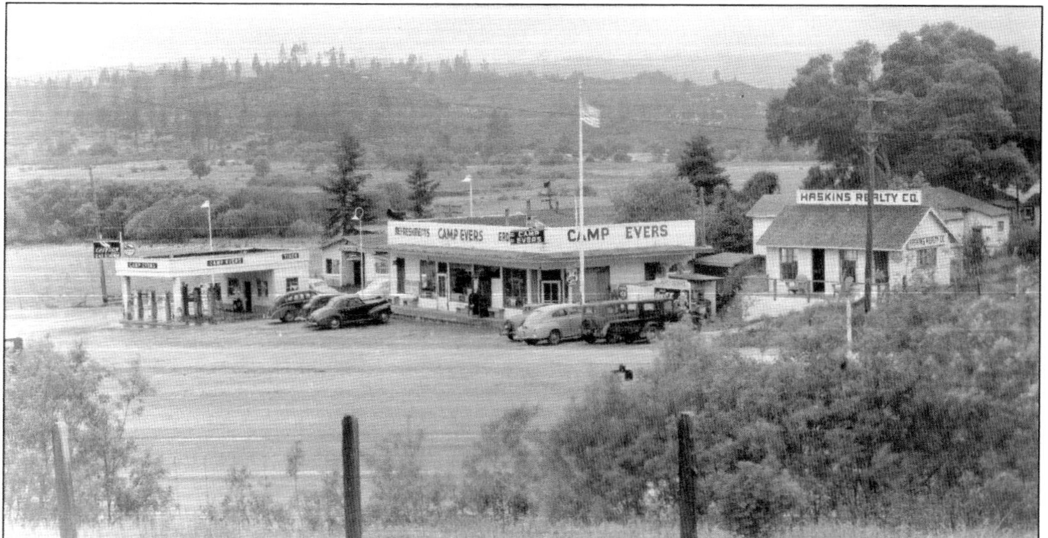


**CAMP EVERS, C. 1945.** In the early 1920s, Finette Locke Shafter sold 28 acres of land to Edward and Caroline Evers. The property was loosely bounded by the then state highway, the old Felton Road (now Bean Creek Road), and today's Mount Hermon Road. The original business consisted of a small grocery story at the south end of the building, a garage with a gas pump, two tourist cabins, and space for tent camping. A dance hall was added later. (Author's collection.)

DANCING

EVERY SATURDAY
EVENING

CAMP EVERS

Santa Cruz-Los Gatos
State Highway
Five Miles From
Santa Cruz

Auto Camp Grounds
High, Level and Dry
Cabins $1 per night

**Camp Evers Notice.** The advertisement shown here is from 1924. With the establishment of the small commercial development, the area came to be known as Camp Evers. Later, 25 acres of the Camp Evers site became the Wesleyan Methodist Campground, then today's Hidden Oaks condominium development. (Author's collection.)

**Butcher Counter.** After the retirement of the Evers in 1946, the property changed hands and grew to include a restaurant, bar, and real estate office. The first rural post office station was established at the center, and both the Greyhound and Peerless bus lines stopped there until the early 1970s. In 1961, Edward Ponza, Battista Erba, and Gene Hopkins opened Camp Evers Market, the first supermarket in Scotts Valley. (Courtesy of the Scotts Valley School District.)

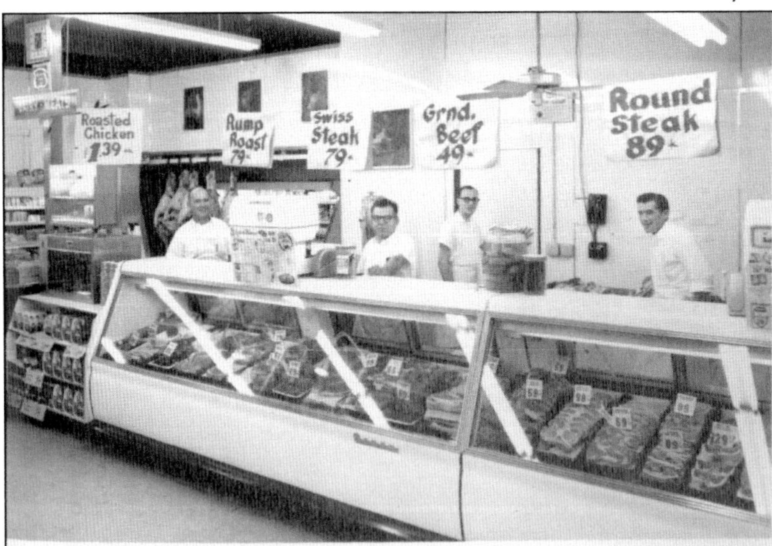

**BEVERLY LODGE.** In 1931, Agnes and William Archibald purchased an eight-acre parcel of land just across from the present Bank of America site. The Archibalds developed the property into the Beverly Gardens & Aviaries, which featured a teahouse, formal gardens, and a bird-oriented specialty shop. The public could view three aviaries with over 200 species of birds, including macaws, ibis, cranes, and wild ducks. (Courtesy of Eric Taylor.)

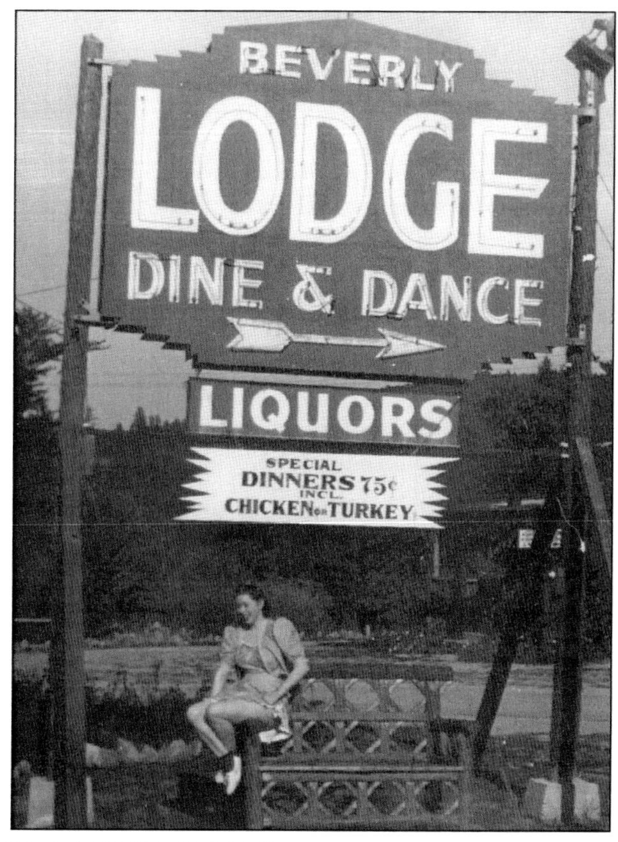


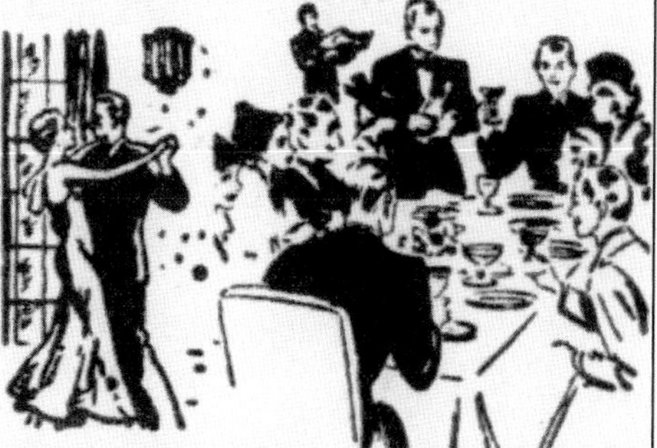


**LODGE ADVERTISEMENT, 1939.** When disease struck their birds, the Archibalds converted the property into a tourist resort and continued to add attractions such as a South American ring-tailed monkey named Ginger, a 14-variety squirrel house, and a restaurant with a Cave Bar. In 1938, John and Dora Sinnhuber purchased the property and operated it until 1944, after which it went through several different owners before closing in 1951. (Author's collection.)

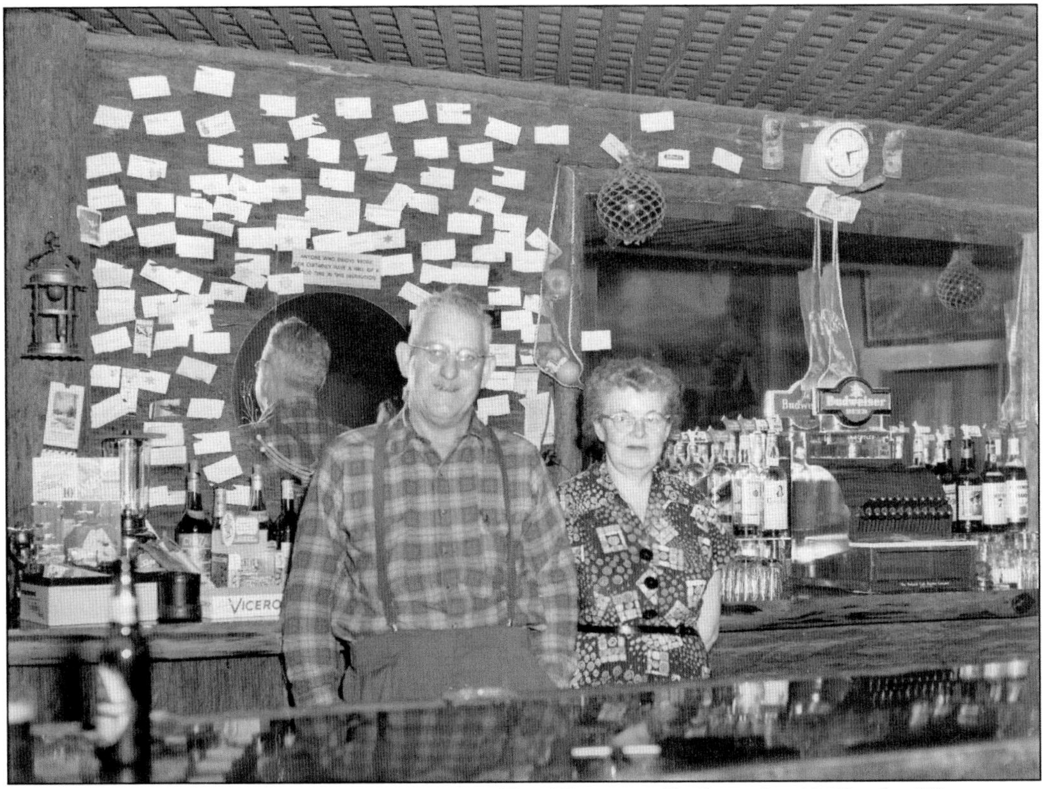

**THE TAYLORS.** Built in the 1940s, the Wawona was a casual German-style tavern located just south of Beverly Gardens. Split off from the Beverly Garden property in 1947, the combination bar-restaurant changed over several times, with Kipp's Welcome Inn, Taylor's Enchiladas, the Rusty Lantern, and finally Malone's in 1980. Carl E. and Ethel Taylor are pictured behind the bar of the Wawona in this c. 1950 photograph. (Courtesy of Eric Taylor.)

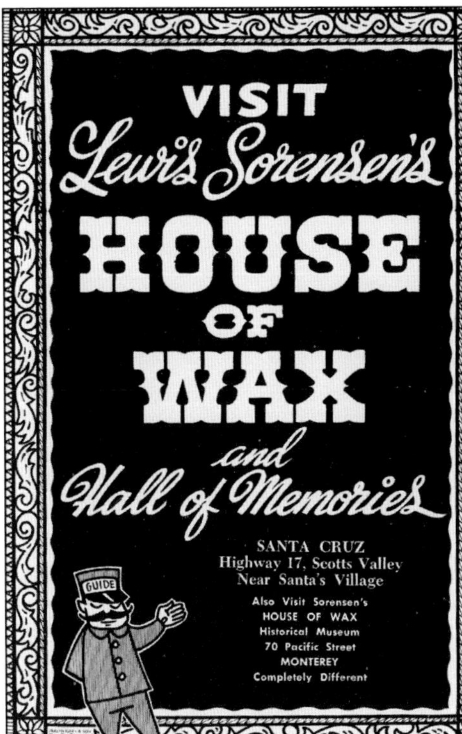


**HOUSE OF WAX.** Built in the early 1950s, the House of Wax was located on the former Beverly Gardens site. Exhibits included Abraham Lincoln, Betsy Ross, and a depiction of a turn-of-the-century one-room schoolhouse. The museum suffered a major fire in 1965 and never reopened. (Author's collection.)

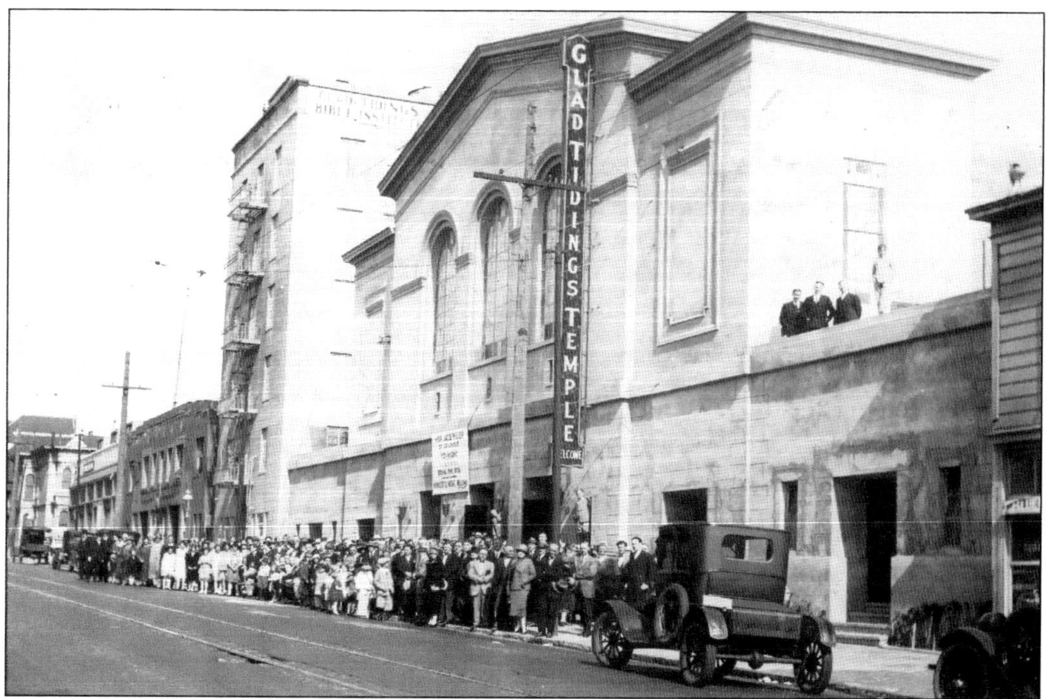


**Glad Tidings Temple.** Developed from a Pentecostal religious outreach program in San Francisco, the Glad Tidings Bible Training School was established by Robert and Mary Craig in 1919 to prepare students for service to Christ. Soon, the school grew too large for the San Francisco location, and in 1950, it was moved to what was then Bethany Park, the Santa Cruz location of an Assemblies of God Summer Campground. (Courtesy of Assemblies of God, Northern California and Nevada District.)

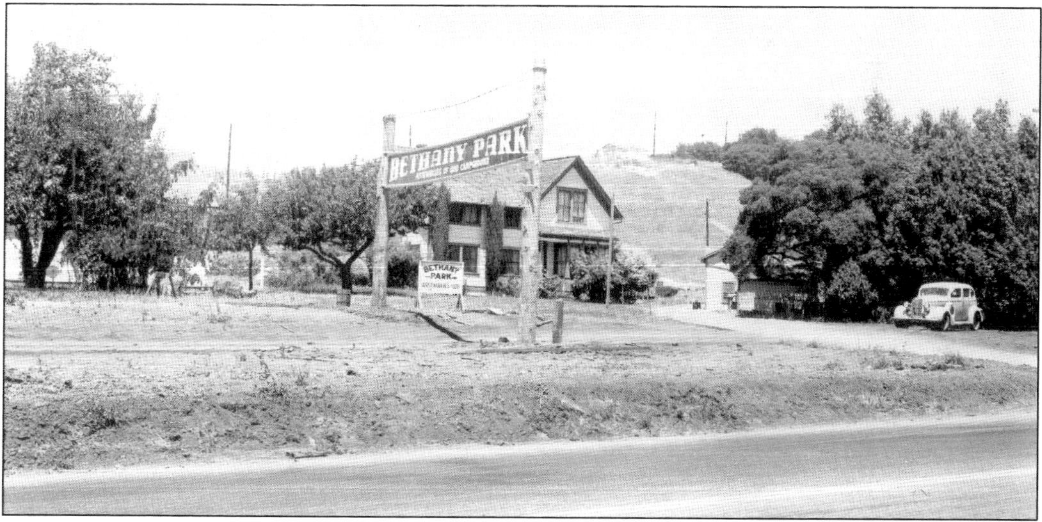


**Highway Entrance.** In 1945, dairyman Don Santos sold 70 acres of land that included a strip of highway frontage, a Victorian-era farmhouse, a barn, and a tamale stand. Access to the property was difficult because of the steep terrain. With war surplus materials, the buildings from the summer camp, limited funds, and faith, the college began to grow. (Courtesy of Assemblies of God, Northern California and Nevada District.)

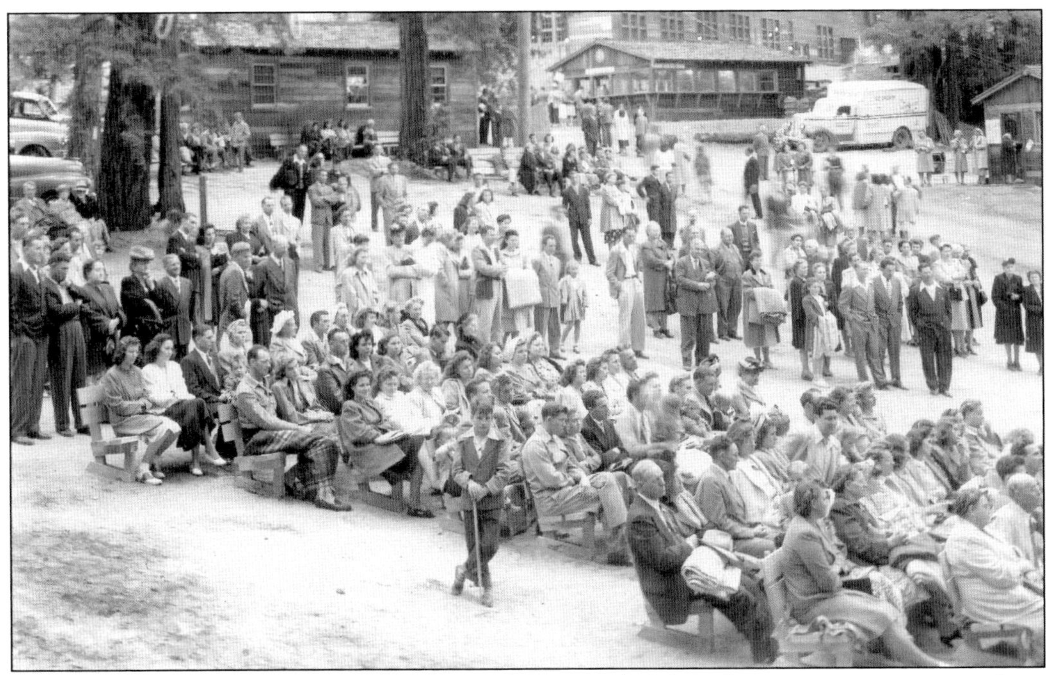

**Camp Meeting.** Large groups of church members attended the religious summer camps, where they slept in tents and small cottages, attended group lectures, and ate in a common dining hall. (Courtesy of Assemblies of God, Northern California and Nevada District.)

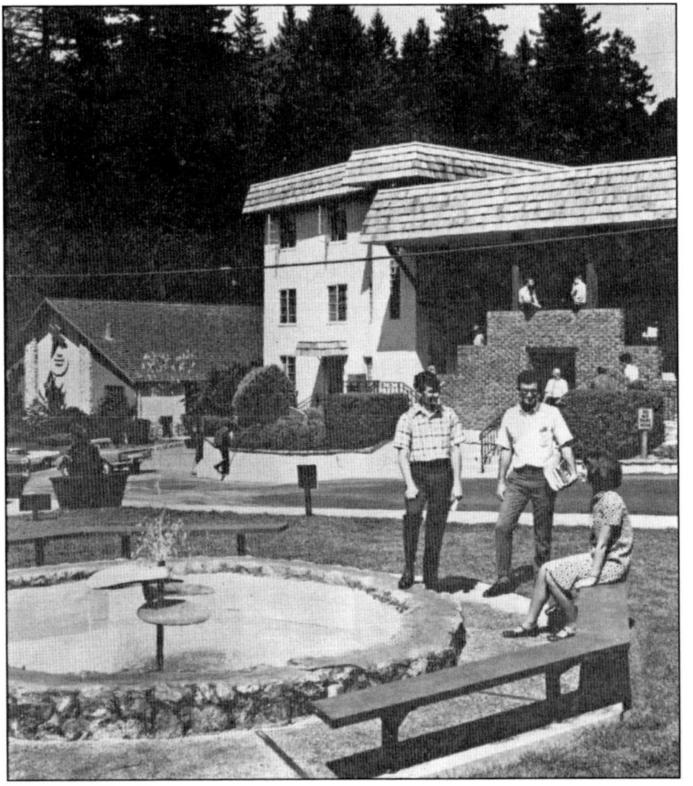

**Bethany College.** While roads, heating, sanitation, and a drinkable water supply were early problems for the new school, solutions were found, and the college went on to build new dormitories and classrooms, along with a chapel, library, theater, gym, administration building, and preschool. Rising costs and dwindling attendance forced the school to close in 2011. In 2014, the 1440 Foundation purchased the former campus. (Courtesy of Assemblies of God, Northern California and Nevada District.)

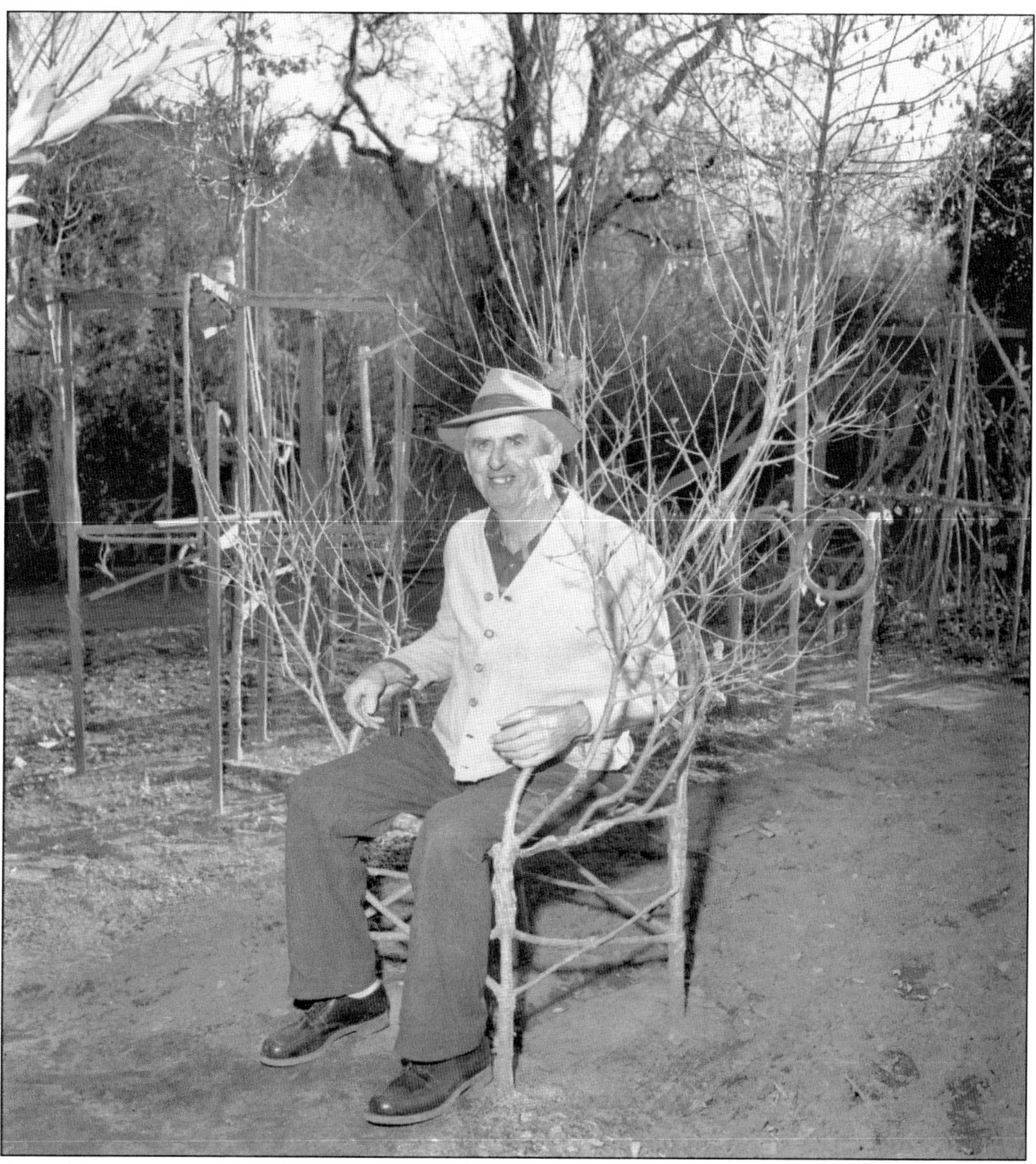

**AXEL ERLANDSON, C. 1950.** Born in Sweden in 1884, Axel Erlandson moved with his family first to Minnesota, then to Hilmar, a Swedish community in the Central Valley near Turlock. A farmer by profession, he had little formal schooling but taught himself auto repair, carpentry, mathematics, and the principles of land surveying. After observing some trees on his property growing together in a hedgerow around his field, he began to experiment using an ancient technique known as pleaching. By the mid-1920s, Erlandson was grafting and shaping tree trunks and limbs into astonishing designs. Over the years, as his technique improved, his wife, Leona, suggested he display the trees. After visiting the Mystery Spot tourist attraction in Santa Cruz with her daughter Wilma in 1945, she thought the unusual attraction would fit the area and proposed Scotts Valley. In 1946, the Erlandsons purchased a three-quarter-acre lot on Scotts Valley Drive for $1,050. The tree removal took over three months, but eventually, four loads of trees were moved the 100 miles to Scotts Valley. (Courtesy of Covello & Covello Photography.)

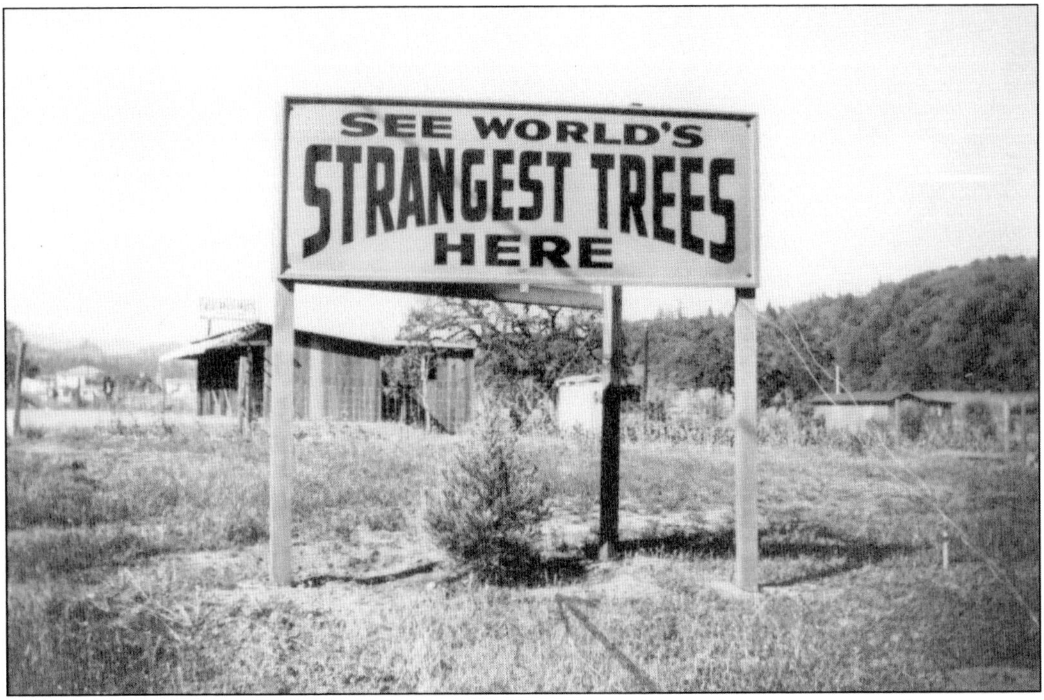

**First Advertisement.** It was Erlandson's daughter Wilma who suggested her father change the name of the attraction from the World's Strangest Trees to the Tree Circus. (Courtesy of Wayne Thompson.)

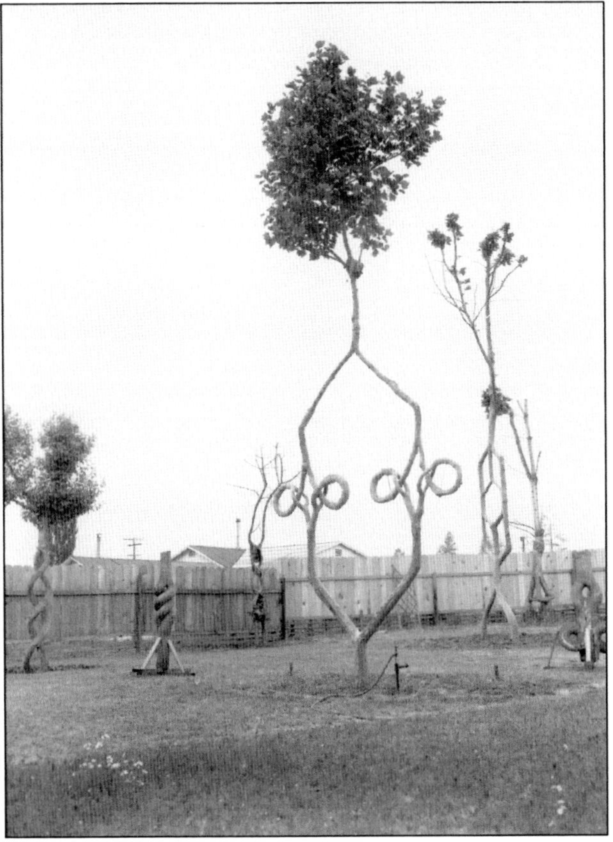

**Early Exhibit.** Replanted with care, the trees resumed growth at the new site, and the exhibit was opened in the spring of 1947. Admission to the attraction was 25¢, plus 5¢ tax. (Courtesy of Covello & Covello Photography.)

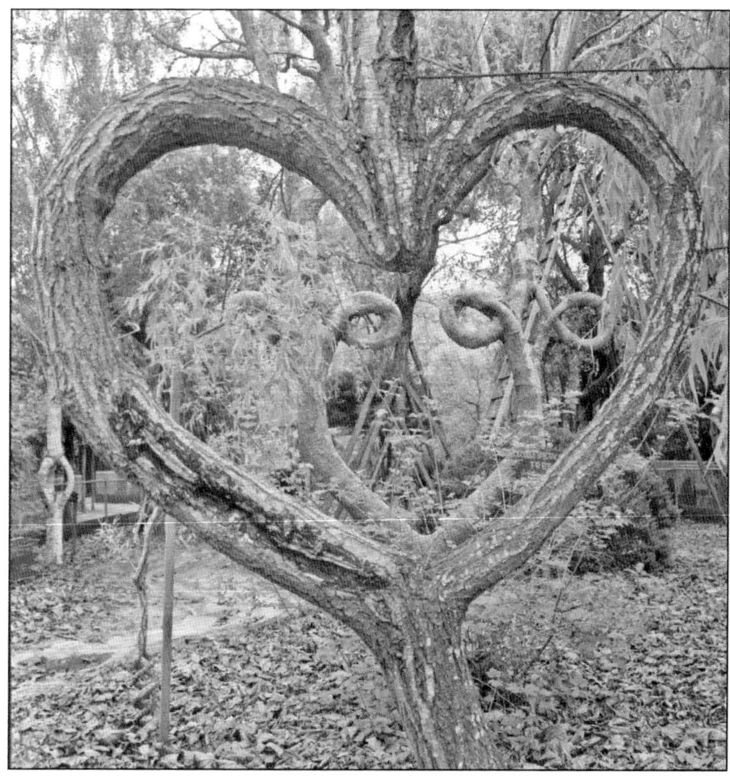

**Heart Tree.** When asked the secret to his success, Erlandson would mysteriously reply, "Oh, I talk to them." (Courtesy of Covello & Covello Photography.)

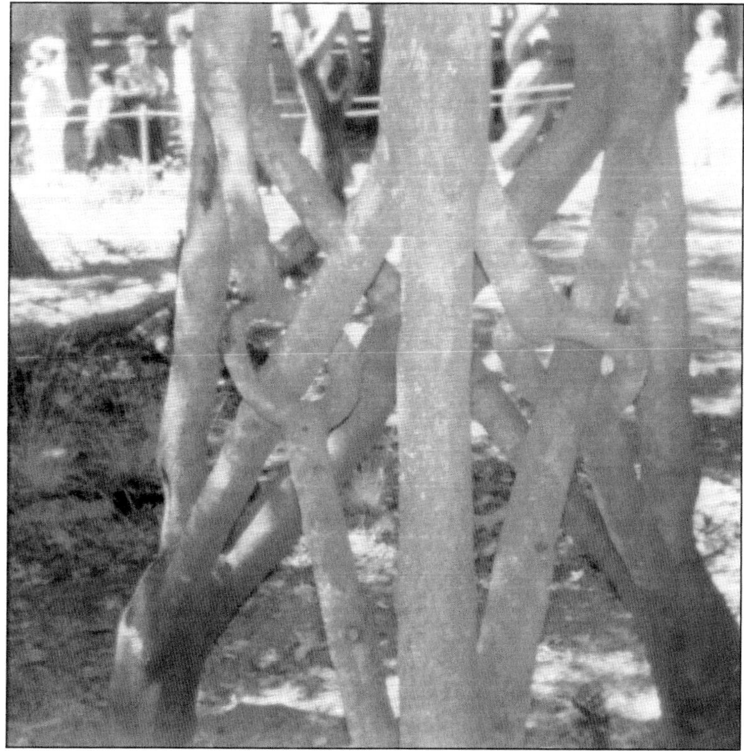

**Water Tower Tree.** Although the attraction had been written up in the *Ripley's Believe It or Not!* news feature 12 times, as well as other publications like *Life* magazine, visitor attendance was never very high due to the rerouting of Highway 17, which bypassed Scotts Valley Drive. (Courtesy of the Scotts Valley Chamber of Commerce.)

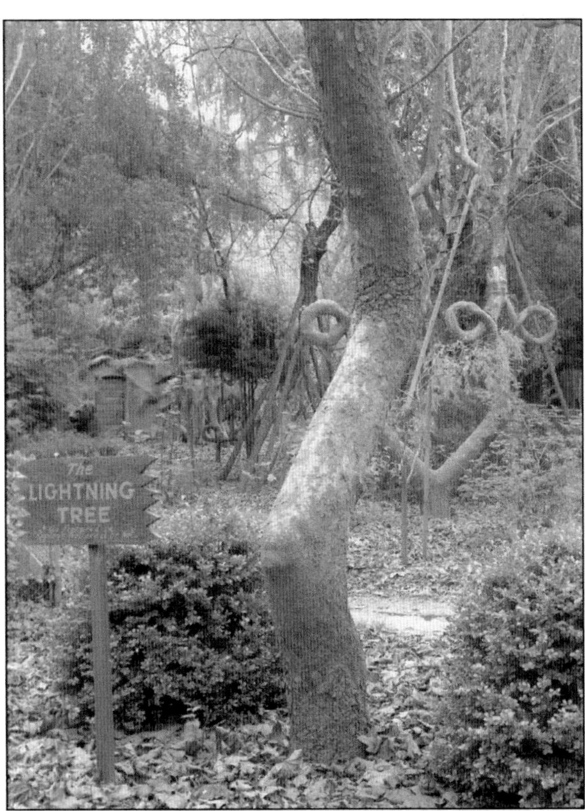


**Zigzag Tree.** Also referred to as the Lightning Bolt Tree, this sycamore was one of the original trees from Hilmar. (Courtesy of Covello & Covello Photography.)

**Needle and Thread.** Known as the Needle and Thread Tree, this ash has interwoven links of living branches. (Courtesy of the Scotts Valley Chamber of Commerce.)

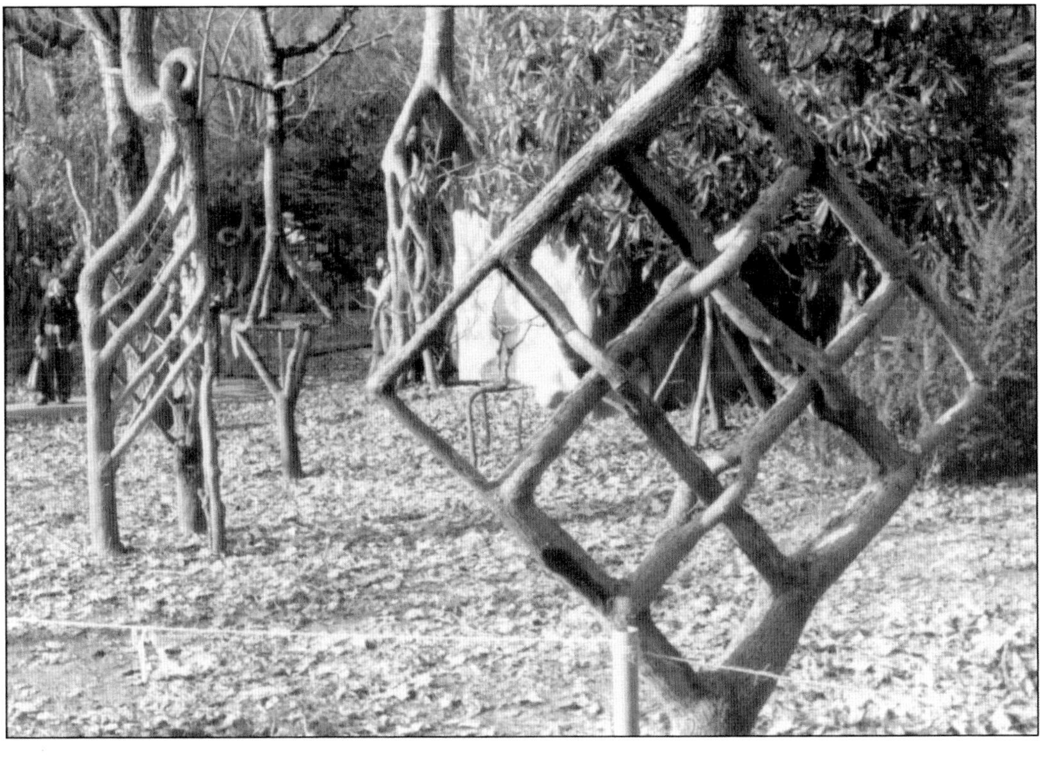

**The Castle.** Erlandson built the small castle at the entrance to the exhibit as a ticket booth and souvenir shop. (Courtesy of the Scotts Valley Chamber of Commerce.)

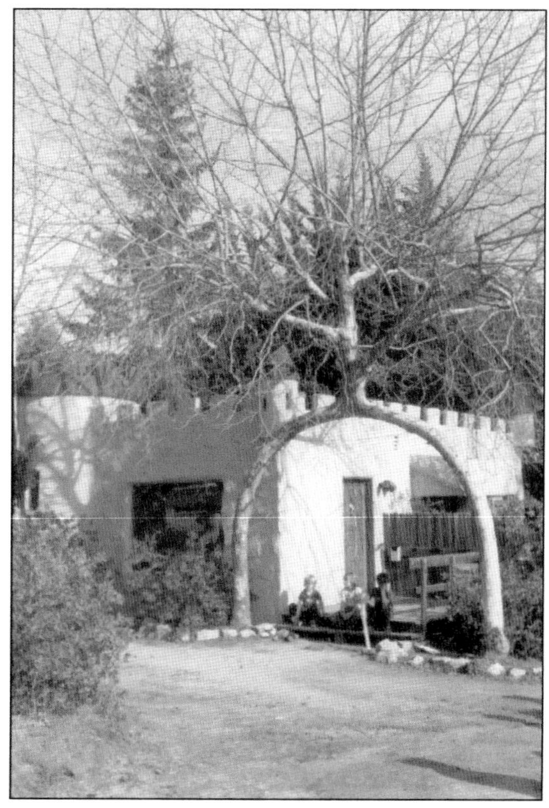

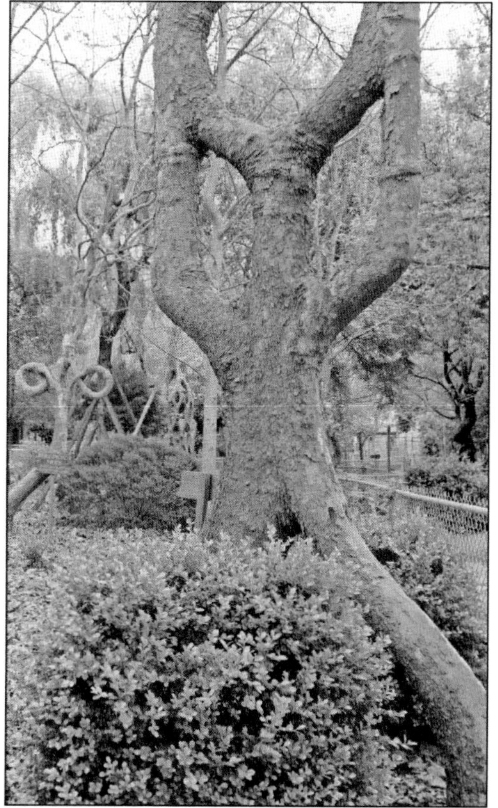

**Totem Sycamore.** By the 1960s, Erlandson had fallen into poor health and tried to find a responsible buyer for his property and trees. In 1963, he sold the property to Larry and Margaret Thompson for $12,000. (Courtesy of Covello & Covello Photography.)

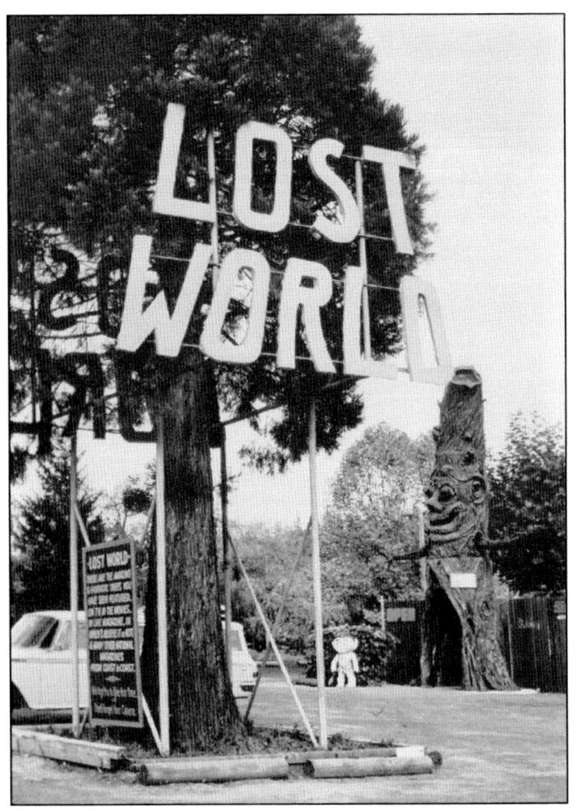


**Lost World.** Inspired by his brother and sister-in-law's tourist attraction called the Trees of Mystery near Klamath, California, Thompson envisioned expanding the Tree Circus into a unique amusement park based on dinosaurs and other mythical creatures and thereby renamed the site Lost World. An additional 40 acres of the Scotts Valley Downs, a former pony cart racetrack, was purchased for expansion behind the old Tree Circus, running west to the freeway. (Courtesy of Eric Taylor.)

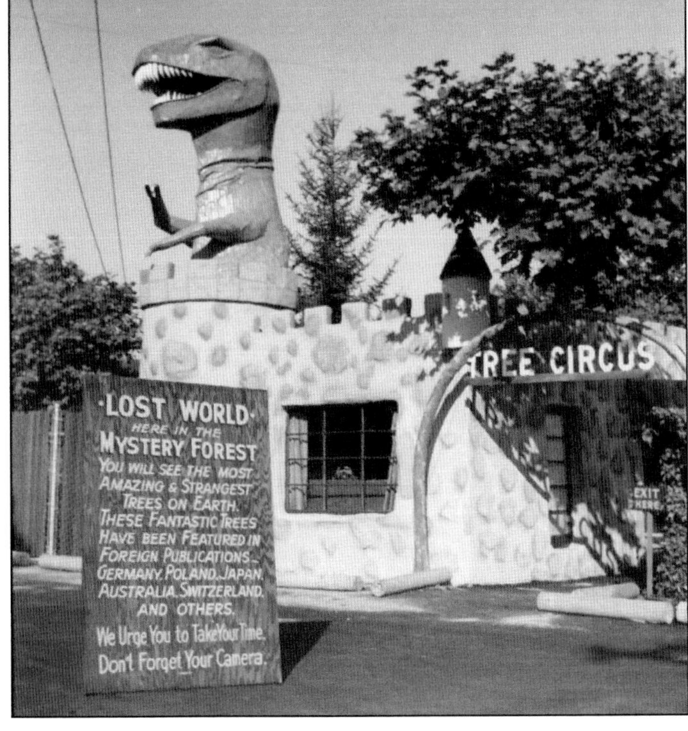


**Entrance.** A large T. rex, which appeared to be bursting out of the turret, was added to the former Tree Circus entrance, and Erlandson's trees became the Mystery Forest. Thompson hired Jack Oehlert from Southern California to construct the 25–30 realistic life-size models of prehistoric animals, which were built of fiberglass over a steel frame. (Courtesy of Eric Taylor.)

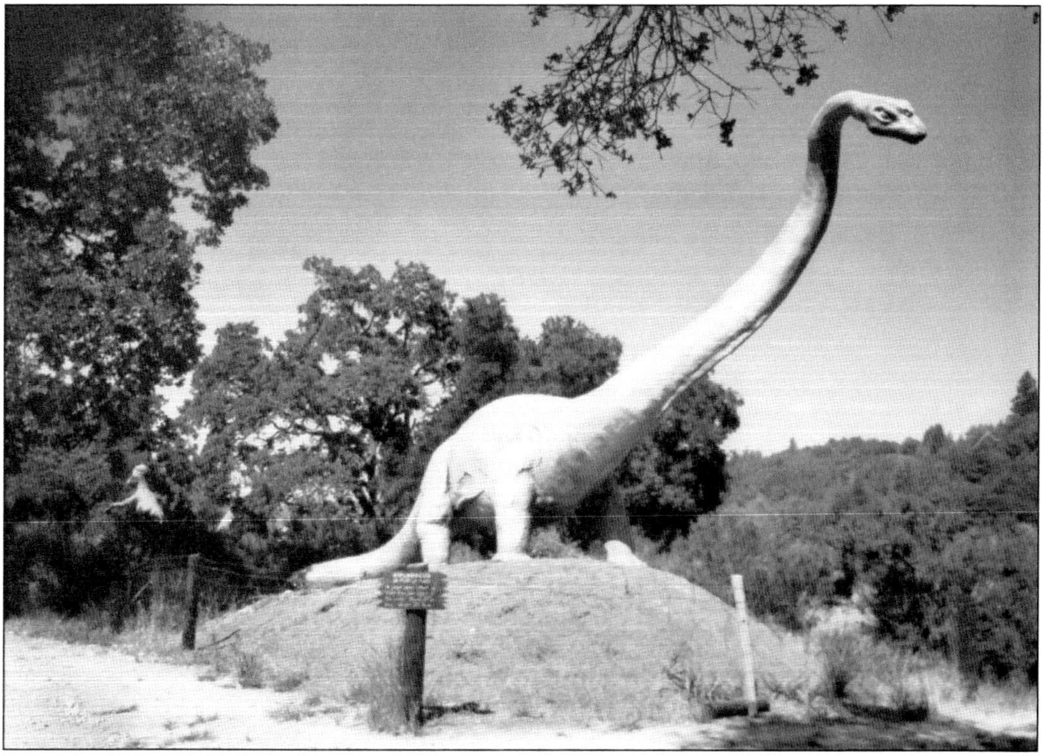

**BRONTOSAURUS.** The large brontosaurus pictured here could be seen from the highway, enticing children of all ages to visit the intriguing exhibit. Other exhibits included a Story Book Land with a dinosaur band and a man-made stream and waterfall. (Courtesy of Eric Taylor.)

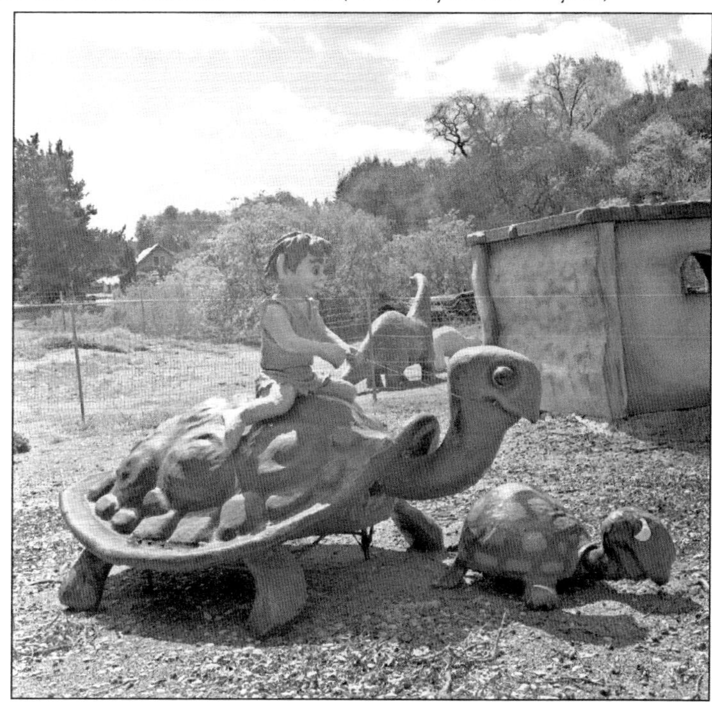

**CAVE BOY.** One of the park exhibits depicted a cave boy attempting to steer a less-than-enthusiastic turtle. A 35-foot animatronic talking tree known as the Gumbi tree and the friendly cave boy also stood watch over the entrance. (Courtesy Covello & Covello Photography.)

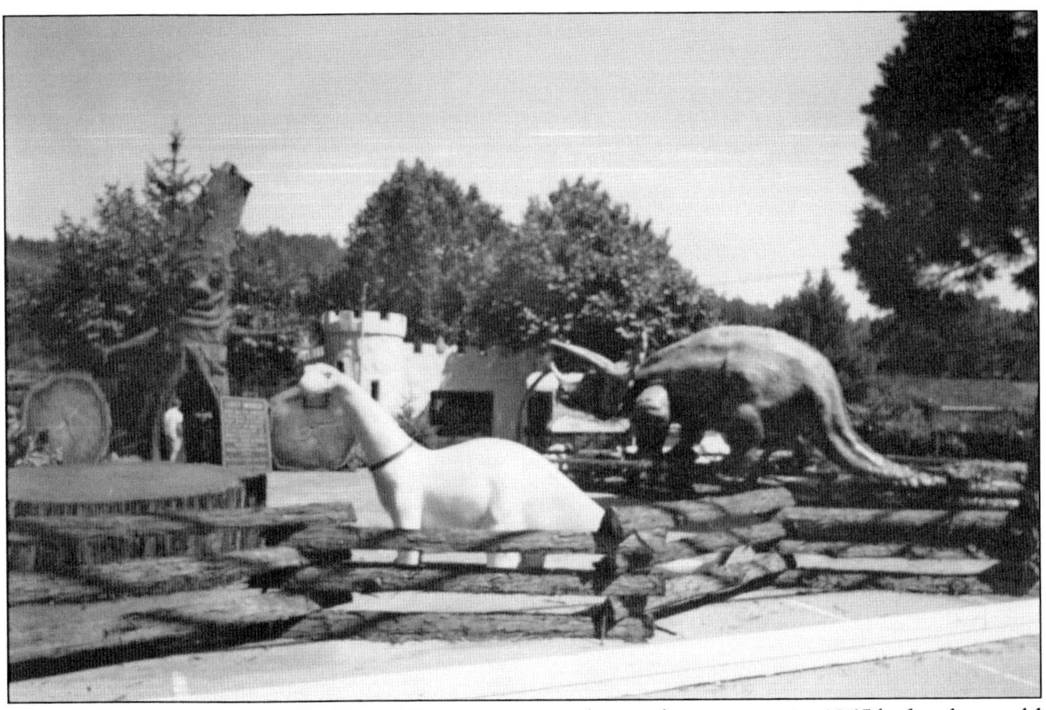

**Entrance Dinosaurs.** Sadly, Larry Thompson passed away from cancer in 1965 before he could complete his vision of the Lost World. His widow Margaret Thompson ran the park after his death for some time but eventually leased the property to others. None of the subsequent operators were able to make a success of the park, and in 1976, the property was sold to Robert Hogan, a local builder-developer. (Courtesy of Eric Taylor.)

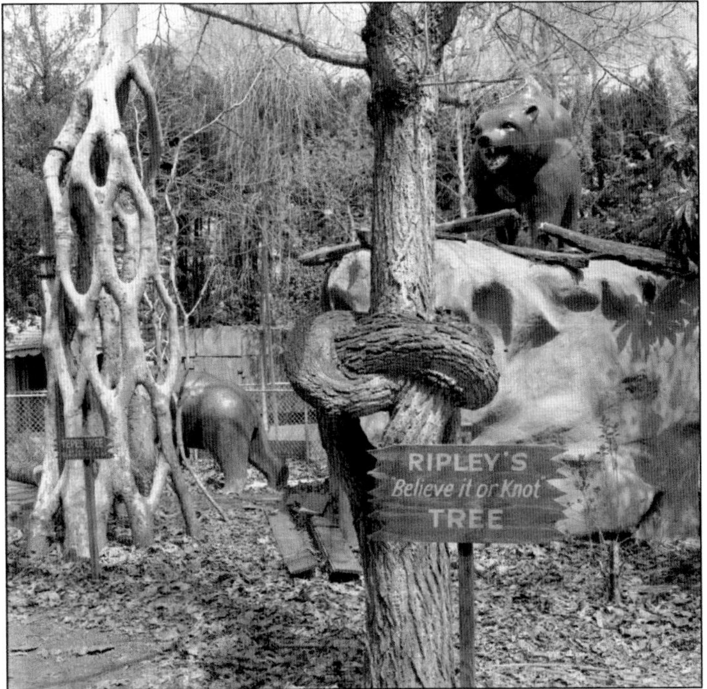


**Believe It or Knot.** In 1979, local landscape architect Joseph Cahill purchased an option to buy the trees from the owner. The Teepee Tree and two Lost World bears can be seen in this photograph. The Thompsons later donated the bears to the City of Scotts Valley. Until recently, they were displayed under a huge oak tree in MacDorsa Park. (Courtesy of Covello & Covello Photography.)

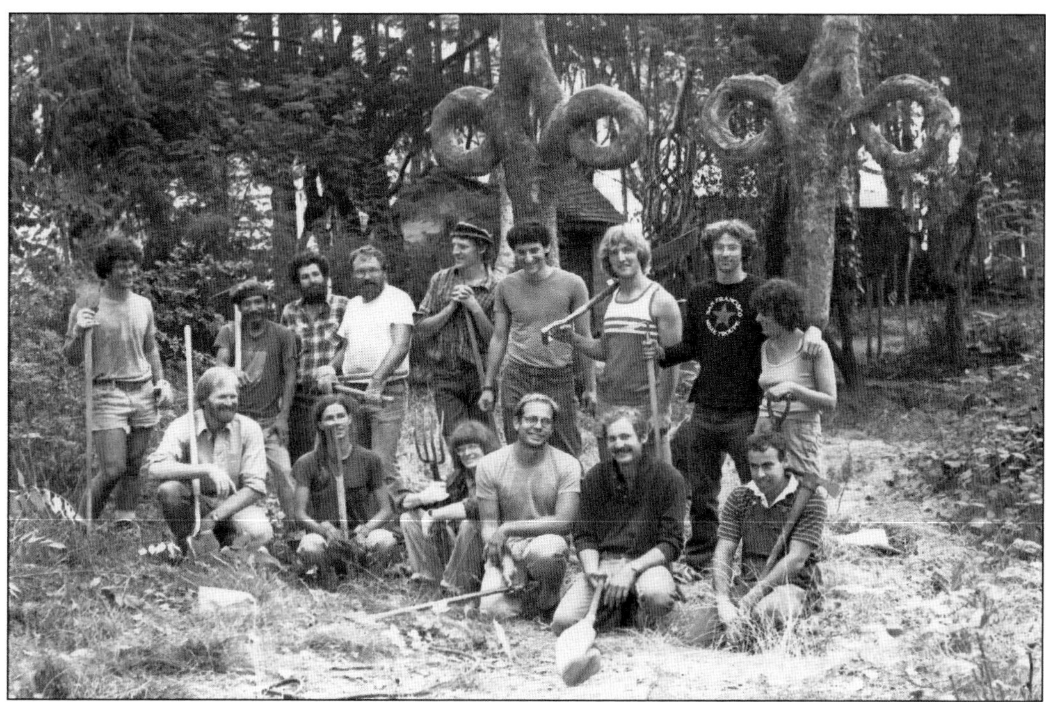

**COMMANDO GARDENERS.** Mark Primack, a Santa Cruz architect who came across the trees in 1983, organized a group of like-minded individuals nicknamed the "Commando Gardeners." They risked trespassing charges to water the remaining 49 trees. (Courtesy of Mark Primack.)

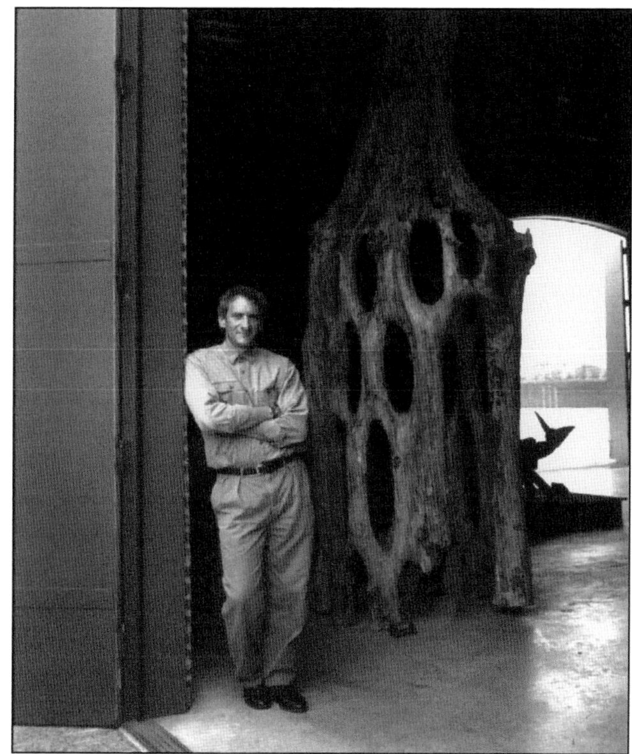

**MARK PRIMACK.** Here, Primack is pictured with the Telephone Booth Tree, now displayed at the American Visionary Art Museum in Baltimore, Maryland. News that the owner of the property wanted to bulldoze the trees led to a hotly contested community-wide debate over property rights versus tree preservationists. In the end, the Scotts Valley Planning Commission voted against their inclusion as heritage trees, and thus, the trees were slated for removal. (Courtesy of Mark Primack.)

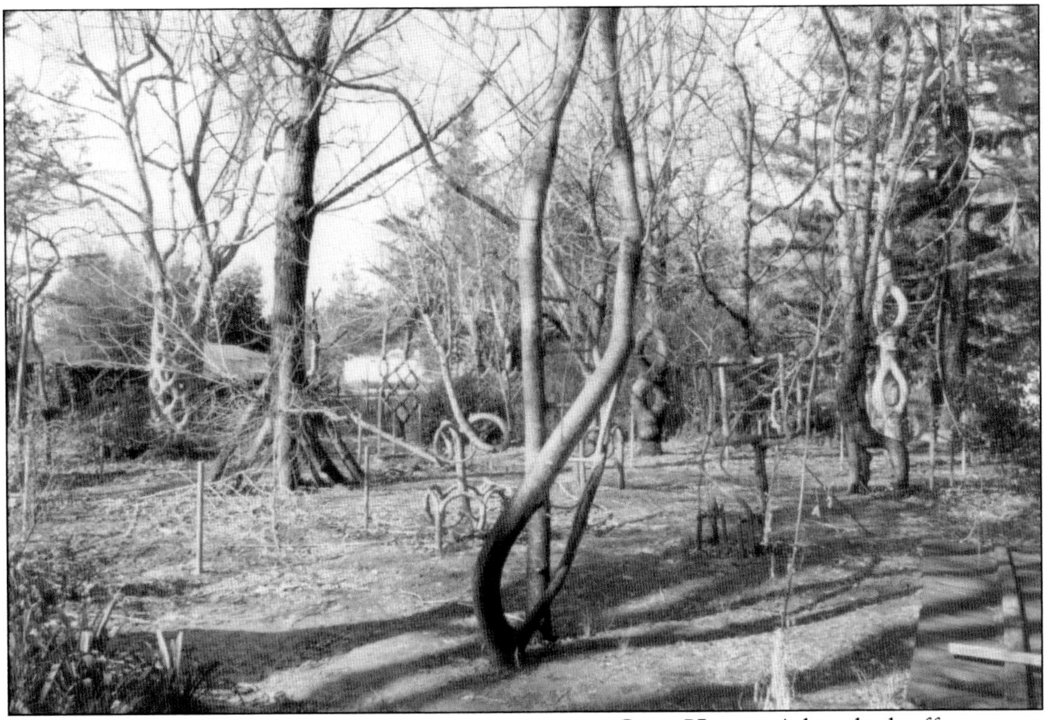

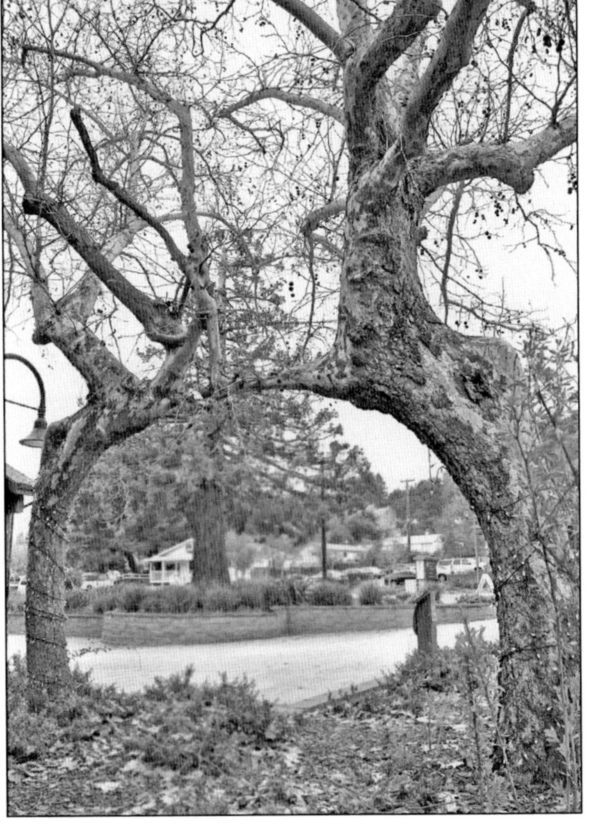

**Open House.** A last-ditch effort was held to raise money for the Circus Trees by holding an open house on Memorial Day weekend in 1980. After several other attempts to move the trees fell through, Michael Bonfante of Bonfante Gardens (now Gilroy Gardens) purchased 25 of Erlandson's trees in 1984. The transportation of the large trees was a costly and detailed endeavor, requiring coordination between local police, highway patrol, CalTrans, and over 100 volunteers. (Courtesy of the Scotts Valley Chamber of Commerce.)

**Remaining Trees.** After the move, the majority of the trees were planted at the Bonfante Gardens Theme Park in 2001. Three original trees from the Tree Circus can still be seen today at the Tree Circus Center on Scotts Valley Drive: the western red cedar out front, the Arch Tree pictured here, and a massive three-legged trunk located on the back patio. (Courtesy of Lucjan Szewczyk/*Press-Banner*.)

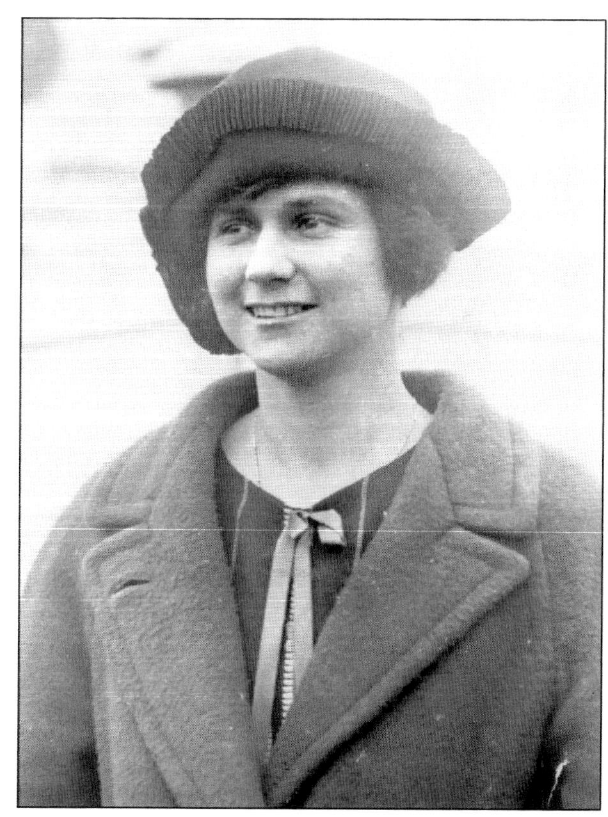

**Marion Hollins.** In 1930, renowned sportswoman Marion Hollins purchased 128 acres on the west side of Carbonera Creek in Scotts Valley for her Vine Hill Farm horse ranch. Hiring well-known architect William Wurster, she built a two-story, 4,830-square-foot barn, owner's quarters, and other outbuildings. Although not well known today, her accomplishments in sports and business rivaled any man of her time. (Author's collection.)

**Young Marion.** Hollins was born in 1913 to a life of luxury and privilege in East Islip, New York. Her father, Harry B. Hollins, owned a large Wall Street stock brokerage firm, and the family lived on an estate on Long Island. She grew up riding, hunting, and playing golf and tennis. Hollins, seen here in white, is 21 years old in this photograph. (Courtesy of the George Grantham Bain Collection, Library of Congress.)

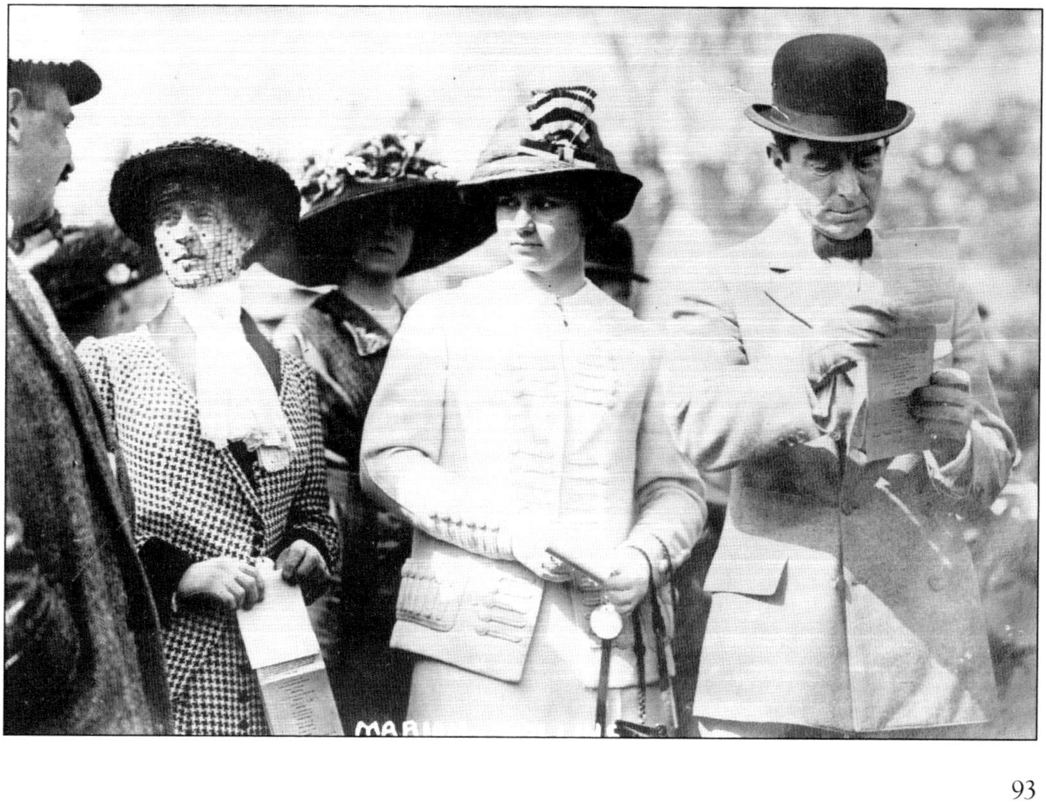

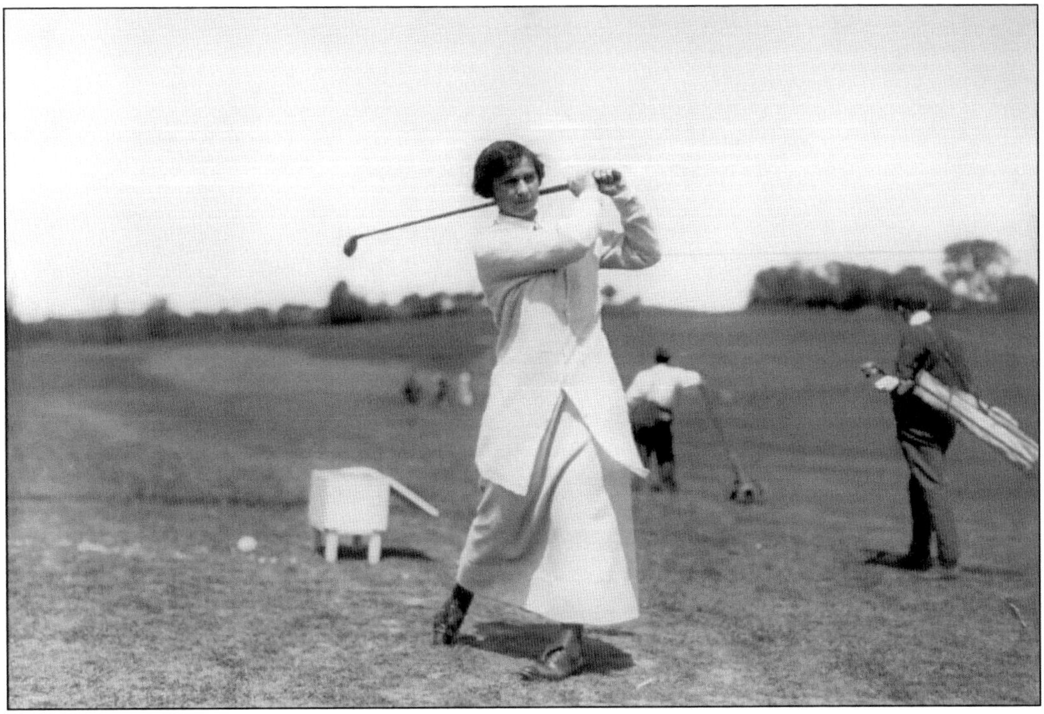

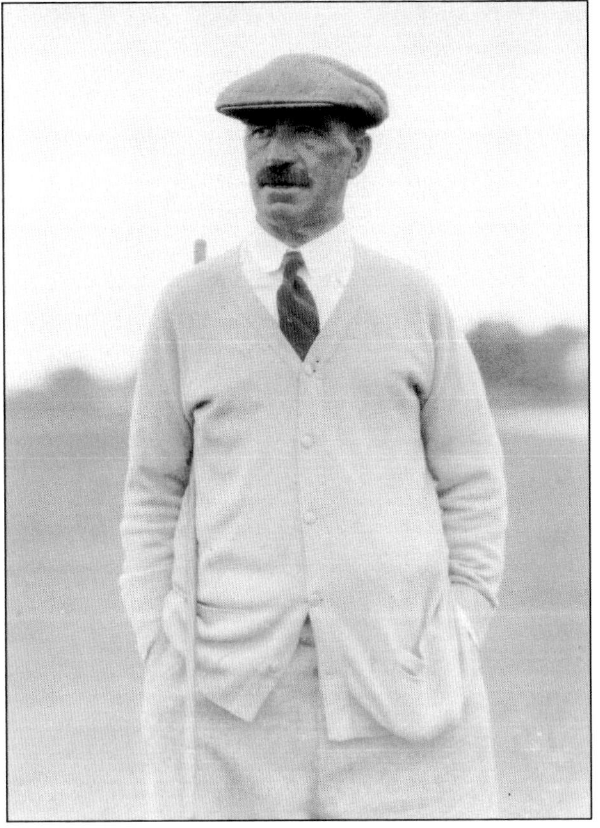

**Golf Champion.** At age 21, Hollins won her first golf championship, and in 1921, she won the Women's National Golfing Championship. Ahead of her time, she promoted and helped build the first championship golf course designed especially for women. In 1923, the Women's National Golf and Tennis Club opened in Glen Head, New York. (Courtesy of the George Grantham Bain Collection, Library of Congress.)

**Dr. Alister MacKenzie.** Recovering from an illness, Hollins came west to California. She started working for Samuel Morse, owner and developer of the Pebble Beach and Cypress Point Golf Courses. While working for Morse, she was responsible for the layout of the famous ocean-side 16th hole. It was at Cypress Point that she first worked with renowned golf course architect Dr. Alister MacKenzie. (Courtesy of the Santa Cruz Museum of Art and History.)

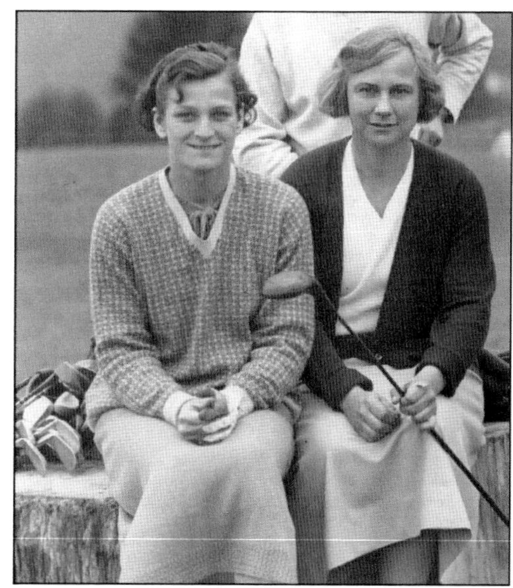

**Golfing Foursome.** In 1928, Hollins received $2.5 million from a $100,000 investment in the Kettleman Oil Corporation. Using her new wealth, Hollins purchased 570 acres of the former Rancho Carbonero and began building the Pasatiempo Golf and Country Club, making her the first known female golf course developer. Shown are Marion Hollins (right) and Babe Didrikson, considered one of the greatest female athletes of all time. (Courtesy of the Santa Cruz Museum of Art and History.)

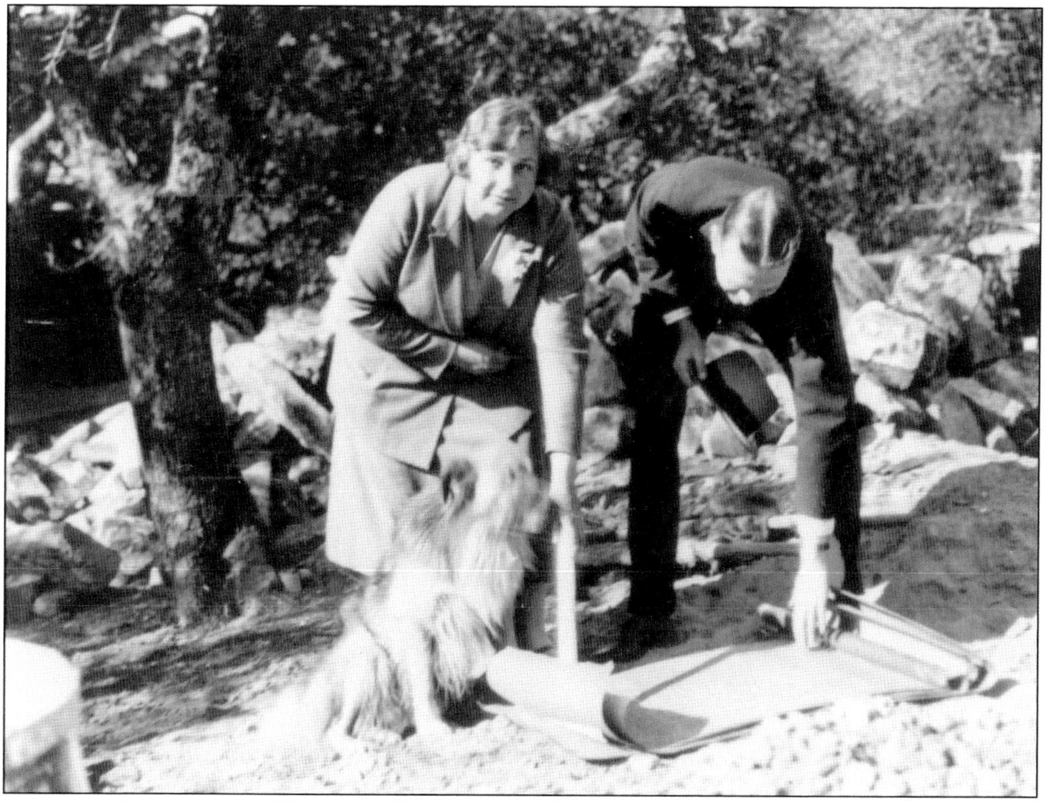

**Marion Hollins and William Wurster.** Hollins hired notable professionals of the day, such as golf course architect Alistair MacKenzie, architects William Wurster and Clarence Tantau, and landscape architect Thomas D. Church, to achieve her vision for the Pasatiempo development, which included an 18-hole championship golf course, a clubhouse, a swimming pool, a steeplechase course, and a beach club at the Santa Cruz Yacht Harbor. (Courtesy of the Pasatiempo Golf Club.)

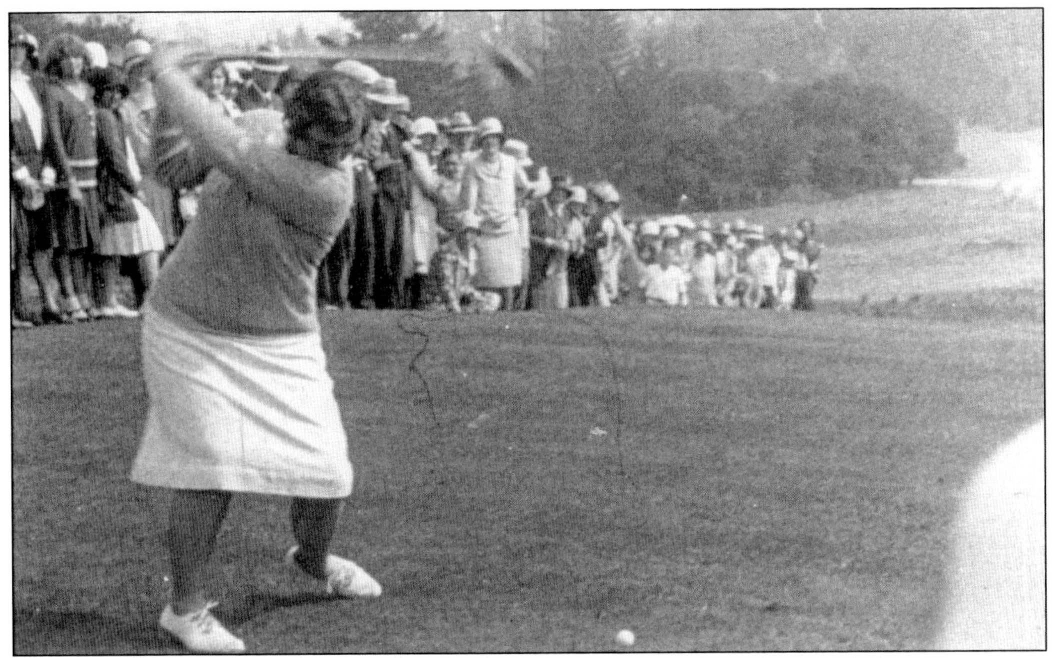

**Teeing Off.** Opening day at Pasatiempo on September 9, 1929, brought over 3,000 spectators to an exhibition match between Marion Hollins, Bobby Jones, Glenna Collett, and Cyril Tolley. Here, Hollins is shown teeing off on that historic day. (Courtesy of the Pasatiempo Golf Club.)

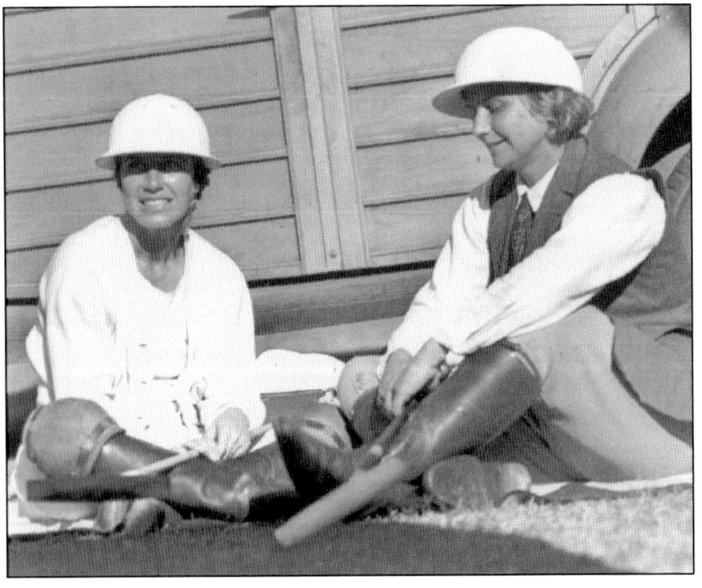

**Hollins and Tracy.** Said to be full of natural exuberance and possess a warm and generous personality, Hollins had many friends. Some of her more notable houseguests while at Pasatiempo included Bobby Jones, Will Rogers, Mary Pickford, Babe Didrikson Zaharias, Spencer and Louise Tracy (pictured, left), Walt Disney, Jean Harlow, Joan Fontaine, and Buddy Rogers. Not only an extraordinary golfer, Hollins also excelled at polo and tennis. (Courtesy of the Pasatiempo Golf Club.)

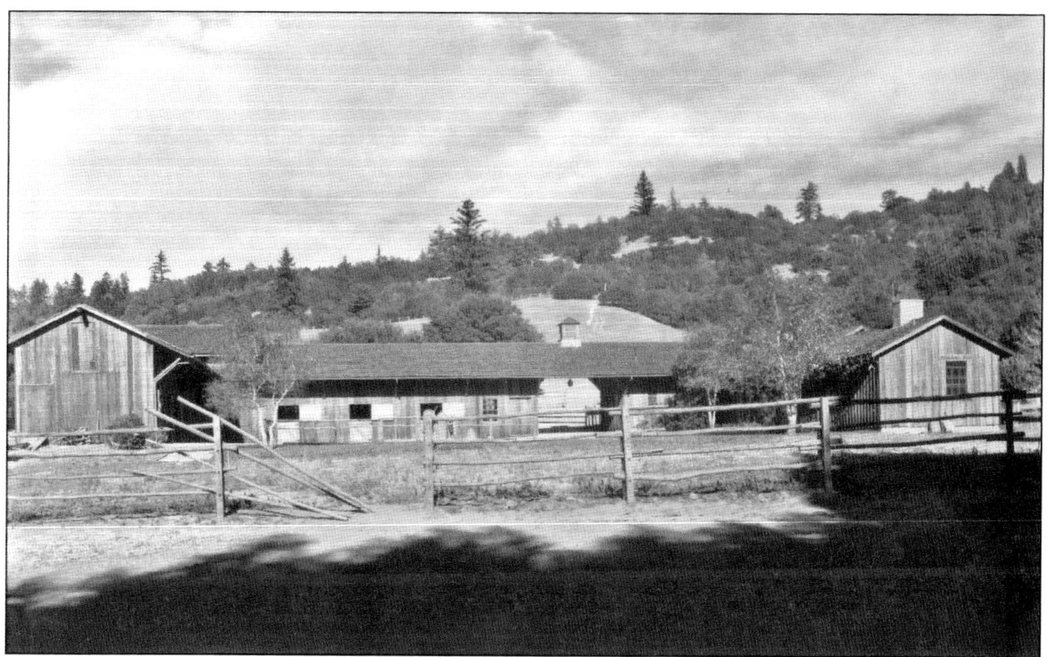

**VINE HILL FARM.** Still involved with horse racing and polo along with Pasatiempo, Vine Hill Farm housed Hollins's racehorses and polo ponies. It was built from local redwood and included a barn with eight large stalls, an owner's residence, a trainer's apartment, and an auxiliary barn and stable. (Photograph by Roger Sturtevant, courtesy of the Oakland Museum of California.)

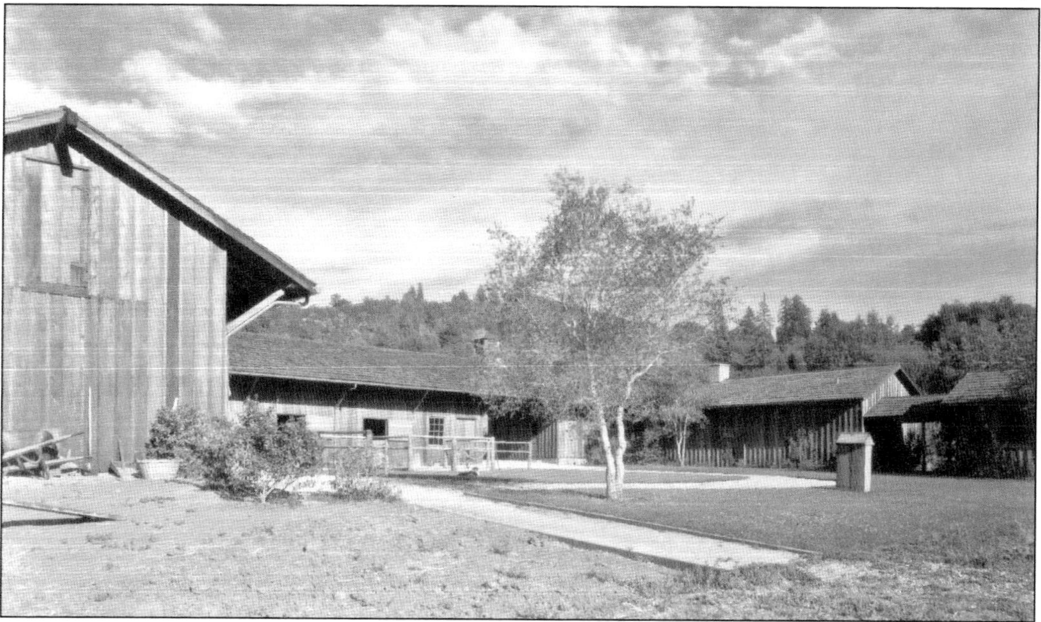

**STABLES AND BARN.** At this time, Hollins was also the team captain of the first Curtis Cup Match, a golf competition between American women and British and Irish women, which the United States won. In 1930, Hollins helped form the Pacific Coast Steeplechase and Racing Association, utilizing the steeplechase course at Pasatiempo. (Photograph by Roger Sturtevant, courtesy of the Oakland Museum of California.)

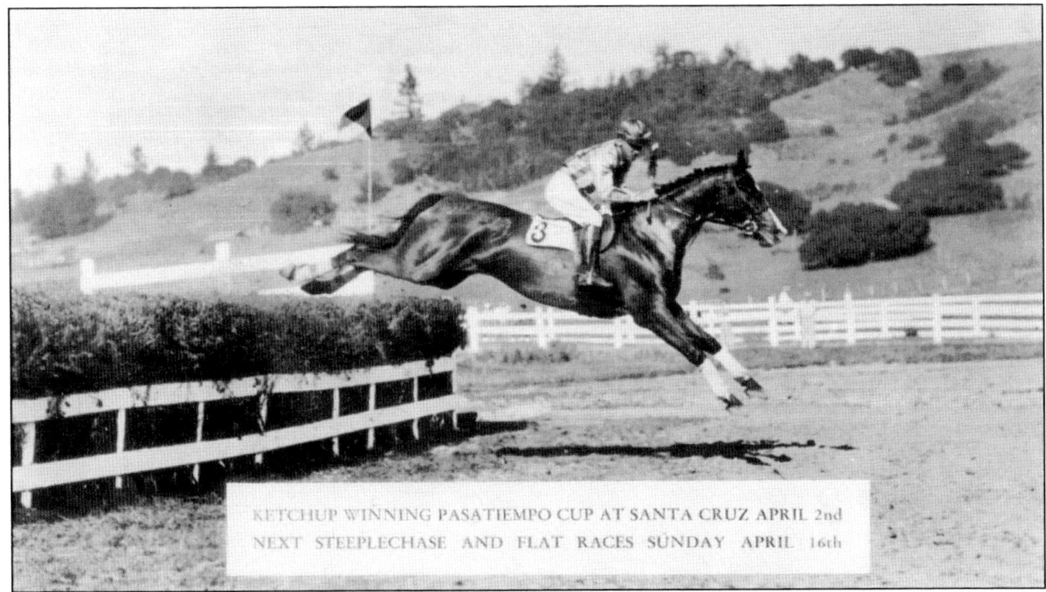


**KETCHUP.** One of Hollins's steeplechase jumpers was named Ketchup. She had two other well-known horses, including Del Fennell and the record-breaking Nevada Queen, whom she purchased for the unheard-of sum of $15,000 in 1931. Due to her lavish spending and numerous real estate investments, Hollins's wealth was nearly gone by early 1937. (Author's collection.)

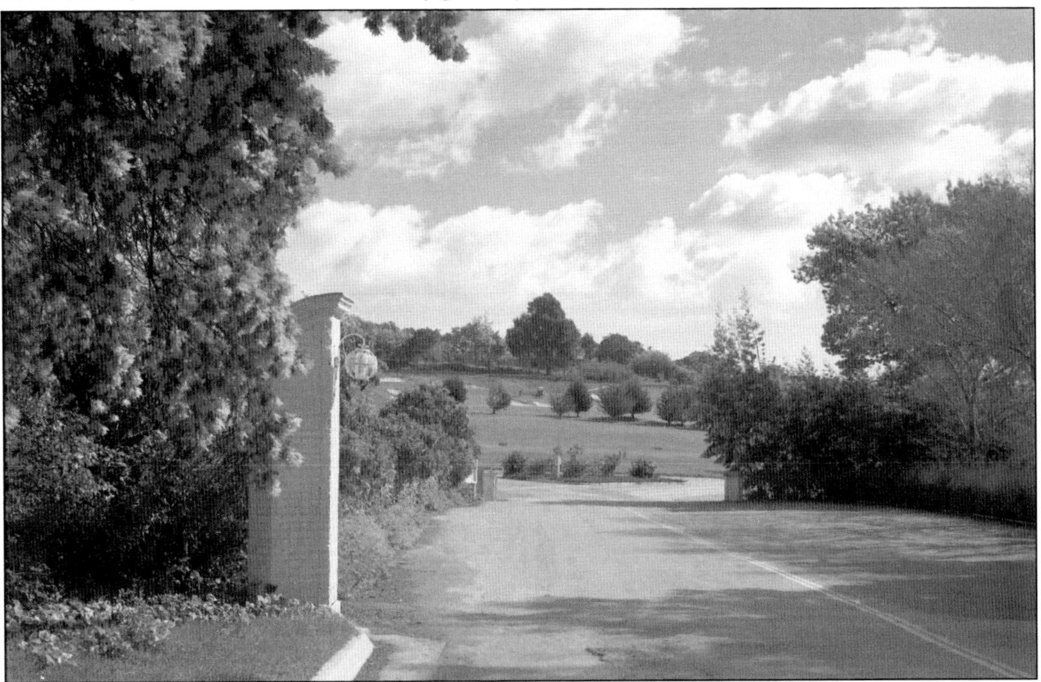

**ENTRANCE TO PASATIEMPO, C. 1960.** To further add to her troubles, Hollins was hit by a drunk driver and suffered a bad concussion that same year. She was forced to sell her beloved Pasatiempo and lost her home on Clubhouse Drive. She moved to Pebble Beach, but it was apparent the car accident had changed her personality. Becoming increasingly ill, Hollins entered a nursing home and died alone in 1944. (Courtesy of Covello & Covello Photography.)

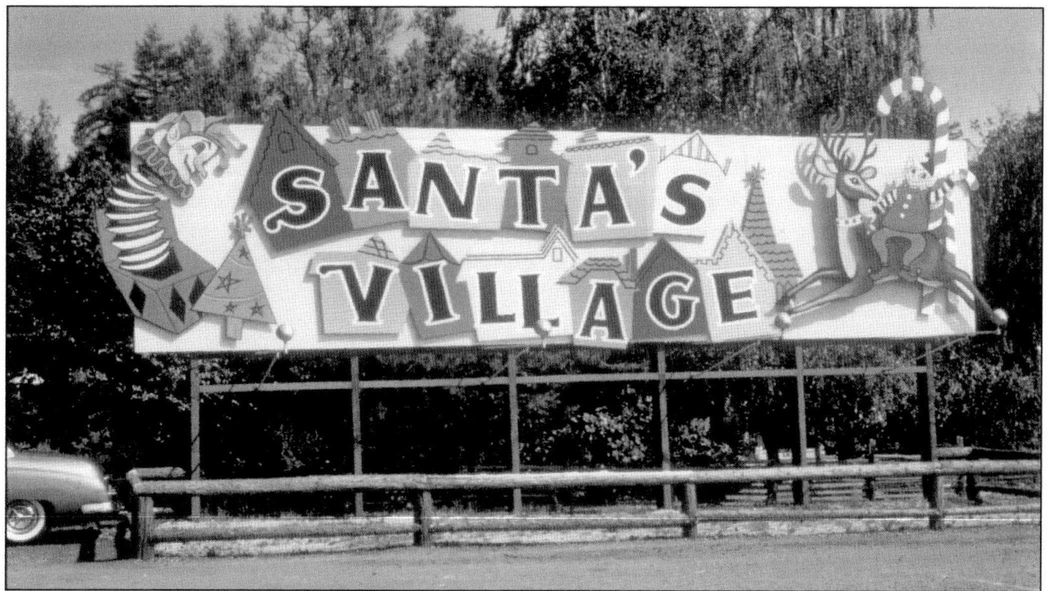


**Santa's Village Sign.** In 1935, Hollins's Vine Hill Farm became Lawridge Farm. In addition to ranching and farming, Robert and Katherine Law bred and trained polo ponies on the property. In 1956, a 25-acre parcel was leased to H. Glen Holland, a Southern California developer who had just opened a Santa's Village near Lake Arrowhead in San Bernardino County in 1955. (Courtesy of Julie Fetter.)

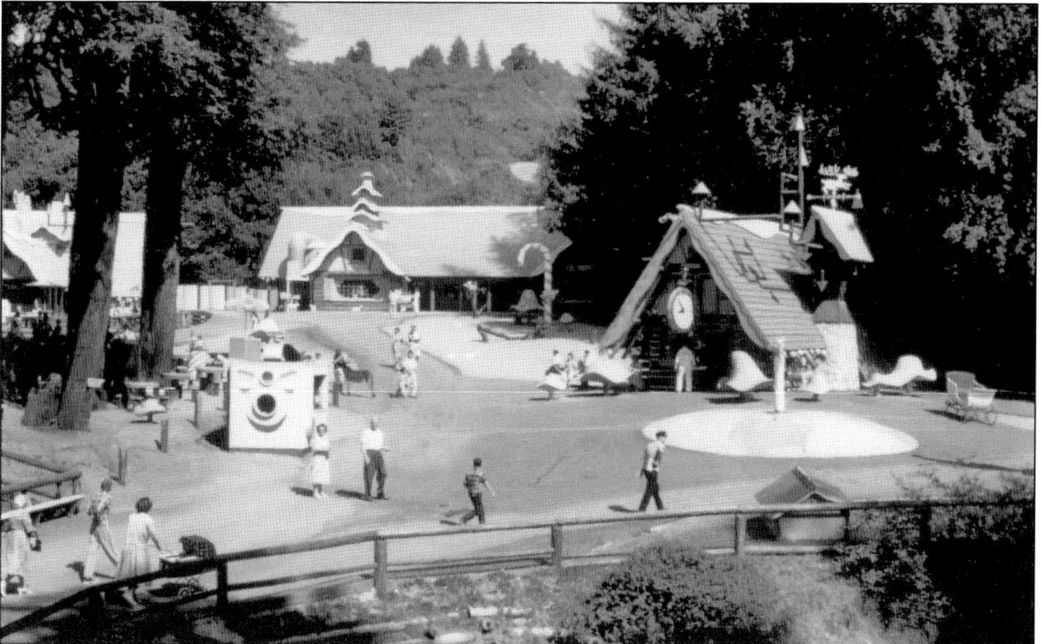

**Santa's House.** Built by contractor J. Putnam Henck, the new Santa's Village opened on May 30, 1957. The entire project took nine months to complete and cost $1 million. Holland went on to develop a third Santa's Village, near Chicago in Dundee, Illinois. The Illinois attraction is the only one still open today, although in a different form as Santa's Village Azoosment Park. (Courtesy of Julie Fetter.)

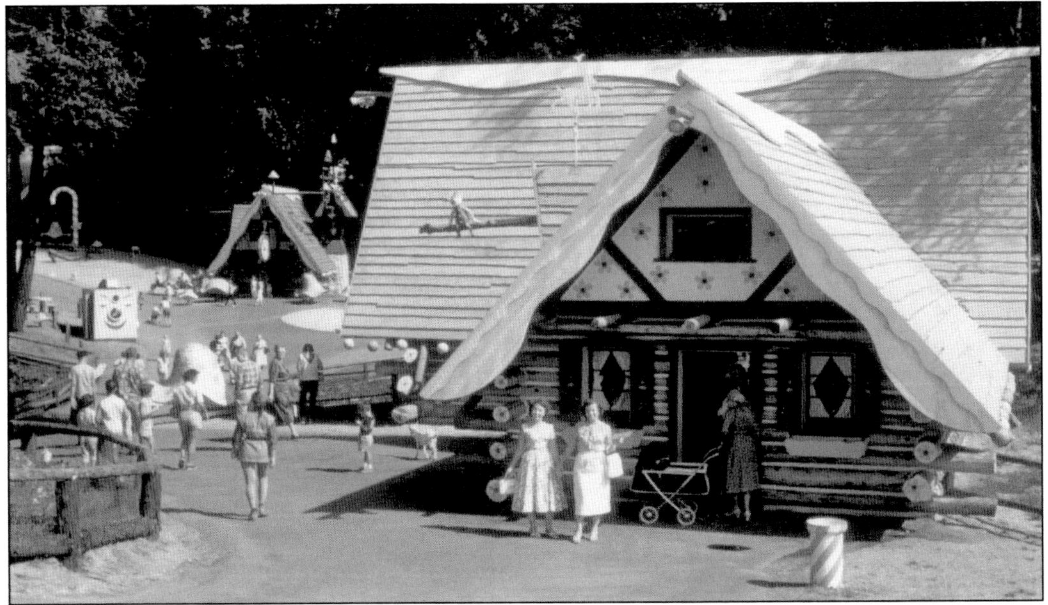

**The Dollhouse.** Santa's Village attractions would grow to include Santa and his sleigh, Alaskan reindeer, a baby petting zoo, a gingerbread house, a candy house, a lollipop tree, a giant jack-in-the-box, a gift shop, and numerous brightly painted cement mushrooms. (Courtesy of Julie Fetter.)

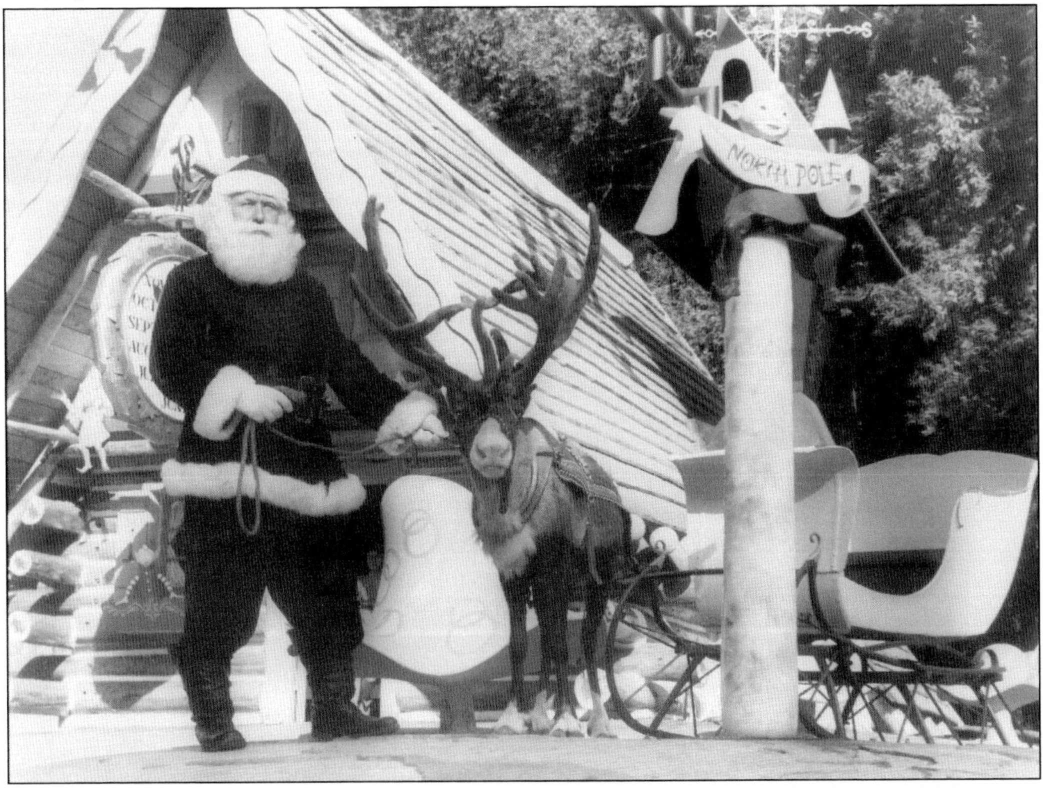

**Santa and Reindeer.** Santa's house included a clock that counted down the days until Christmas and a frozen North Pole, which stood outside. (Author's collection.)

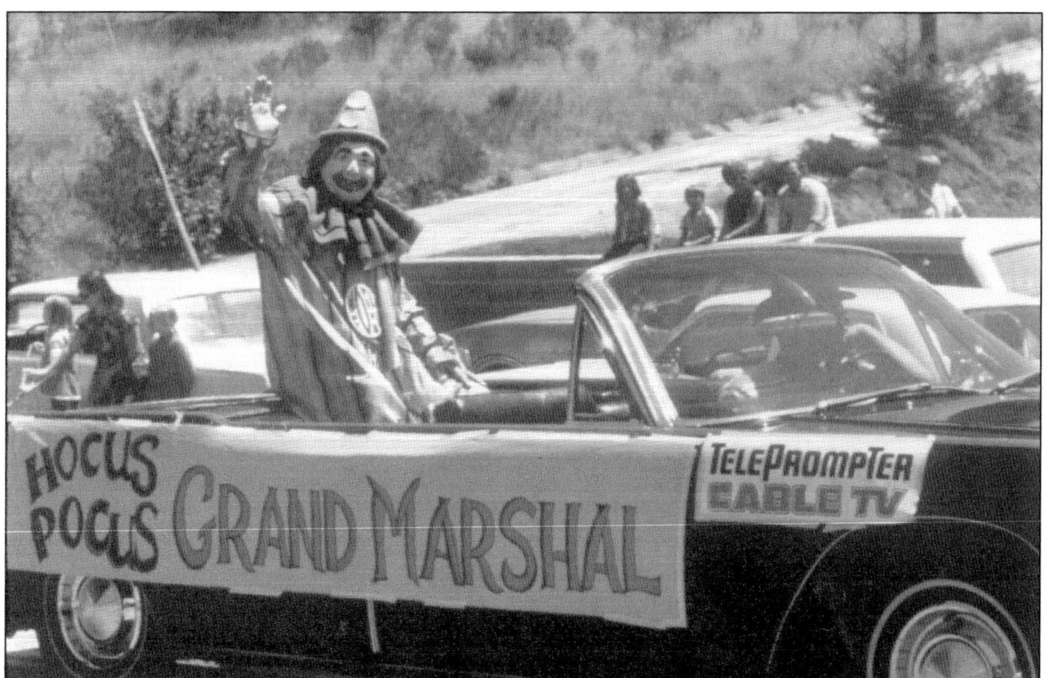


**HOCUS POCUS.** The first official Santa Claus of the park was Carl Hansen, who came from the San Bernardino Santa's Village. Later, Ben "Tiny" Litrenta succeeded Hansen as the new Santa. Alma Ragon, community volunteer and wife of the fire chief, took the part of Mrs. Claus. Here, Carl Hansen is the grand marshal for a Scotts Valley Days parade. (Courtesy of SVHS.)

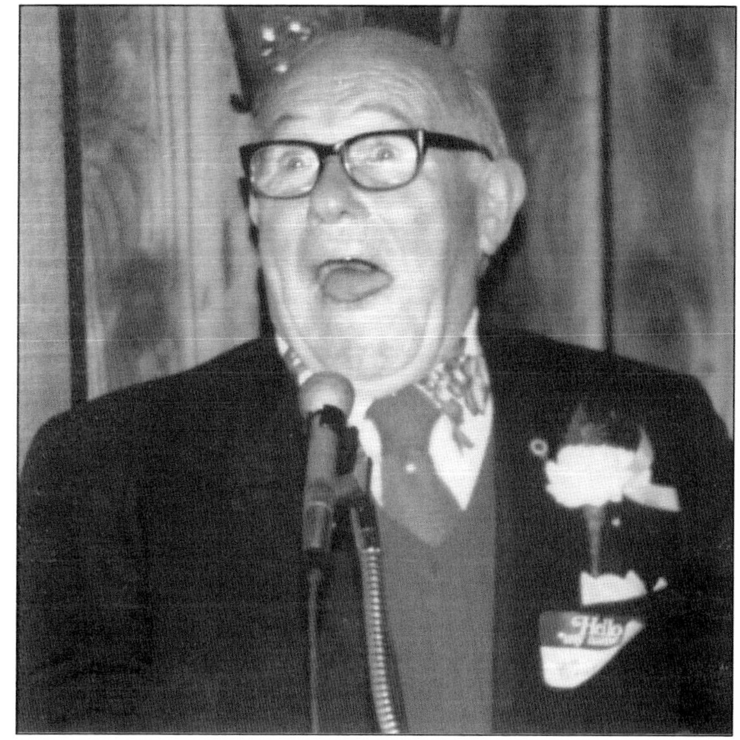

**CARL HANSEN.** Hansen worked at the Scotts Valley location for eight years, then left for a starring role in his own *Hocus Pocus* television program. In 1995, a community park off Whispering Pines and Lundy Lane was named in his honor for his work as a tireless community volunteer and beloved entertainer. (Courtesy of the Scotts Valley Chamber of Commerce.)

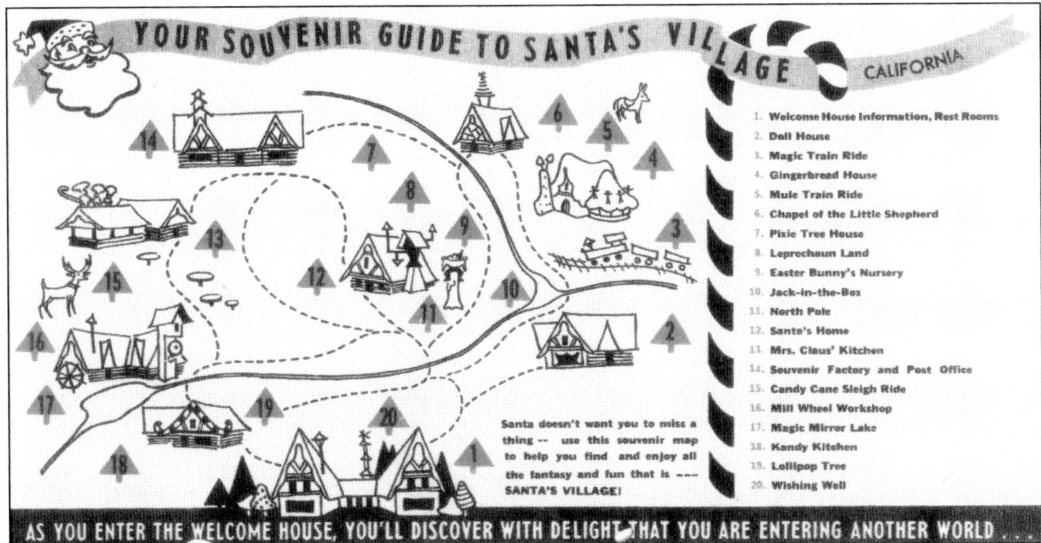


**SOUVENIR MAP.** Declining attendance forced the owners to sell Santa's Village in 1966; however, the property was leased back and continued to operate. Noorudin Billawalla, the new owner, purchased the entire Santa's Village property for $615,000 in 1977. He had planned to create a complex akin to Knott's Berry Farm, with a hotel, shopping center, and amusement park rides, but the City of Scotts Valley rejected his proposal. (Author's collection.)

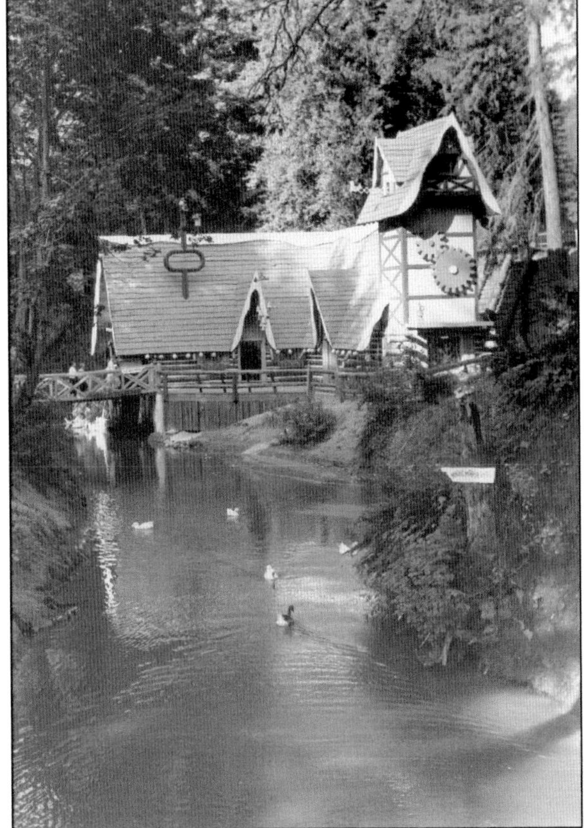

**SANTA'S WORKSHOP AND POND.** Santa's Village later became the Village, a large complex that sold arts and crafts items. The venue was finally closed for good in 1979 and went through several owners, including the City of Scotts Valley. Two former Santa's Village buildings have been dismantled and moved to Sorensen's Resort in Hope Valley near South Lake Tahoe. (Author's collection.)

**The Old Barn.** As the current owners of Santa's Village land had no immediate plans for development, Marion Hollins's polo barn went back to its original use. Caretaker John Strong and his family lived on-site for many years and raised Arabian horses. The property then stood vacant for some time. (Courtesy of Julie Fetter.)

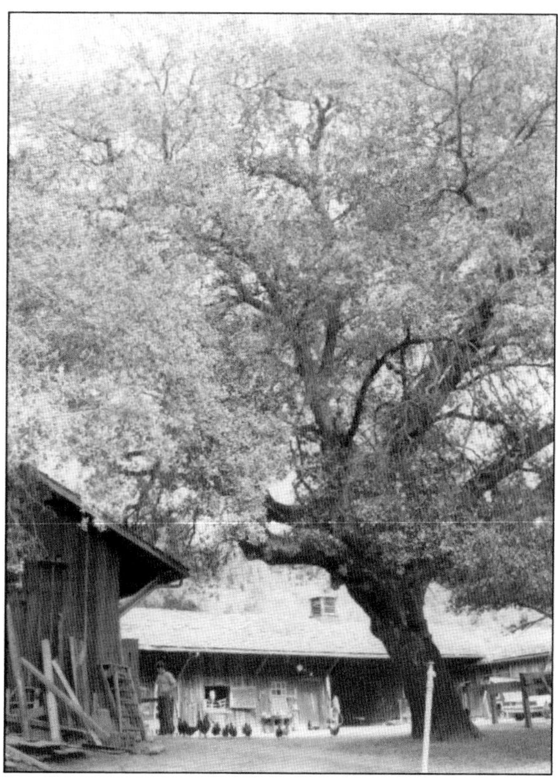

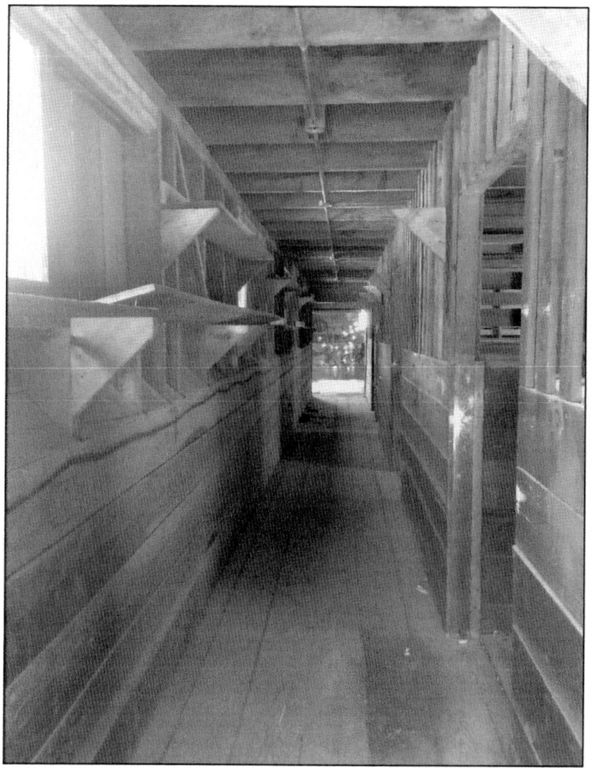

**Interior View.** In this interior view of the polo barn from 2014, the horse stalls can be seen to the right. (Author's collection.)

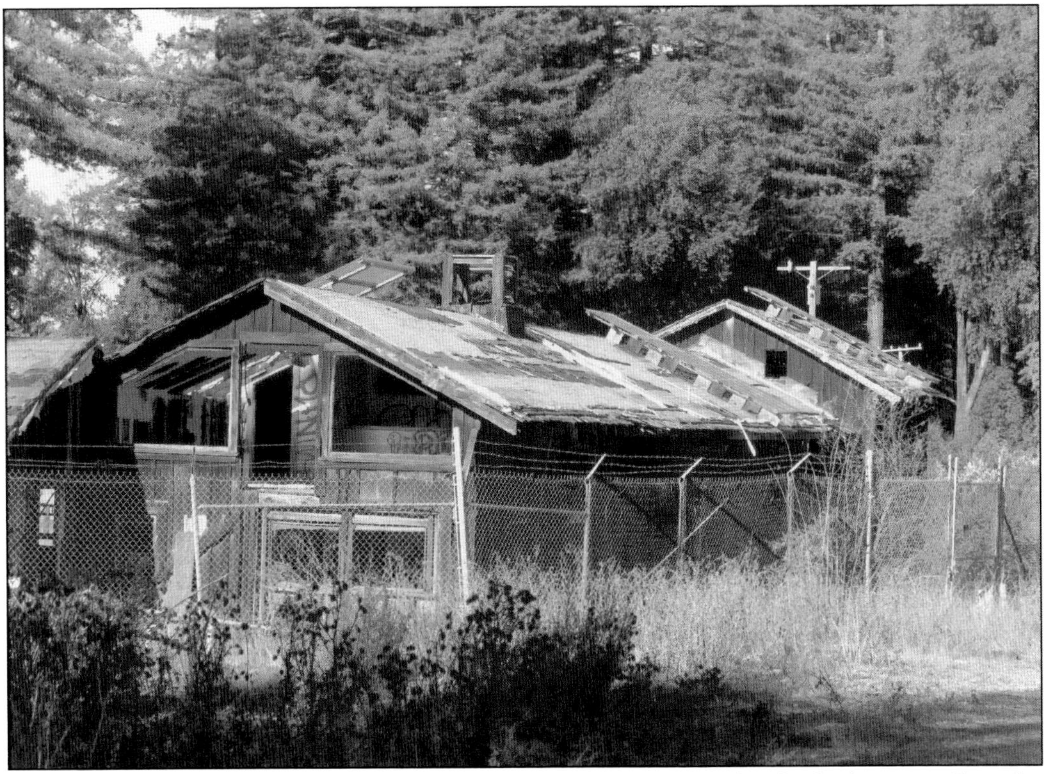

**A Sad End.** Years of neglect and vandalism under absentee ownership had taken its toll on the barn, as seen here. Despite a prior arrangement to move and partially rehabilitate the Hollins barn, an agreement in 2014 allowed the owner to demolish the structure. (Author's collection.)

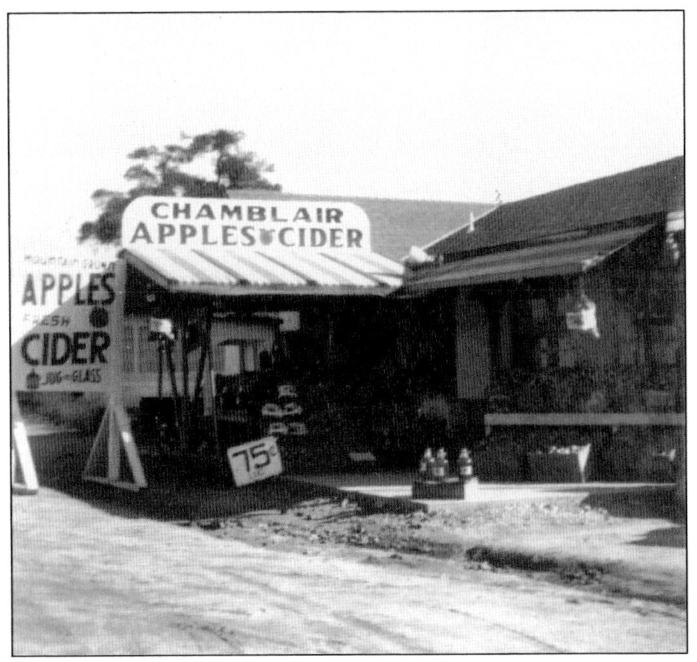


**The Cider Mill.** For many, a trip through Scotts Valley was not complete without a stop at the Cider Mill. Owners A. Ernest Blair and James S. Chamberlin ran the stand on Scotts Valley Drive from 1945 to 1962. Two generations of the Blair family have operated the 30-acre apple farm off Granite Creek Road, originally part of the pioneer Waite farm. (Courtesy of Chuck Blair.)

**Scotts Valley Motel.** During the 1940s through the 1960s, many small owner-managed motels lined Scotts Valley Drive, often with an attached café or sandwich shop. Constructed in 1948, the Scotts Valley Motor Court is the oldest remaining motor court, although the small cabins are now monthly rental units. (Photograph by the author.)

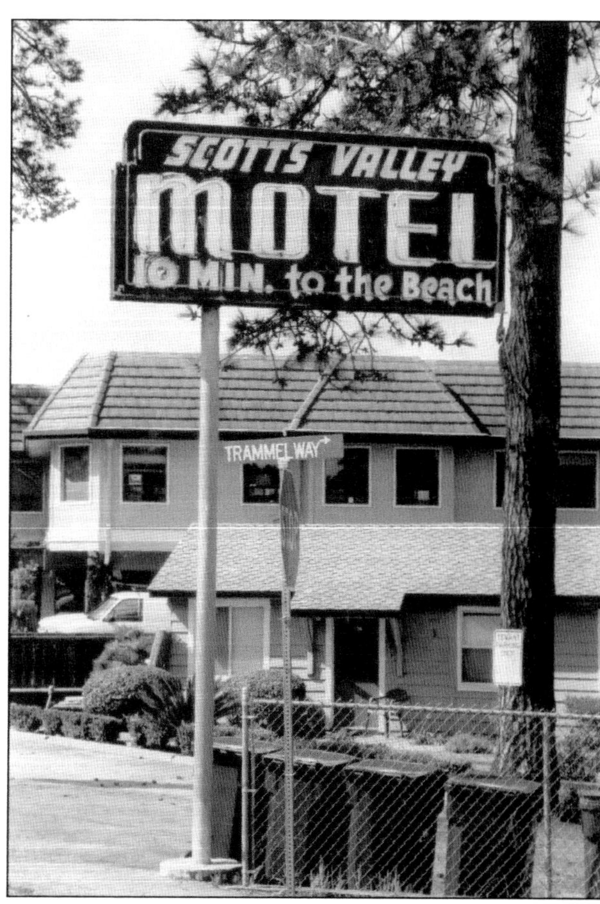


**Mission Springs.** In 1926, the Swedish Evangelical Missionary Association of California purchased a 49-acre site off Lockhart Gulch Road for the eventual construction of the Mission Springs Conference Grounds. The area was rumored to be part of a former Indian village situated near the headwaters of Zayante Creek. The missionary association purchased the site from the family of Sam Lockhart. (Author's collection.)

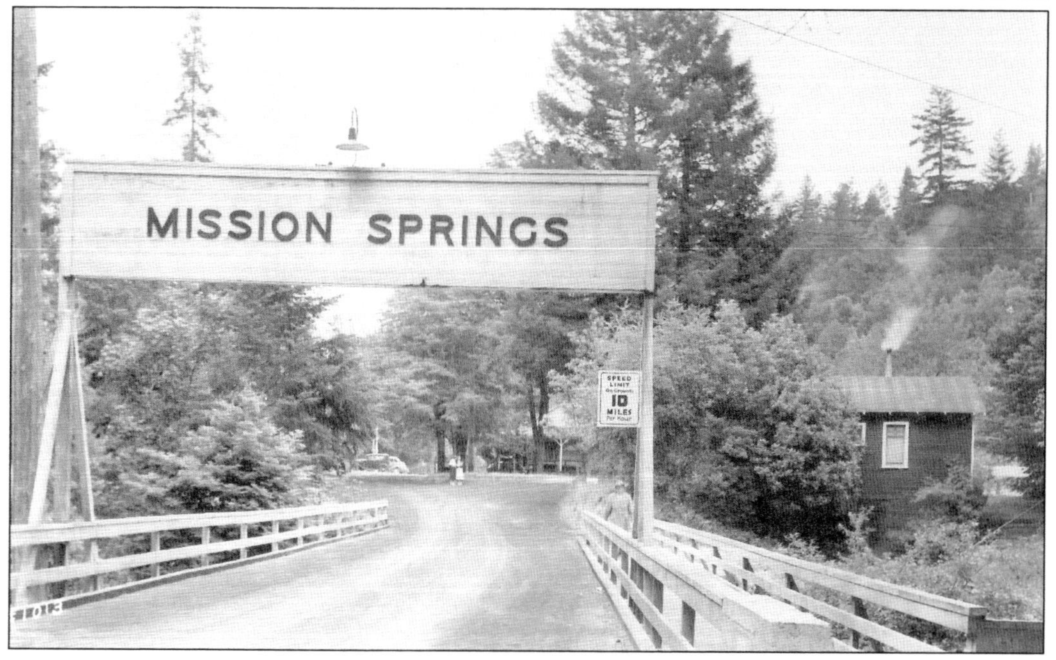

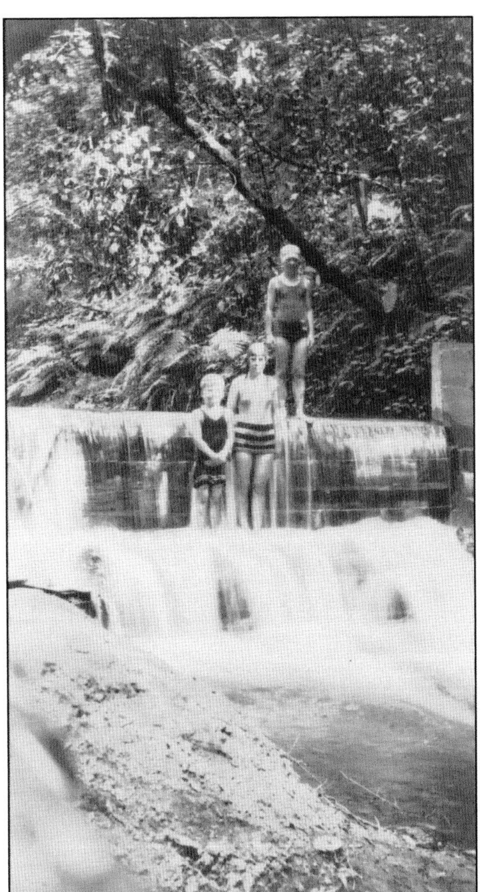

**Bean Creek.** While the 1920s and 1930s brought religious camps to Scotts Valley (Mission Springs, Bethany Park, Camp Redwood Glen, and Camp Westlyn on Bean Creek), many families also bought summer homes in Scotts Valley. The Edwards family built their summer cabin above Bean Creek in the early 1920s and dammed up the creek for a swimming hole. This photograph is from 1928. (Courtesy of Peggy Edwards.)

**Gordon's Chuck Wagon.** Serving lunches from $1.00 and dinners from $2.75 (not including a beverage or dessert), Gordon's Chuck House was a longtime Scotts Valley landmark located on the corner of Whispering Pines, Mount Hermon Road, and Scotts Valley Drive. Torn down in the late 1960s and replaced by the Union 76 gas station, the pioneer Hendricks home was also close to this site. This photograph was taken around 1950. (Courtesy of Ronnie Trubeck.)

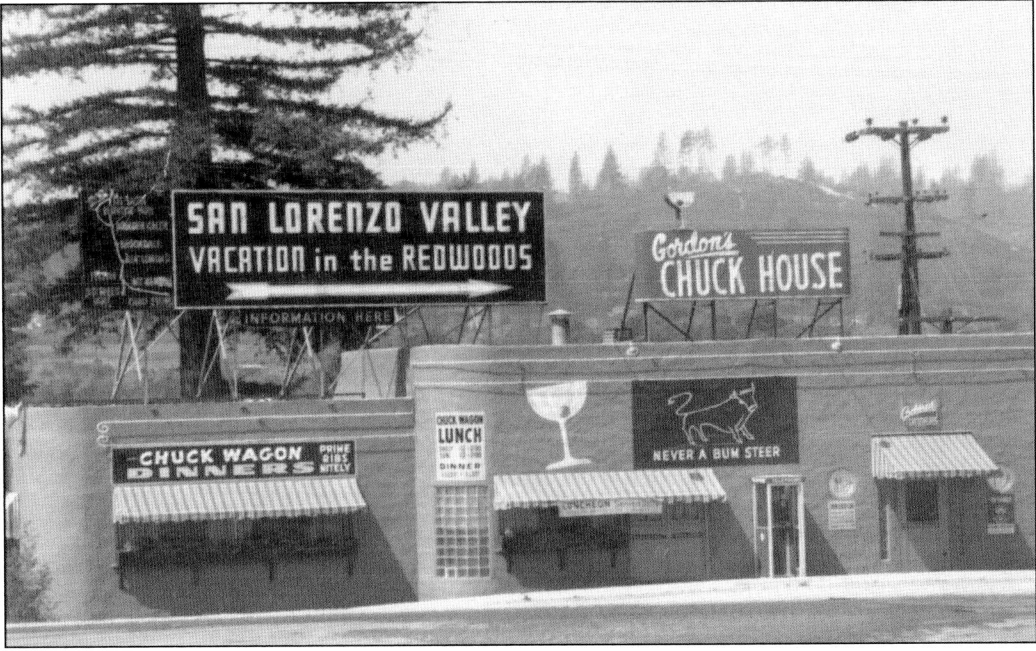

# *Six*

# A City Grows Up

It took the threat of a proposed memorial park and cemetery to spur Scotts Valley residents to begin the difficult process of city incorporation. The idea of incorporation had been discussed many times but had been abandoned due to the unpopularity of extra tax assessments and disputes over the areas to be incorporated. With the City of Santa Cruz threatening to annex the Sky Park Airport, plus the proposed cemetery project, it seemed a good time to push for local control. To spearhead that process, the Scotts Valley Property Owners Association came into existence in 1960, with Agnes Lewis as president.

After extensive study groups, committee meetings, and spirited public forums, the incorporation measure went to the ballot on April 14, 1964. The proposal passed with the narrow margin of 344 for and 323 against. The results were challenged in court for the next two years until the case was finally heard in the state's district court of appeal. The challenged votes were whittled down, but city incorporation still held the majority vote. As for the proposed cemetery, the developer never appeared at the final hearing and the use permit expired.

On August 2, 1966, the first elected officials for the new city took office. Bill Graham was elected mayor, winning a coin toss with C.R. Roberson, who became vice mayor. M. Willis Lotts took his seat as an elected council member. The other two elected council members, Ken Stacy and Dave Alford, had moved out of the city limits during the two-year challenge period, so Paul Couchman Jr. and James Kennedy were appointed to replace them.

At the time, the current water district manager, Friend Stone, known as "Stoney," was appointed the first city manager. In a 1971 newspaper interview, he explained his vision for Scotts Valley: "Just another city is not our aim. Our plan is a well-balanced city with enough business revenue to pay for city government, enough industrial enterprise to furnish jobs to those who want to live in the area and enough green belt areas scattered around within this so we don't get crowded."

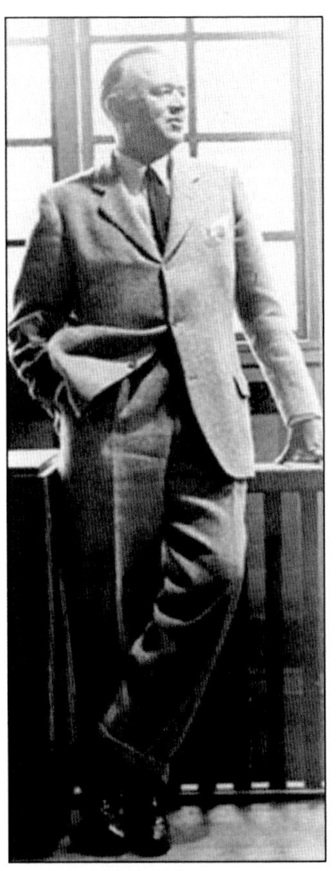

**William Wurster.** In addition to designing hundreds of homes in the Bay Area, including several at Pasatiempo and the Hollins barn in Scotts Valley, William Wurster was responsible for the Bank of America Center in San Francisco, the Cowell and Kresge Colleges at UC Santa Cruz, Merritt College in Oakland, and Ghirardelli Square in San Francisco. Wurster Hall at UC Berkeley is named for Wurster and his wife, Catherine Bauer. (Courtesy of the Thomas D. Church Collection, Environmental Design Archives, University of California, Berkeley.)

**Gregory Farmhouse.** Built in 1928, Wurster's Gregory Farmhouse near Canham Road in Scotts Valley is considered the prototype for the California ranch style. His award-winning concept included a revolutionary open design, which carefully incorporated natural views, utilized appropriate building materials for the site, and created spaces that could be used for a variety of uses. (Courtesy of the Thomas D. Church Collection, Environmental Design Archives, University of California, Berkeley.)

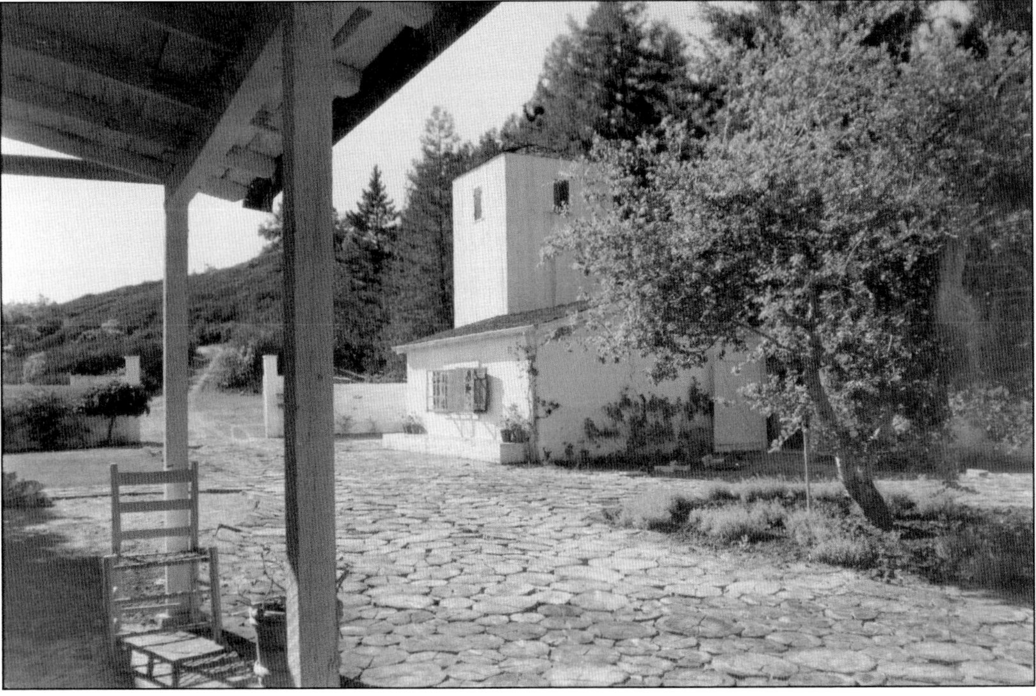

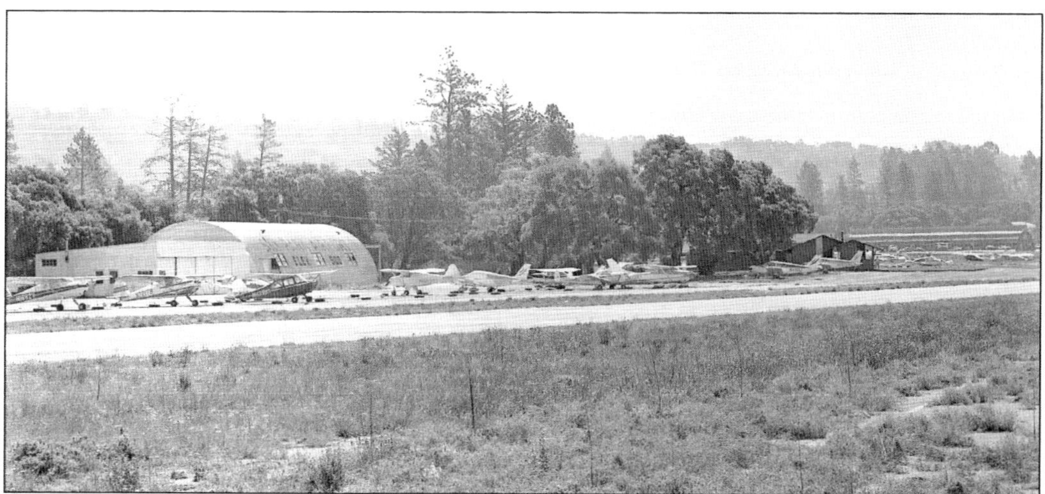

**Sky Park Airport.** In 1946, Jack and Lola Graham leased land for a private landing strip on their property off Mount Hermon Road, which was part of the original Locke dairy. In 1947, operators Wayne Voights and Jack Wilson opened a flight school that trained returning World War II veterans under the GI Bill. (Courtesy of Norman Burns Photography.)

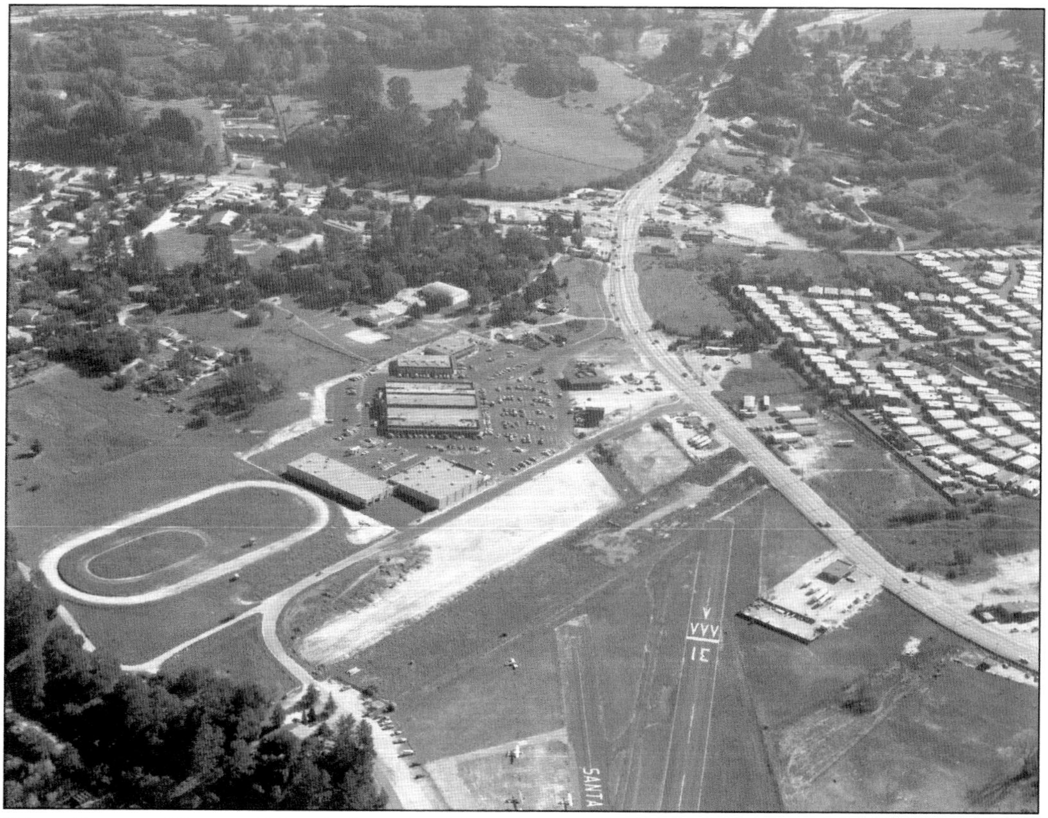

**West Scotts Valley.** The flight school lasted until 1949. For a short time after that, George Brady ran his Piper Aircraft dealership at the airport. This aerial view of west Scotts Valley taken in 1976 shows the partial runway of the Sky Park Airport, the California Pony Racing Track, and the King's Village Shopping Center. (Courtesy Covello & Covello Photography.)

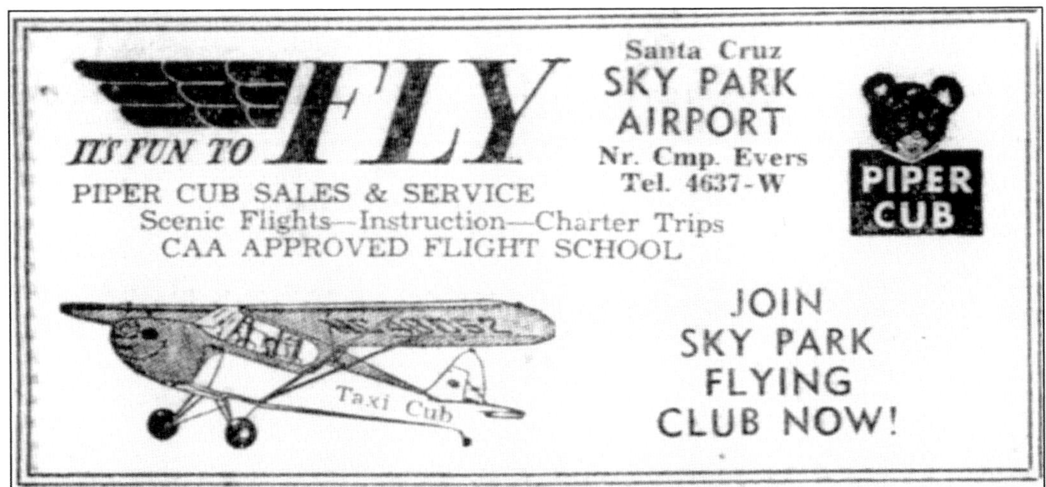


**SKY PARK ADVERTISEMENT.** From 1951 to 1965, Russell and Esther Fields Rice ran the operations of Sky Park Airport. Both licensed pilots, they had previously operated the city of Santa Cruz's airport in Capitola. Jack Johansen was the resident aircraft mechanic. At the height of airport operations, some 60 planes and three flying clubs made Sky Park their home base. (Author's collection.)

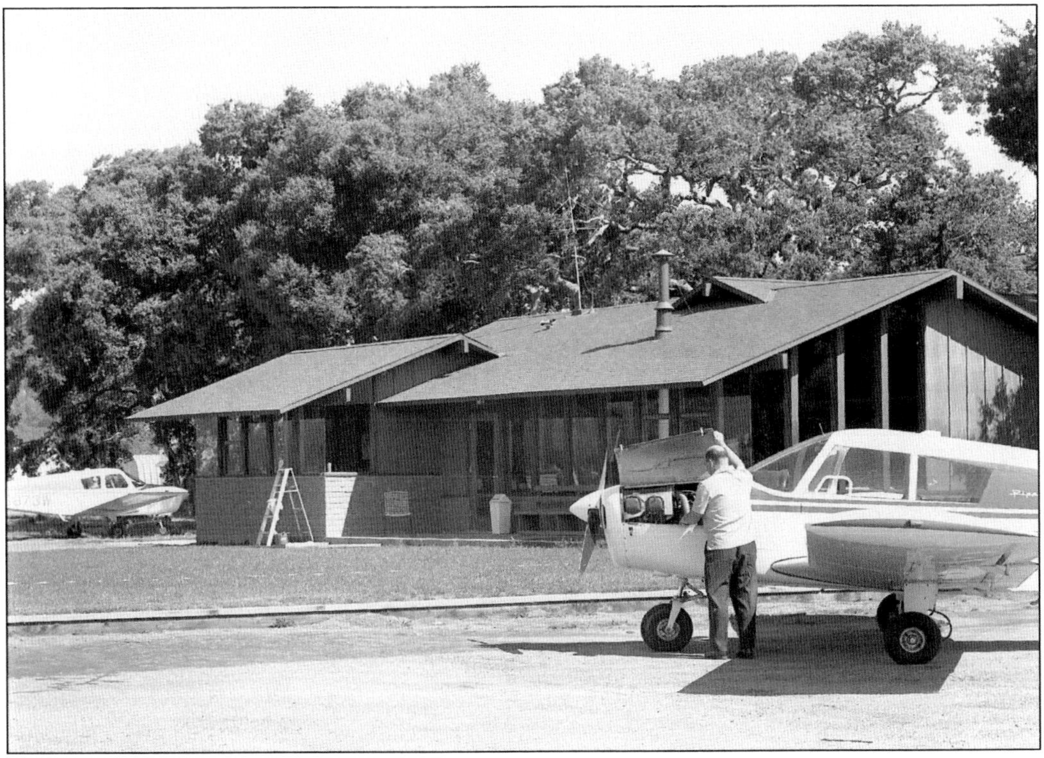

**TERMINAL BUILDING.** In 1968, a $45,000 terminal building was added, which later became the Scotts Valley Parks and Recreation Administration Building. Many pilots recalled the dangerously strong updrafts at the end of the runway during takeoffs. In 1981, Steve Wozniak, cofounder of Apple, crashed his Beechcraft Bonanza at Sky Park. Wozniak and the three passengers aboard suffered injuries. (Courtesy of Norman Burns Photography.)

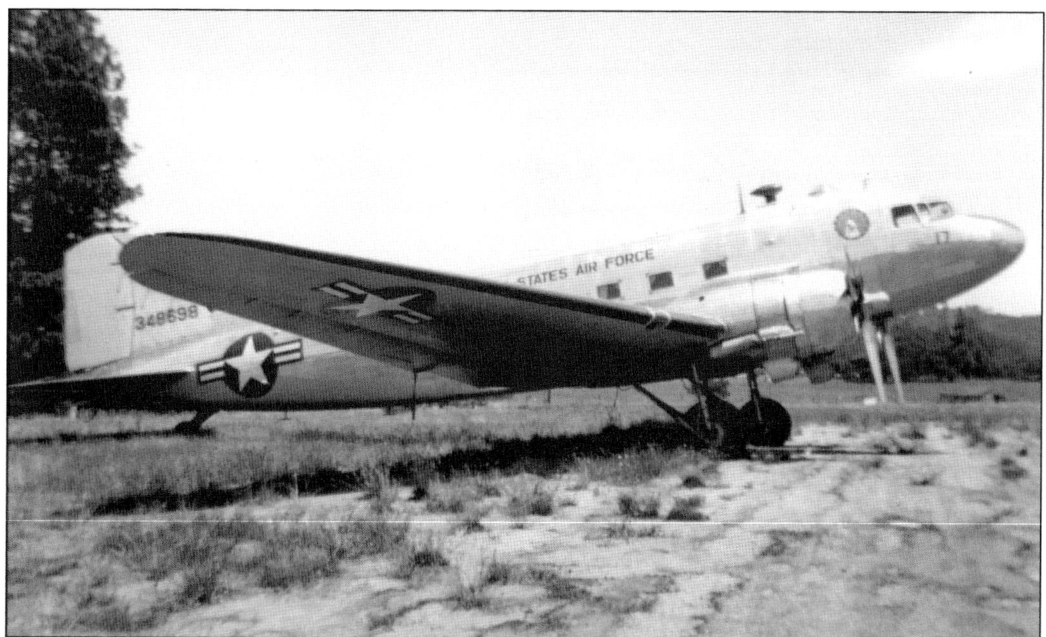


**AIR FORCE C-47.** Weighing in at 30,000 pounds, this C-47 was the heaviest plane to land at Sky Park. The landing left a groove on the runway for which the Air Force was sent a bill for $550. (It is not known whether the Air Force actually paid.) In 1962, the City of Santa Cruz purchased the airport site and later annexed the property. On January 1, 1983, the airport closed. (Courtesy of Catherine Seapy.)

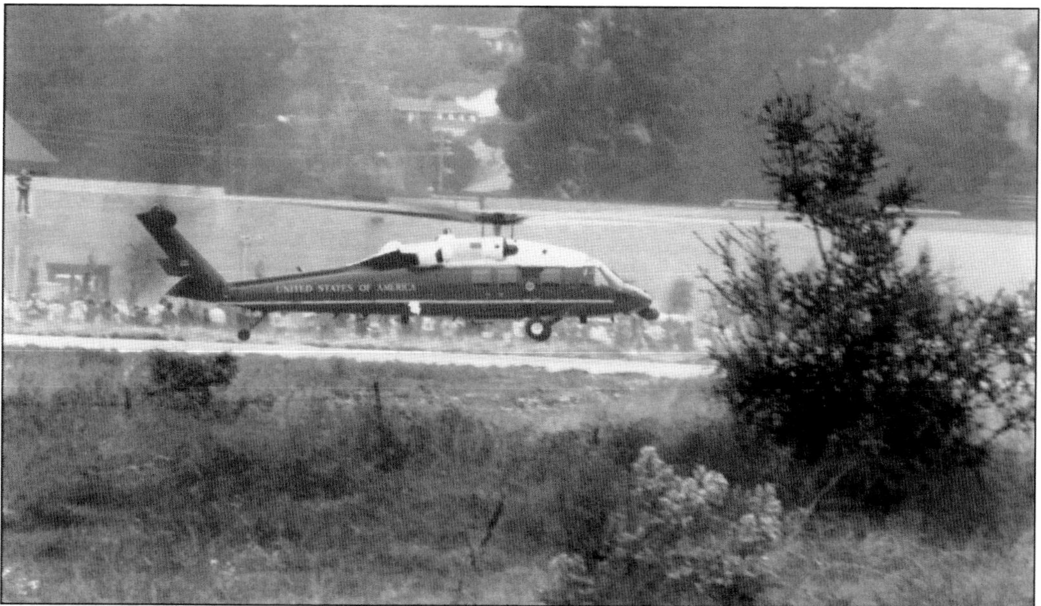


**PRESIDENTIAL HELICOPTER.** In 1989, Pres. George H.W. Bush flew into Sky Park to inspect the damage from the Loma Prieta earthquake. In 1990, the City of Scotts Valley began the process of transforming the old airport land into a town center development to be completed with restaurants, shops, offices, a town green, and residential units. (Courtesy of the Scotts Valley Police Department.)

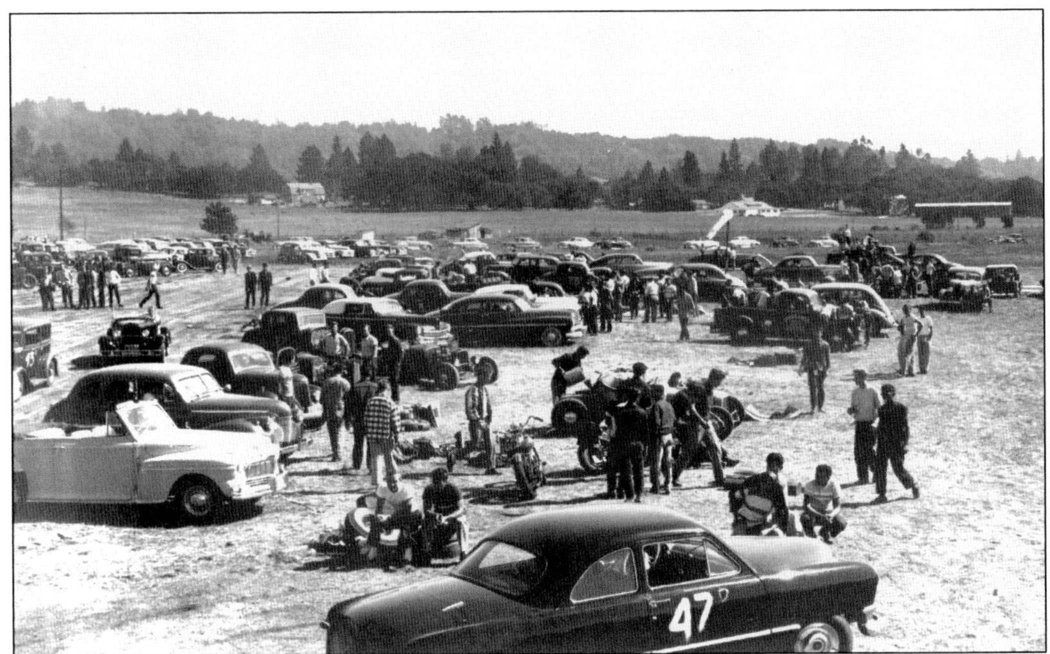


**DRAGSTERS AT SKY PARK.** In September 1950, a group of speed enthusiasts gathered at the Sky Park Airport, then a privately owned airstrip. Using insurance coverage from the Cal-Neva Roadster Association, they held what is believed to be the first "legal" drag races in Northern California. (Courtesy of SVHS.)

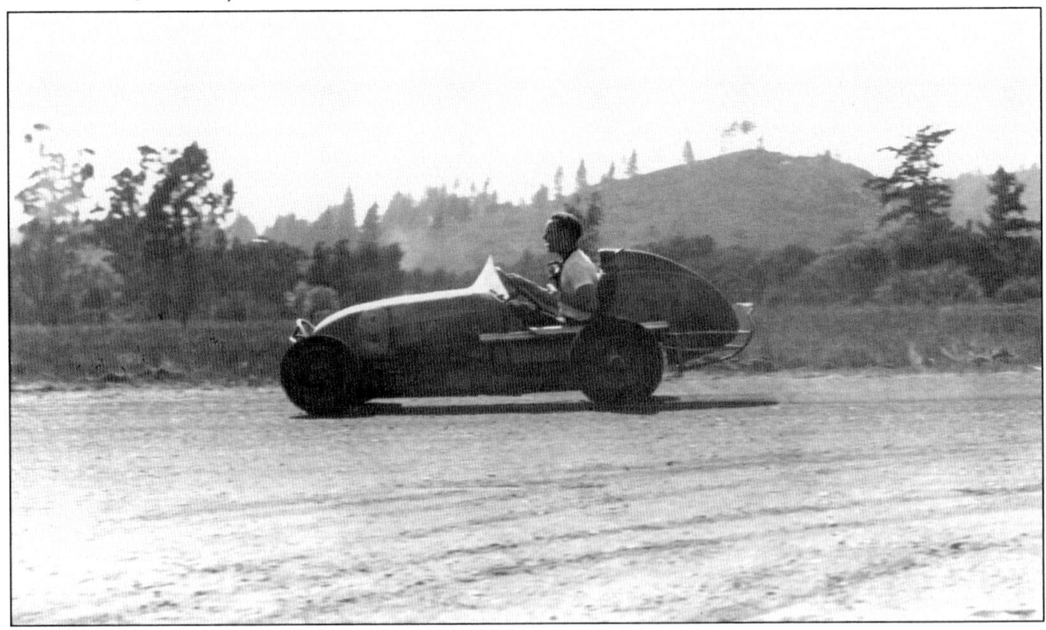

**RACER.** Older cars, often from the 1920s and 1930s, would be stripped down to only the essential parts to reduce weight, and new parts would be added or substituted for additional speed. With an estimated 2,000 spectators, drag racing clubs, such as the Slo-pokes, Gear Jammers, Cam Snappers, Clutch Busters, Cam Twisters, Oakland Smokers, and Sacto-Flyers, entered the timed races. (Courtesy of SVHS.)

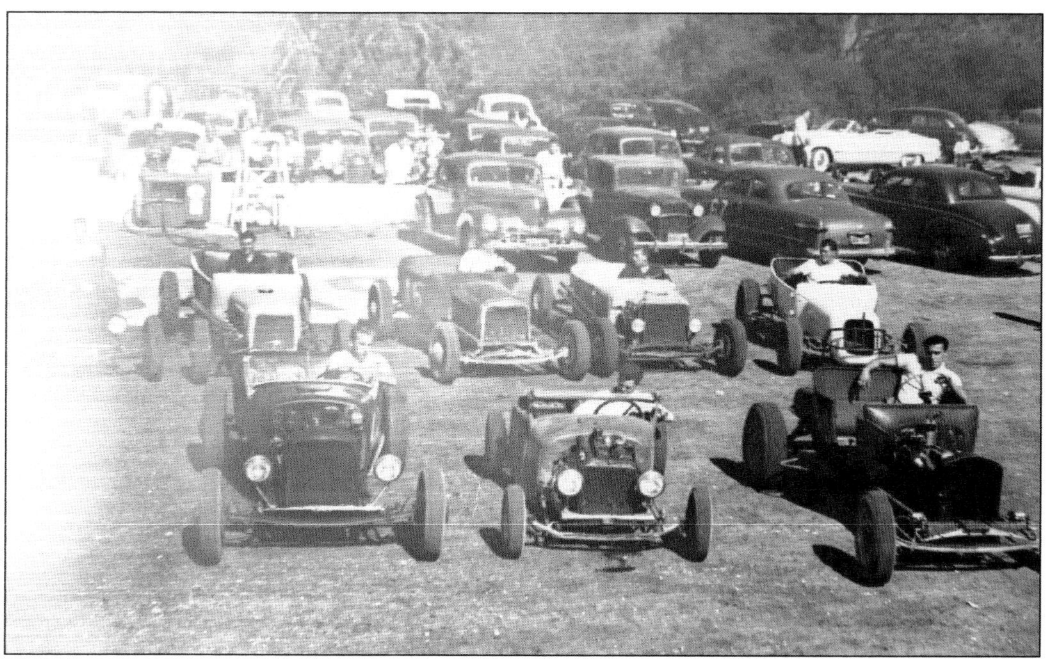

**Waiting Dragsters.** The officers of the two Santa Cruz Dragster Clubs, the Slo-pokes and the Cam Snappers, made arrangements for the race. The highway patrol reportedly announced, "No one would be cited if they left the airport grounds in a safe and orderly manner." (Courtesy of SVHS.)

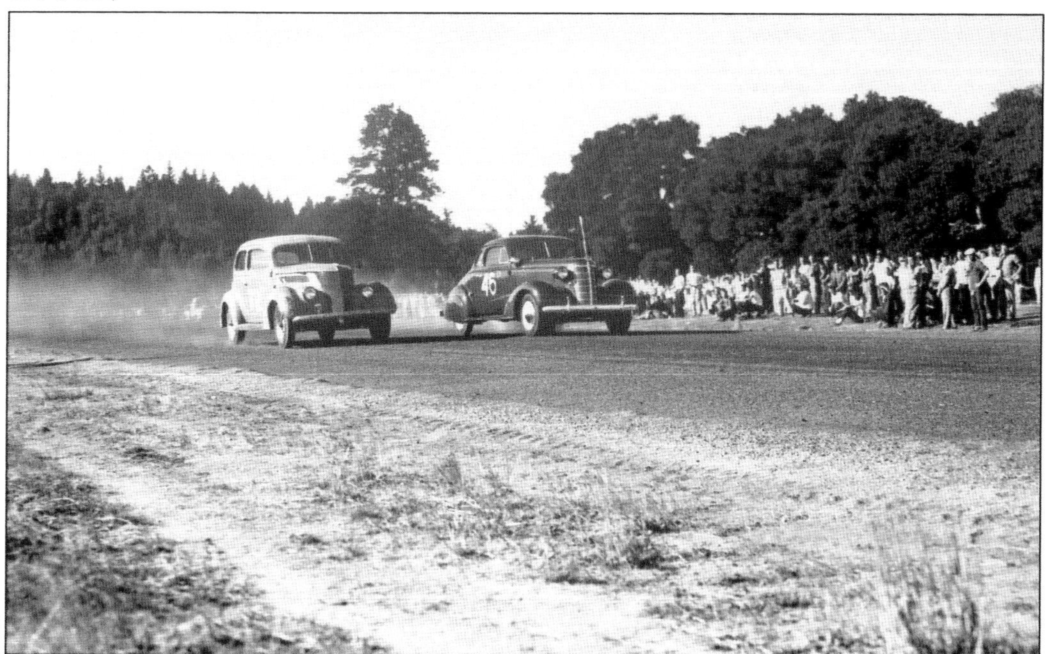

**Racing Heat.** Marked with hand-painted numbers, the cars paired off to race. The winners went back to race again until a final champion of each class was established. Donated trophies were awarded to the top time holders, and that night, the Sky Park management held a dance in one of the aircraft hangars for the public. (Courtesy of SVHS.)

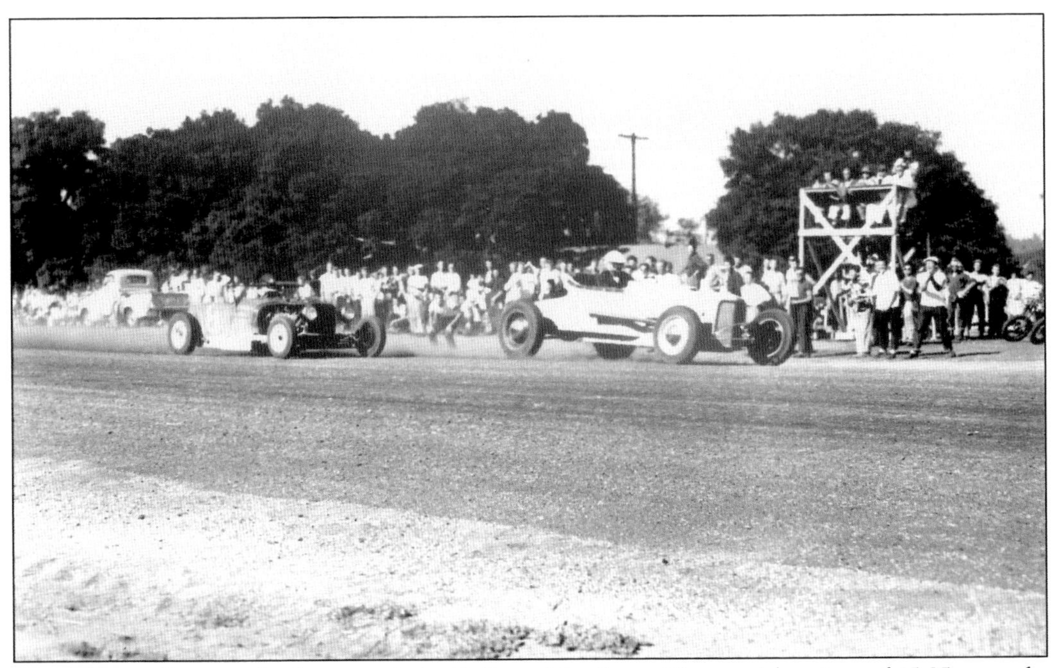

**Kelley over Gilbert.** In this race, Brice Kelley of the Sacto-Flyers, with a time of 15.35 seconds, wins over ? Gilbert of the Foothill Roads, who had a time of 16.96. (Courtesy of SVHS.)

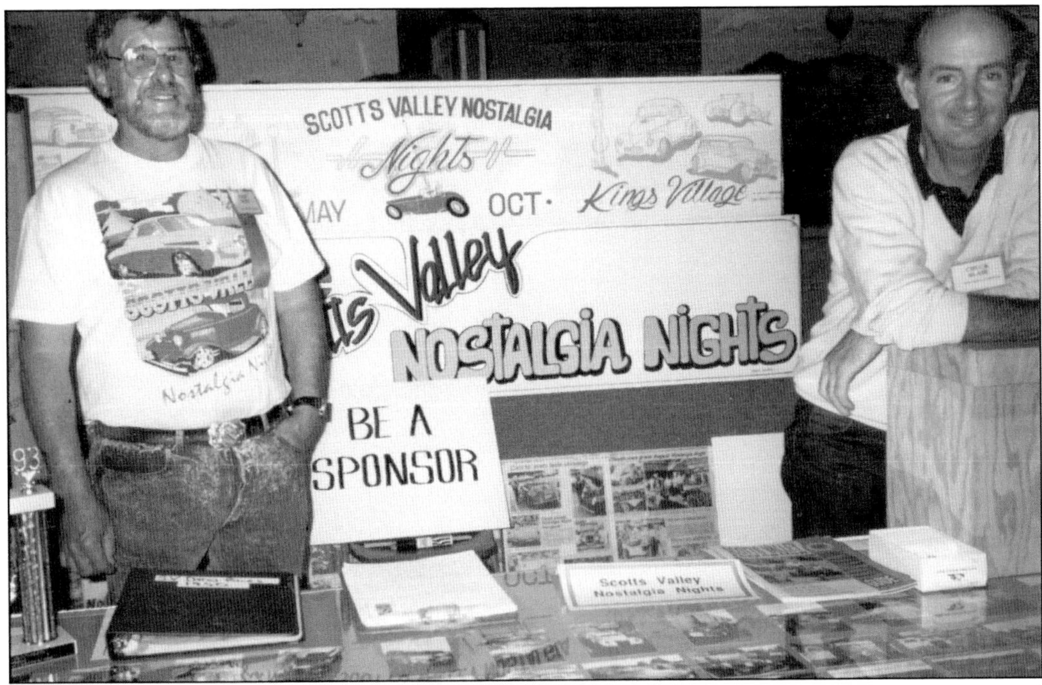


**Nostalgia Nights.** For 14 years, the Scotts Valley Lions Club and other volunteers organized Nostalgia Nights. Founded by local resident Vern Hart, who also assisted the original Sky Park drag races, the event showcased custom cars of all types and raised money for local nonprofits. Tireless community volunteers Vern Hart (left) and Chuck Blair are shown here. (Courtesy of the Scotts Valley Chamber of Commerce.)

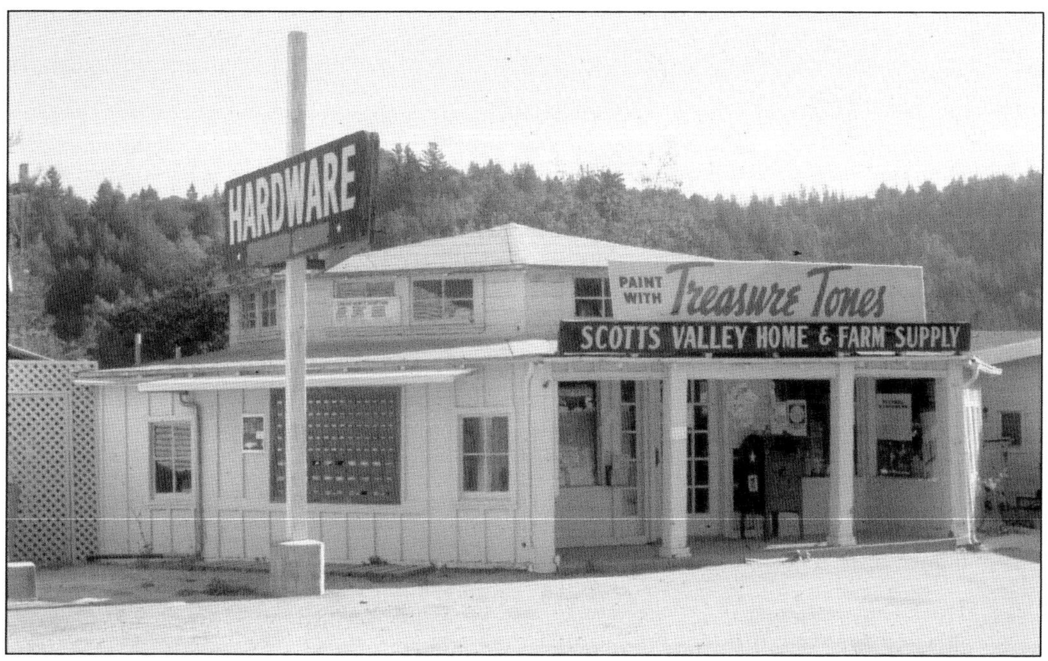


**THE OCTAGON.** From 1947 through 1973, Helen and Herman Nanna operated Scotts Valley's first branch post office within her Scotts Valley Hardware and Farm Supply Store on Scotts Valley Drive. The octagonal building shown here was a former bird aviary moved from Beverley Gardens because of a postwar shortage of new building materials. Nanna was a well-known Scotts Valley businesswoman, and her store and post office station became an unofficial community center for residents. (Courtesy of Charlene Duval.)

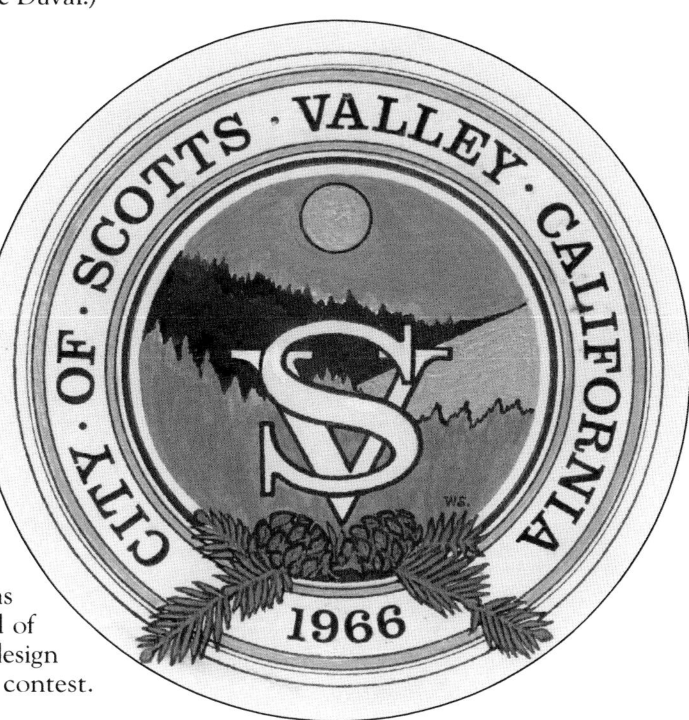


**CITY SEAL.** Early on, there was some question as to the correct punctuation of the city name, whether it should be Scott's Valley or Scotts Valley. After discussion, the city council decided the name of the city should reflect all the Scott descendants, not just Hiram Scott, and the town became officially known as Scotts Valley. This official seal of Scotts Valley was the winning design of Wendell Simons in a 1966 contest. (Courtesy of SVHS.)

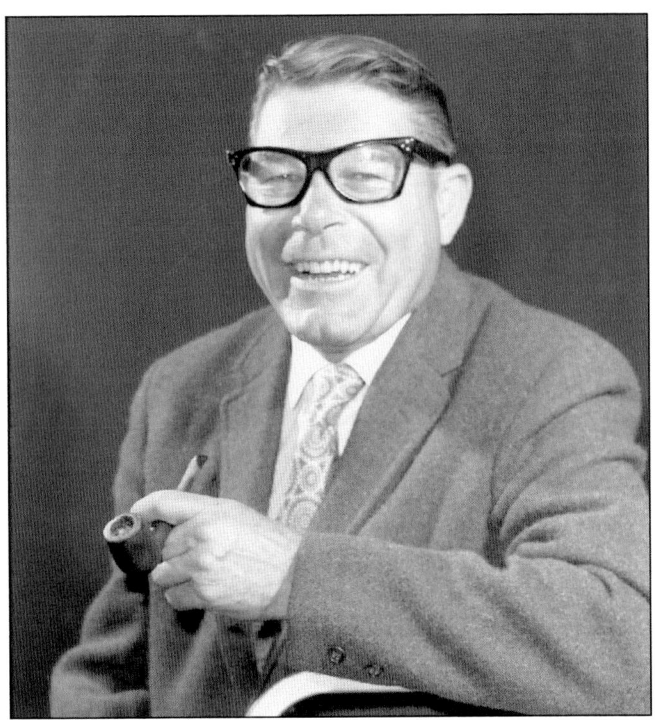

**Bill Graham, c. 1967.** Scotts Valley's first mayor, Bill Graham, was the son of Jack and Lola Graham, longtime Scotts Valley residents. The elder Grahams owned a portion of the old Locke dairy off what is now Mount Hermon Road. Bill and his father operated a building supply and a sand and cement aggregate plant roughly where today's McDonald's restaurant is located. Graham also developed the Spring Lakes Mobile Home Park. (Courtesy of Norman Burns Photography.)

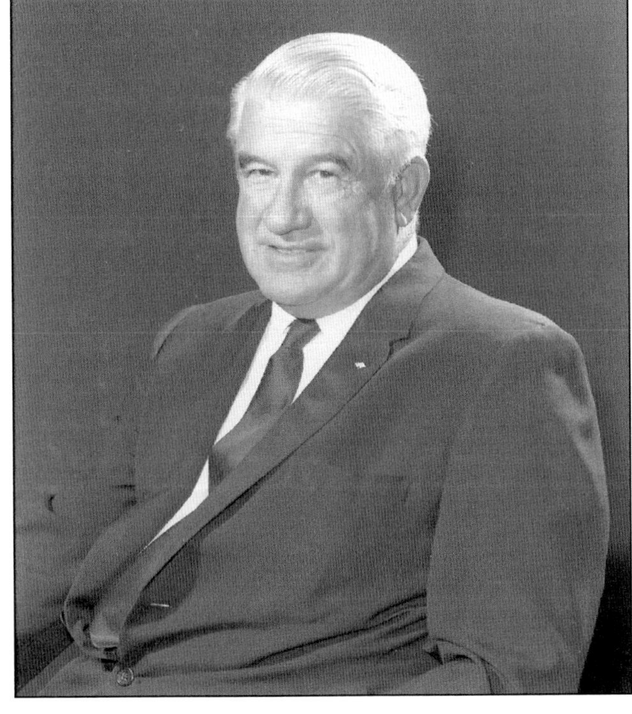

**Friend Stone, c. 1967.** Known somewhat as a horse trader, Friend Stone possessed a can-do attitude as city manager that was just what the fledgling city needed. To save money, Stone, as city manager, also temporarily became city clerk, city planning director, and police commissioner to fill positions that were legally required by law. He became nationally known for a brief time by shrewdly purchasing three obsolete government-guided missiles for $95 each to use as street culverts, fuel tanks, and manhole covers. (Courtesy of Norman Burns Photography.)

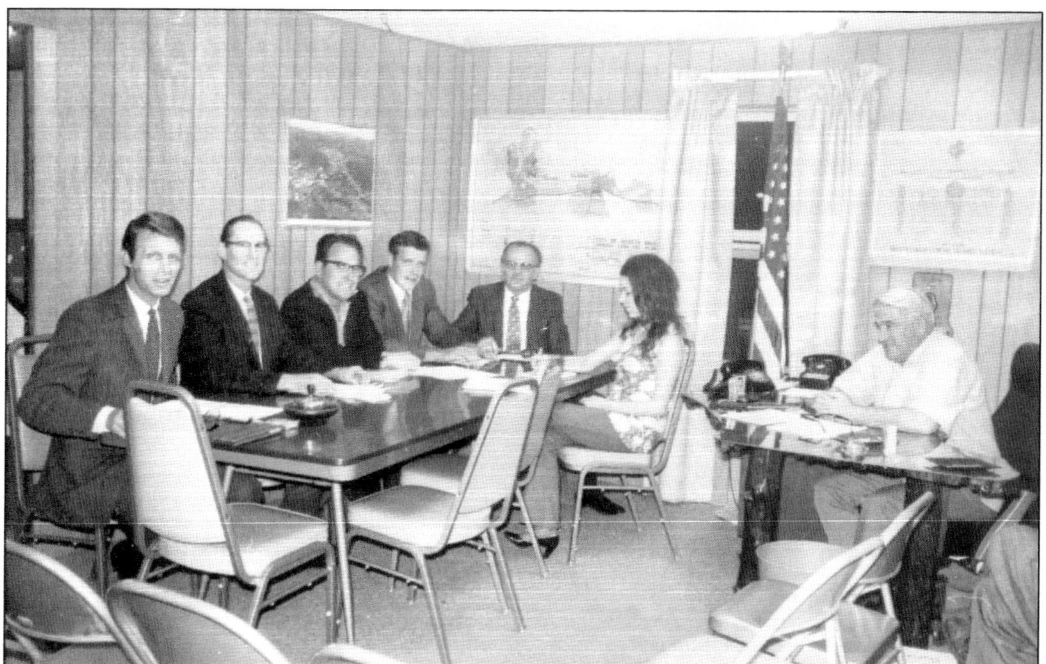

**City Council, 1971.** From left to right are council members Walter Shulte, Paul Couchman Jr., C.R. Roberson, James Kennedy, Mayor M. Willis Lotts, secretary Donna Berri (now Lind), and city manager Friend Stone. The first city offices were located with the Water District on Scotts Valley Drive, next to the Gold Cup Café. Lind is the current mayor of Scotts Valley. (Courtesy of Donna Lind.)

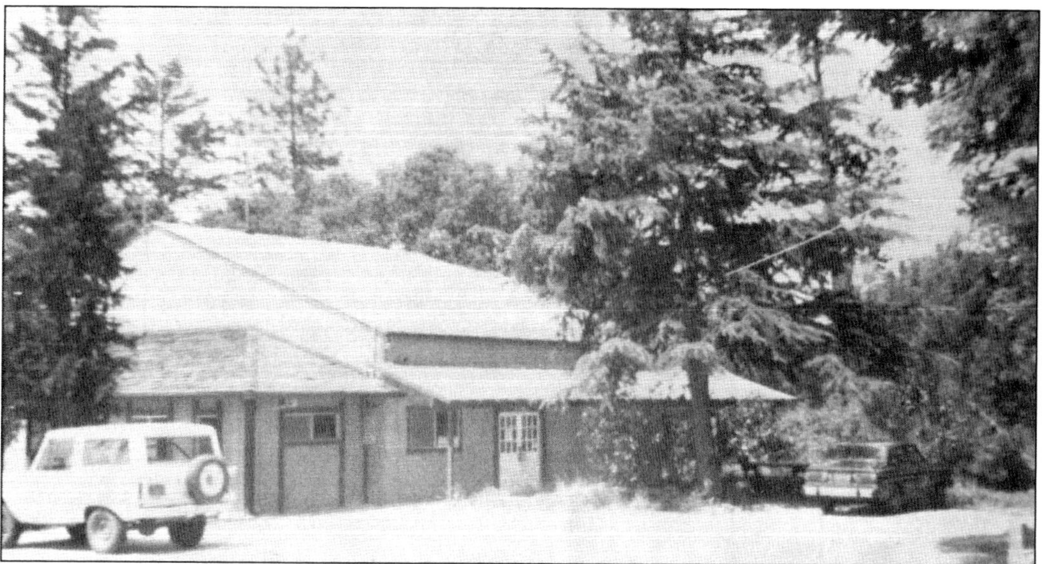

**Second City Hall.** In need of more space, the city hall and one-man police department were moved from Scotts Valley Drive to an old farmhouse in the Sky Park area around 1967. After five years in the aging building, a nearby airport hangar was adapted for use as the next city headquarters. In 1987, the current city hall on Civic Center Drive, adjacent to the Scott House and MacDorsa Park, was completed. (Courtesy of Jay Topping.)

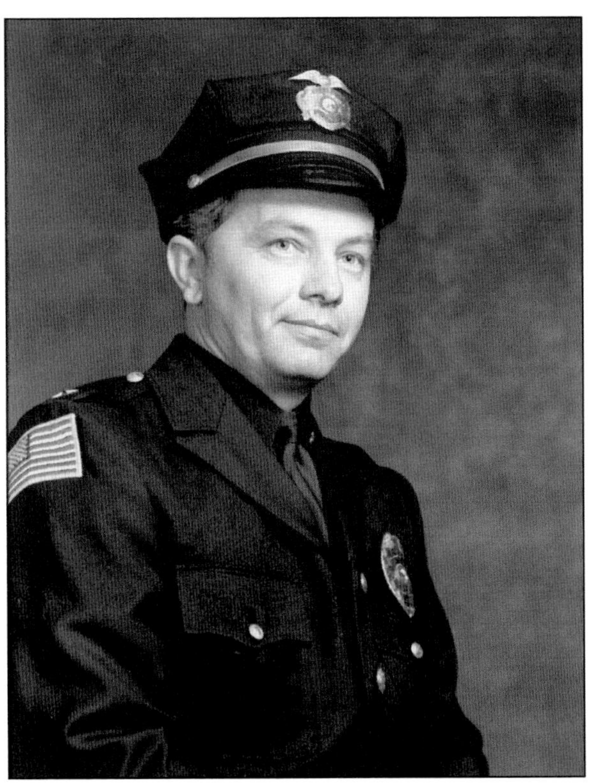

**Chief Pittenger, c. 1967.** Scotts Valley has had only five police chiefs: Gerald Pittenger (pictured), Stephen Walpole, Thomas Bush, Steven Lind, and John Weiss. (Courtesy of Norman Burns Photography.)

**First Police Car.** Driven by current police chief John Weiss in the 2015 Scotts Valley Fourth of July parade, the 1967 Ford Galaxy Police Interceptor replicates the original "Unit One" driven by Chief Pittenger. (Photograph by the author.)

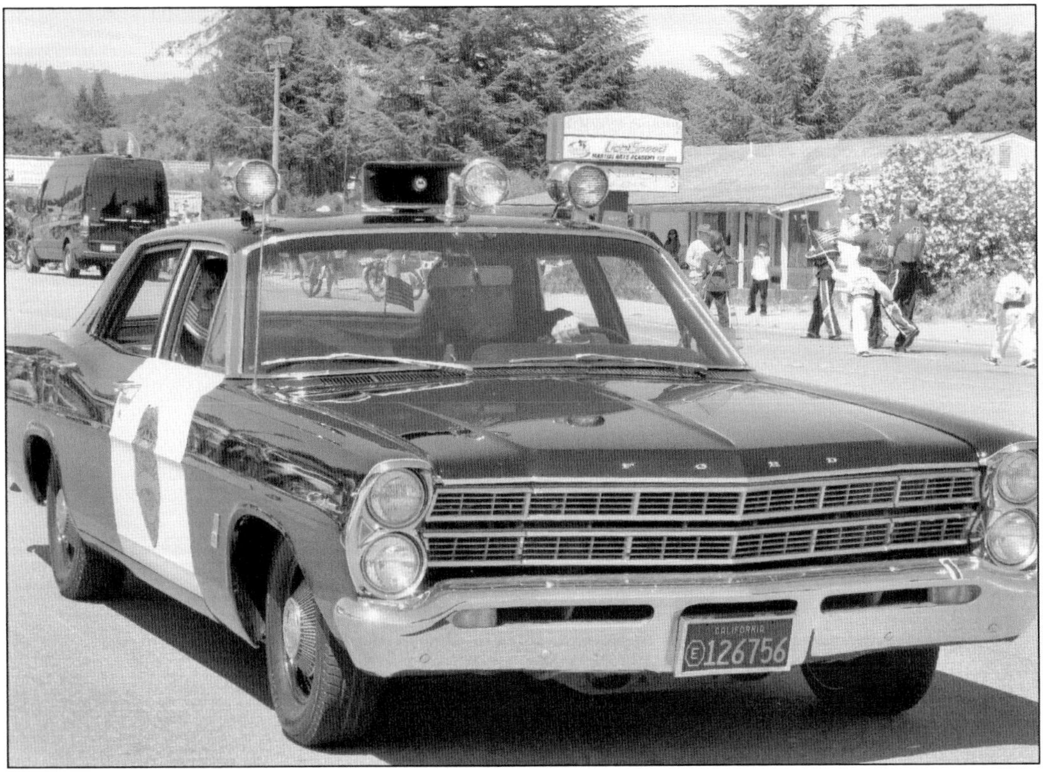

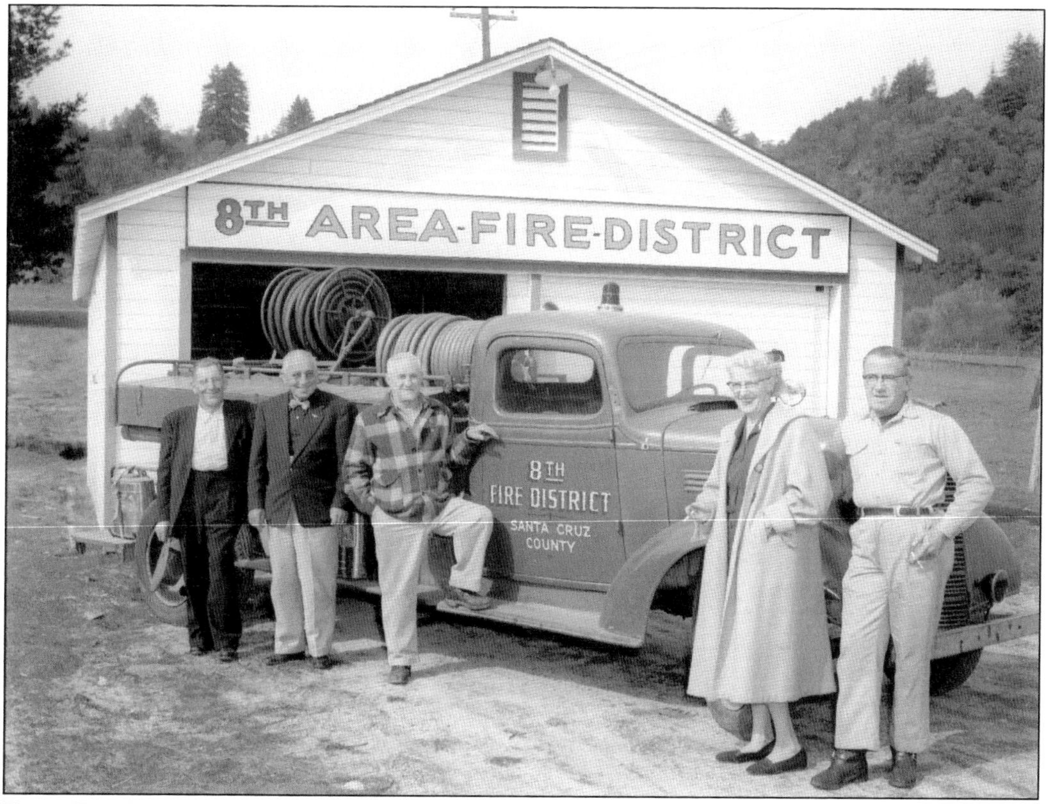

**EARLY FIRE DISTRICT.** Formally organized in 1942, the Eighth Area Fire District originally consisted of both the Scotts Valley and the Branciforte areas. Volunteer firefighters used a refurbished 1937 Chevrolet dump truck affectionately known as "Old Faithful." A phone tree summoned volunteers. Standing in front of Old Faithful in 1955 are, from left to right, commissioners DeForrest Mocker, Frank Souza, and Lawrence "Pop" Dixon, secretary Gladys Dixon, and Chief Lloyd Ragon. (Courtesy of Covello & Covello Photography.)

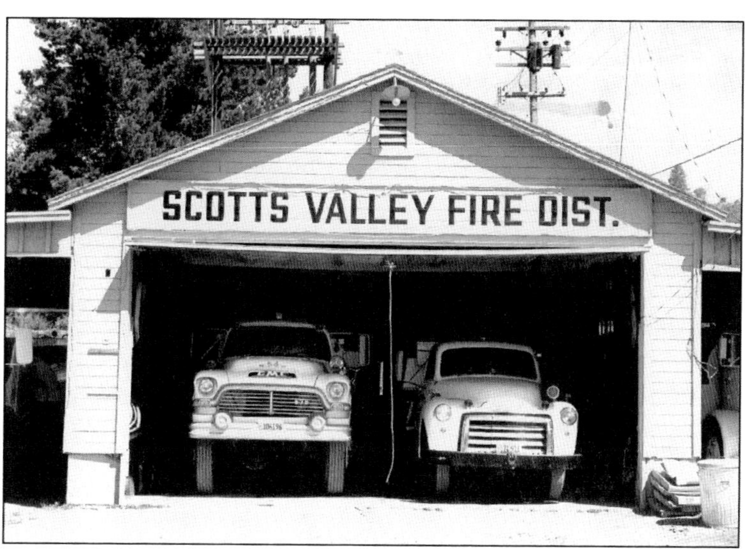


**FIREHOUSE, 1956.** In 1956, a new firehouse was built on Scotts Valley Drive, now the current office of Scotts Valley Rockery. With an all-volunteer staff, fire chiefs Battista "B.J." Erba, Lloyd Ragon, and Everett "Sparky" Taylor ran the fire district until 1972, when C. Bruce Scott began as the first full-time fire chief. (Courtesy Covello & Covello Photography.)

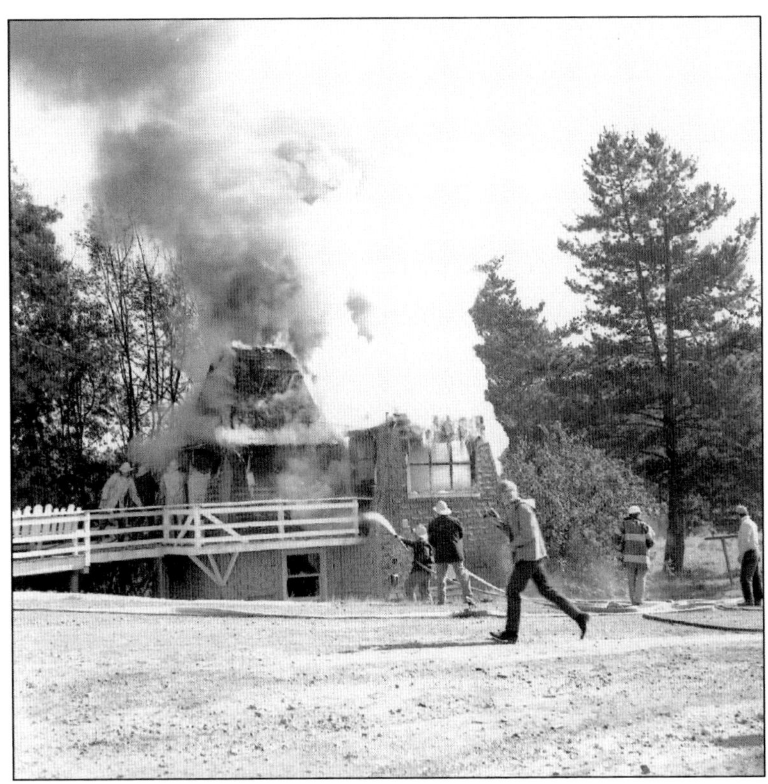

**PRACTICE BURN.** Here, the fire district conducts a practice burn on Anderson's Old Mill Café on Scotts Valley Drive. As of 2016, the Scotts Valley Fire District, under Chief Daniel Grebil, is equipped with four fire engines, a water tender, a hazardous material response vehicle, two fire stations, and 35 shift firefighters. (Courtesy of the Scotts Valley Fire Department.)

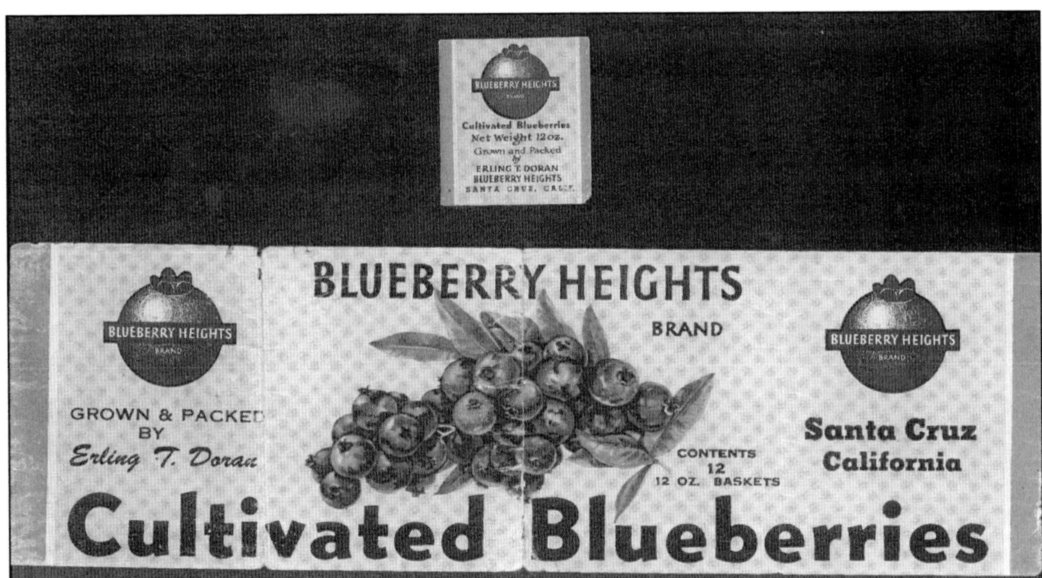


**BLUEBERRY LABEL.** Today, only the street names of Blueberry Drive and Blueberry Court hint at Scotts Valley's past, when it was once widely known for blueberry production. Blueberry farms could be found off Mount Hermon Road, near Camp Evers, and off Lockwood Lane. Workers were paid 12¢ a basket; however, many pickers, usually young people, found they ate more than they harvested. (Courtesy of Catherine Seapy.)

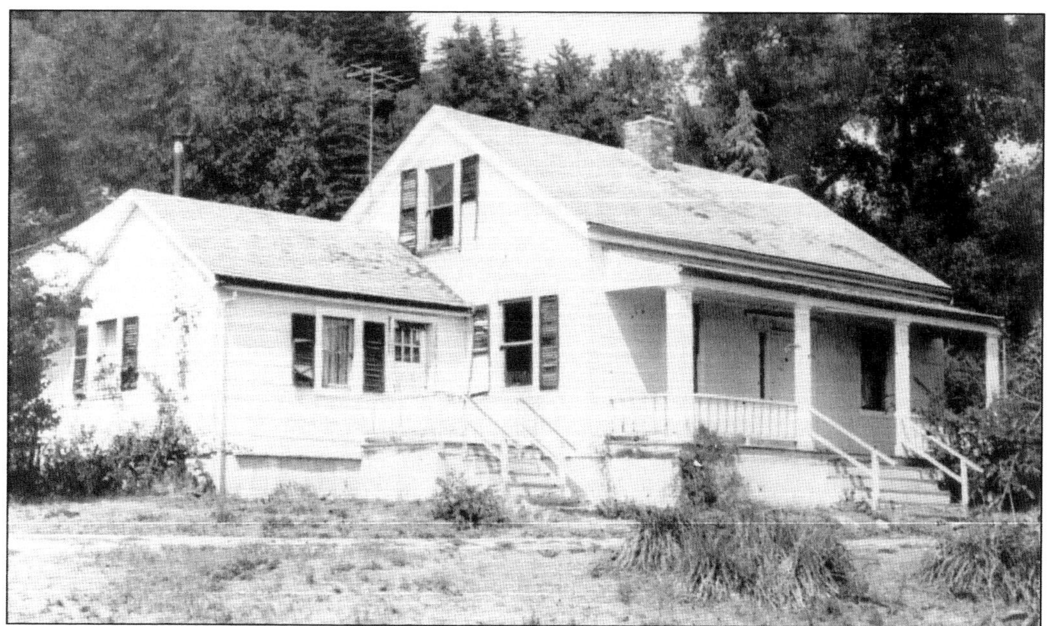

**Before Restoration.** When plans for a large mixed-use development failed in 1975, developers Arch MacDonald and Steve Dorsa donated a five-acre parcel to the City of Scotts Valley that included the Scott House. MacDonald and Dorsa also agreed to sell the city an additional four and a half acres that later became the city hall and police department site, along with MacDorsa Park, location of the Scott House. (Courtesy of SVHS.)

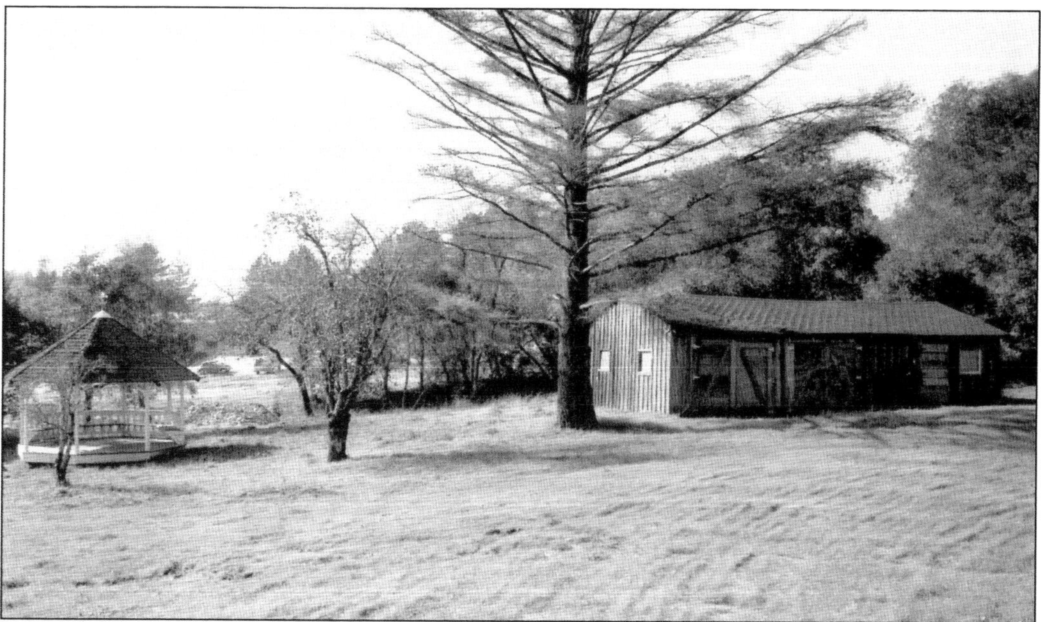

**Scott House Garage.** After the Scott House was moved around 1936, a combination garage and shed was constructed from recycled lumber from the old Scott outbuildings. Marcie Claussenius lived in the Scott House for 41 years, the longest of any resident. The garage was demolished sometime in the late 1970s to allow for the development of the park. The gazebo shown here was moved to the park from the Pinnacle Pass Shopping Center. (Courtesy of SVHS.)

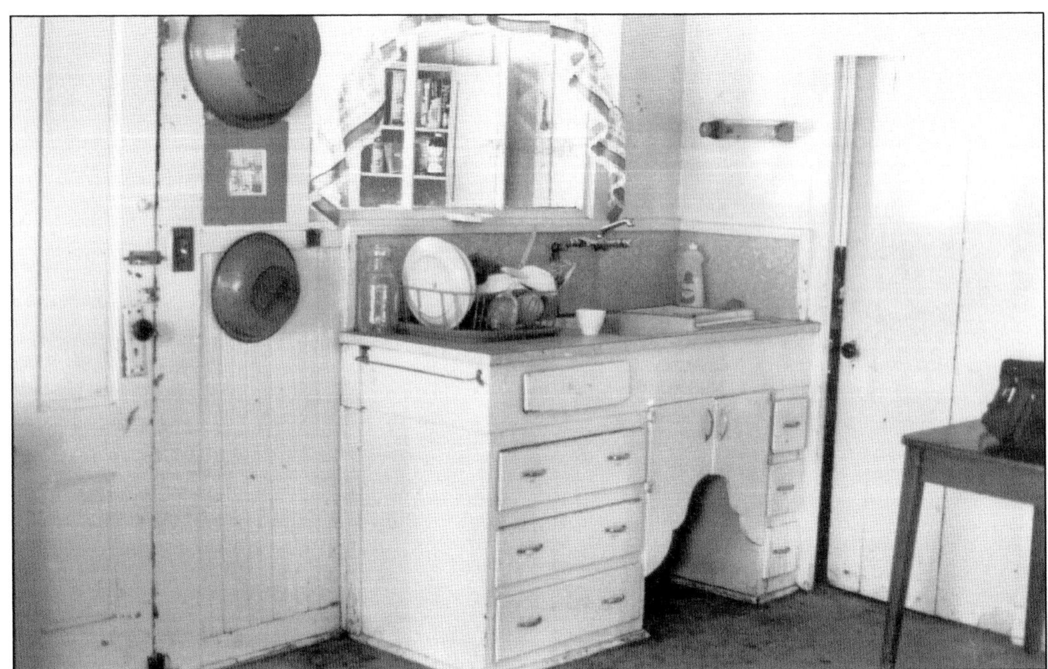

**OLD SCOTT HOUSE KITCHEN.** In 1977, the newly formed Scotts Valley Historical Society helped place the Scott House in the National Register of Historic Places. It proved to be a daunting task, as the historic home needed much work. First, the later nonhistorical additions were removed and a new foundation was added. Later work included earthquake bracing, new siding, rewiring of the electrical system, new roof and gutters, and interior work. (Courtesy of SVHS.)

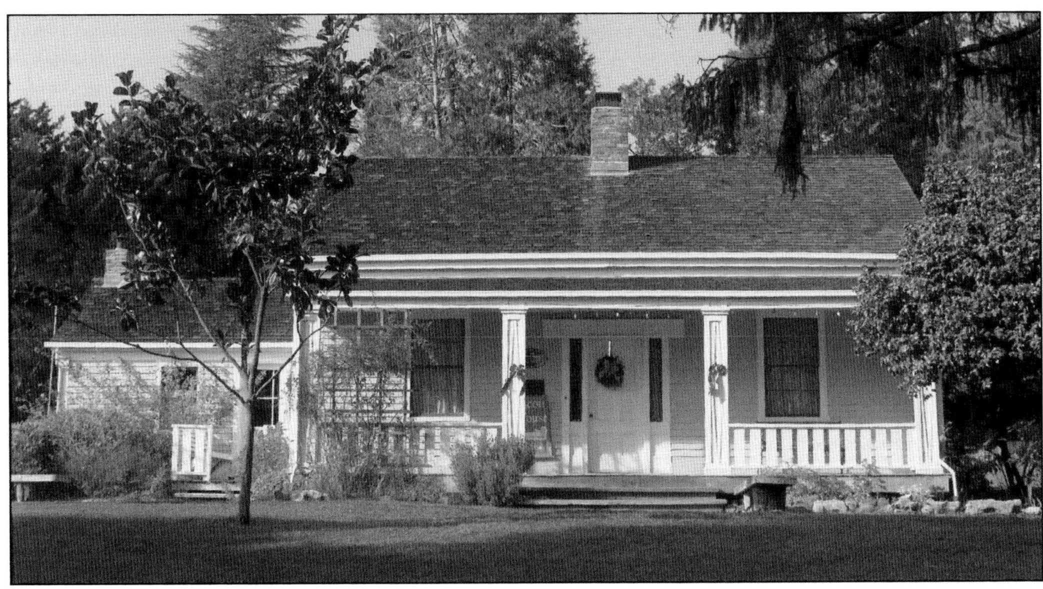

**SCOTT HOUSE, 2003.** In 2003, the Scott House celebrated its 150th birthday. Still going strong, the Scotts Valley Historical Society has future plans to build a new multipurpose historical museum to include interpretive exhibits to increase the public's knowledge of the vast amount of Scotts Valley prehistory and history. (Courtesy of SVHS.)

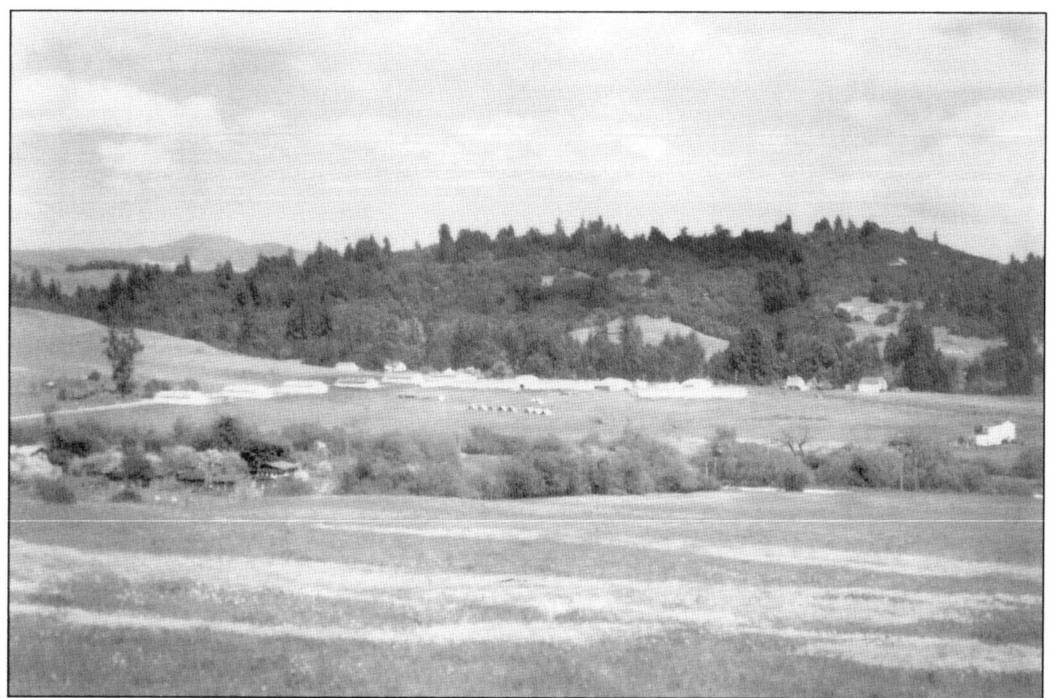

**Mission Hatchery.** Built on 32 acres at the north end of Scotts Valley in 1939, the Mission Hatchery raised chicks at the present-day site of the Vineyards Housing Development. The chicken houses gradually fell into disrepair and were abandoned. In 1967, a group of hippies settled into the dilapidated buildings. Eventually, they were removed—with some difficulty—through the efforts of the new city council. (Courtesy of SVHS.)

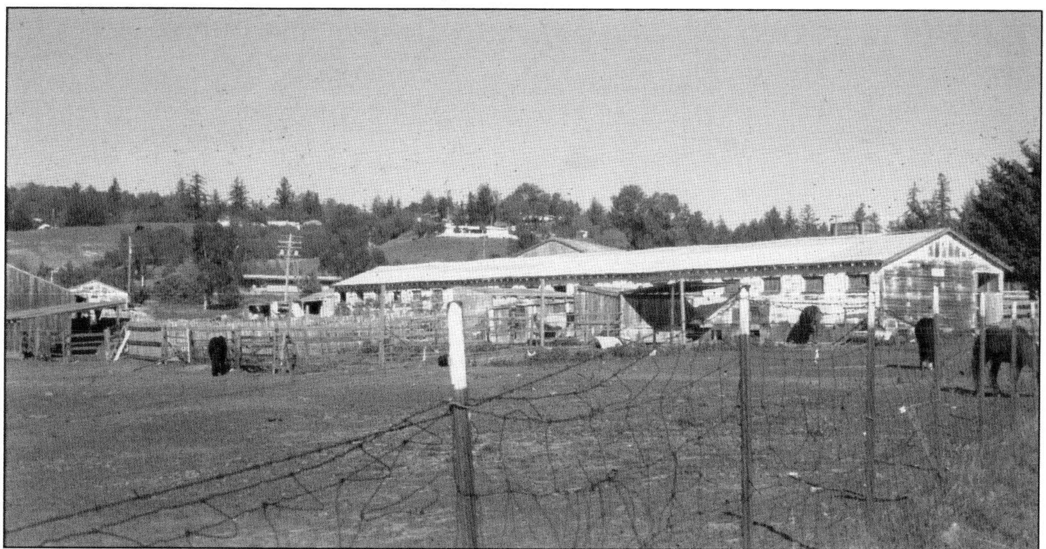

**Billawalla's Ranch.** An extension of Scotts Valley Days, the first outdoor historical reenactment and extravaganza was staged in 1976 to tell the history of Scotts Valley and the United States. The Cavalcade, as it came to be known, was held on developer Noorudin Billawalla's property, the former chicken hatchery. The west end of Vine Hill Elementary School can be seen to the mid-left of the photograph. (Courtesy of Charlene Duval.)

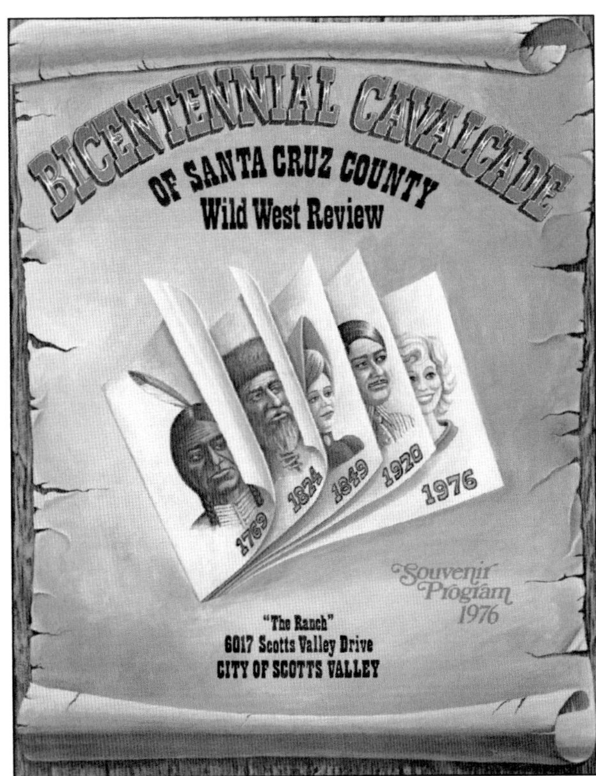


**Cavalcade Cover, 1976.** The two-hour show included a cast of more than 250 performers, with singers, dancers, Indians, pioneers, Mexican bandits, founding mothers and fathers, and even a reenactment of a Western gunfight. Animals used in the show were longhorn steers, oxen, camels, water buffalo, sheep, goats, cows, horses, burros, and mules. (Author's collection.)

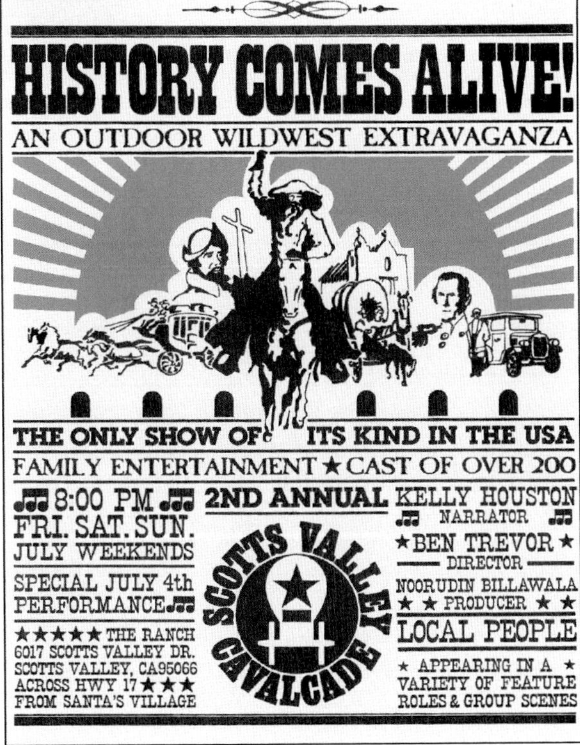


**Cavalcade Cover, 1978.** In later years, the reenactment grew more elaborate and included an actor playing General Patton, an Army tank with a 105-millimeter gun (on loan from the National Guard), and a "flying saucer" inflatable display balloon (used in the "Moon Landing" scene) that was 18 inches in diameter and 8 inches in height. Three Cavalcades were staged in total. (Author's collection.)

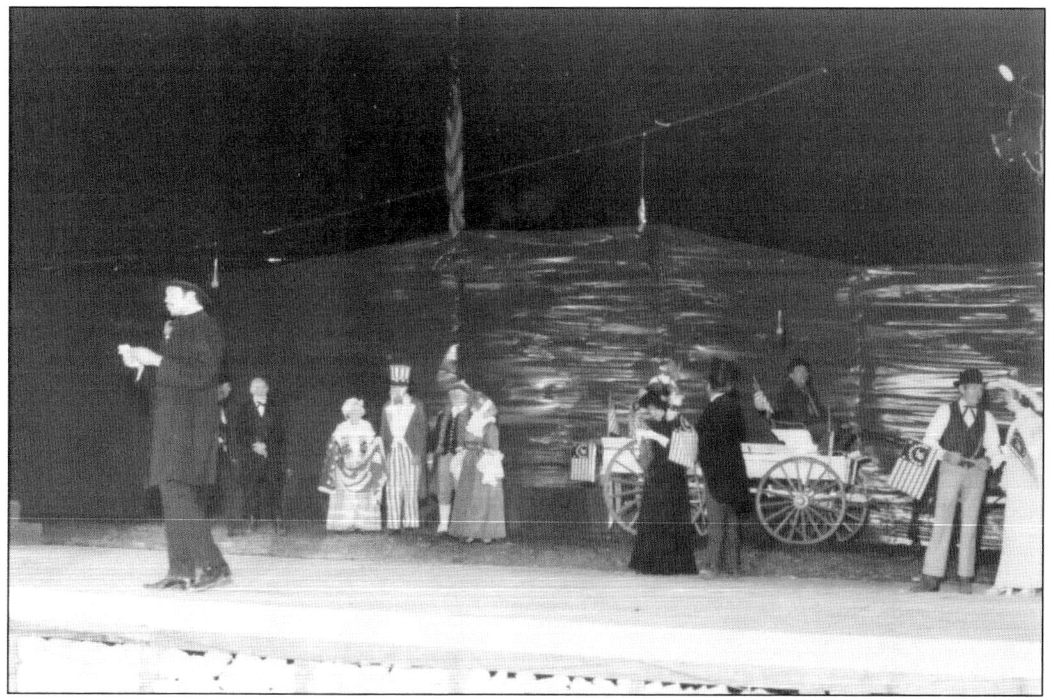

**Cavalcade Stage.** Narrator Kelley Houston tells the story of the nation's founding. (Courtesy of SVHS.)

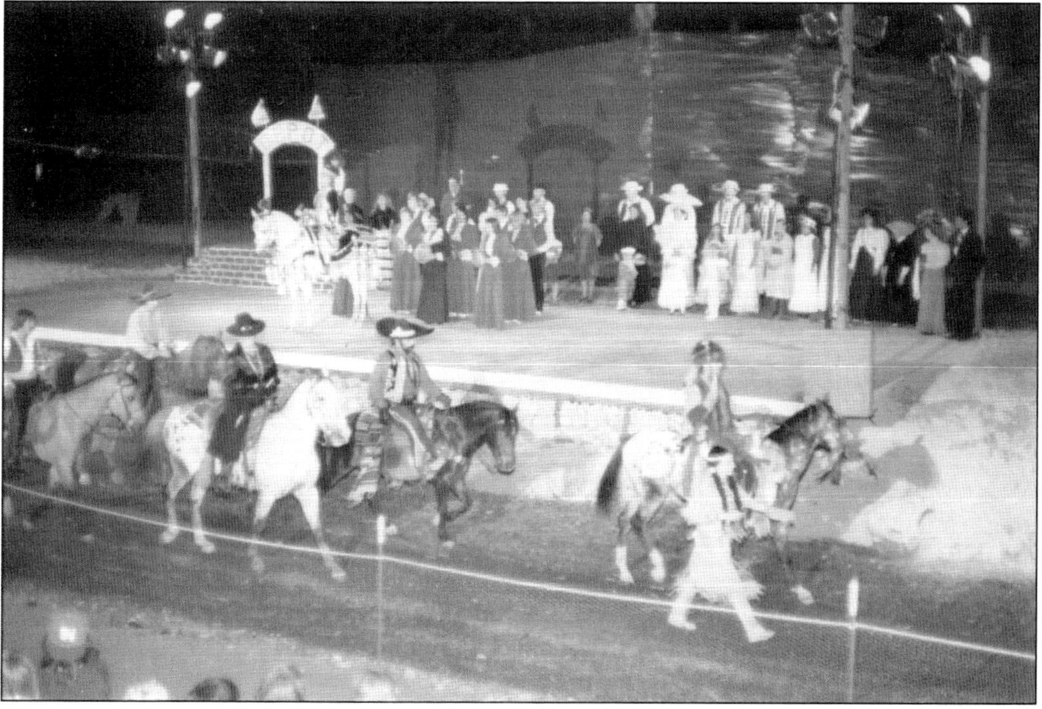

**Cavalcade Scene.** As part of the show, Indians and vaqueros file past a crowd of townspeople waiting at the train depot. (Courtesy of SVHS.)

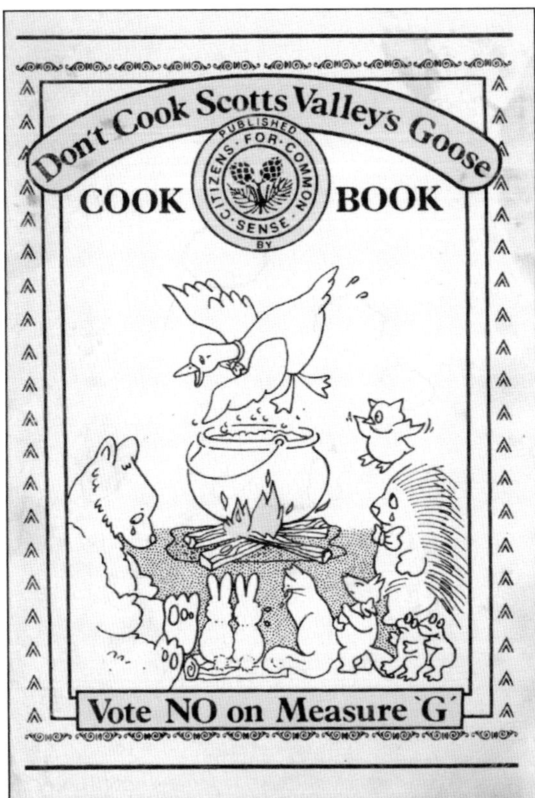


**FUNDRAISING COOKBOOK.** In 1982, a group of concerned residents calling themselves the Committee for Orderly Growth qualified Measure G for the ballot. This was a plan to limit annual growth of residential homes and commercial and industrial square footage. In response, an opposing Measure H, sponsored by Citizens for Common Sense, was also qualified for the ballot. On Election Day, neither measure received the necessary majority votes to pass. (Author's collection.)

**TRIP TO SACRAMENTO.** In 1999, residents opposed to the building of 145 homes on the Glenwood placed Measure O on the ballot. After a contentious campaign, 61 percent of the voters turned down the development. A later Measure M, with a reduced development of 49 homes, won approval by 68 votes in 2002. Below, Glenwood Open Space advocates went to Sacramento to support the purchase of Glenwood land. (Courtesy of Paul Nord.)

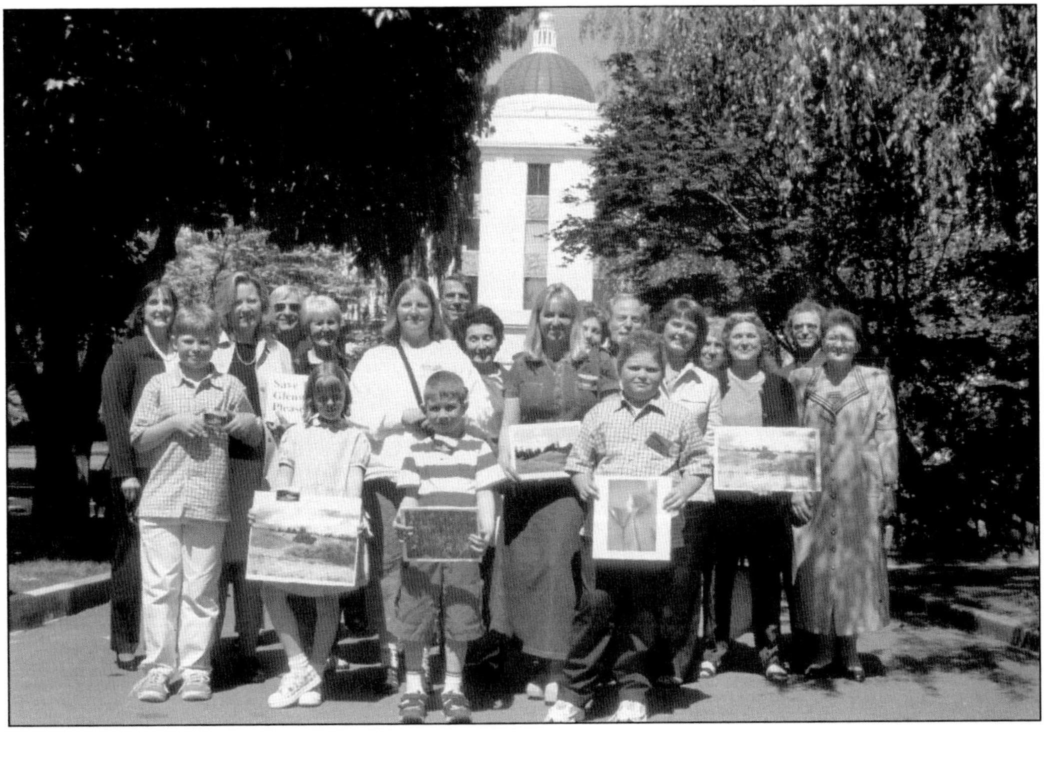

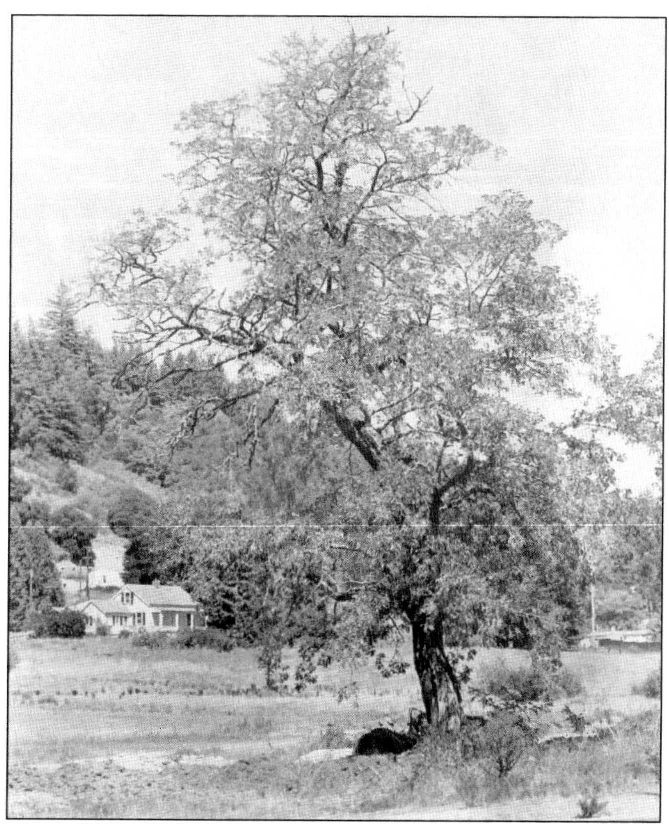

**Scott House.** This is the Scott House as seen from Scotts Valley Drive in the 1960s, after its move. (Courtesy of the Santa Cruz Museum of Art and History.)

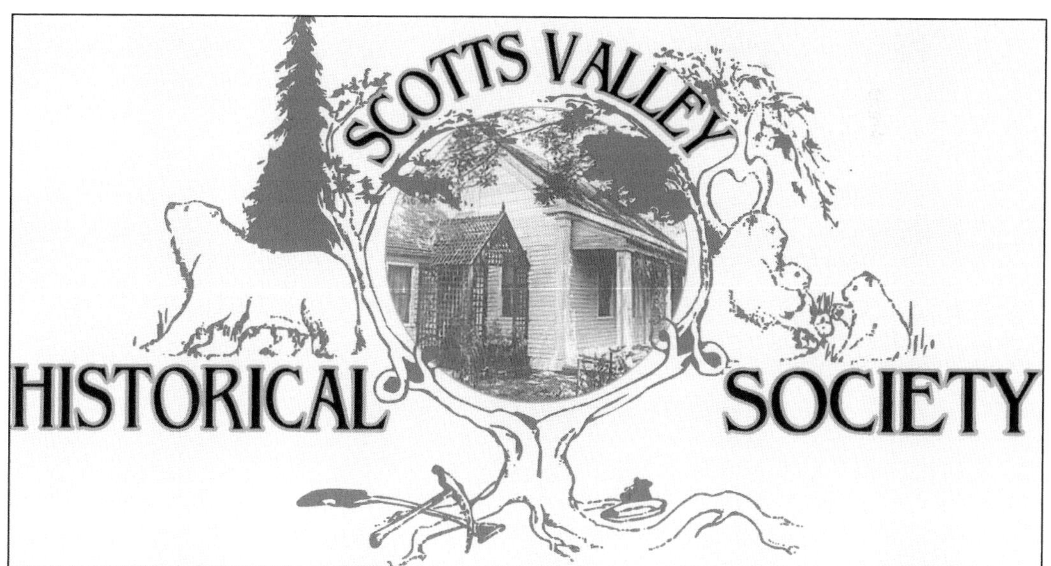


**Scotts Valley Historical Society.** For more information on the Scotts Valley Historical Society or to schedule tours of the Scott House, please contact the author at the address listed in the acknowledgments or write to the Scotts Valley Historical Society, One Civic Center Drive, Scotts Valley, CA 95066. (Courtesy of SVHS.)